Praise for *We Don't* [D0451483]

"*We Don't Talk Anymore* is a wise, clearly written, and helpful book for parents and adult children who are going through the trauma of estrangement. It is a great contribution to the important, but still relatively new, field of advice for families trying to reckon with this painful topic. I highly recommend it."

—*Joshua Coleman, PhD, author of* When Parents Hurt

"This well-focused book addresses so well the cataclysmic schism that often fractures the unity of an intact family. Dr. McCoy gives a glimpse into very real family dynamics of broken relationships with poignant clinical scenarios. Her expertise as a family counselor and therapist provides the reader with soothing treatment and practical approaches to understand and move forward to heal and mend these now fragile relationships. The author provides up-to-date research to document current counseling techniques, including research on epigenetics. This book is a must for any parents or adult children who have lost their relationships with each other."

—*Charles J. Wibbelsman, MD, clinical professor of pediatrics, University of California, San Francisco*

WE DON'T
TALK
ANYMORE

Also by Kathy McCoy, PhD

The Teenage Body Book

WITH CHARLES WIBBELSMAN, MD

Understanding Your Teenager's Depression: Issues,
Insights, and Practical Guidance for Parents

Purr Therapy: What Timmy and Marina
Taught Me about Life, Love, and Loss

Aging and Other Surprises

Making Peace with Your Adult Children

The Secrets of My Life: A Girl's Self-Discovery Journal

Growing and Changing: A Guide for Preteens

WITH CHARLES WIBBELSMAN, MD

Solo Parenting: Your Essential Guide

Changes and Choices: A Junior High Survival Guide

Life Happens

WITH CHARLES WIBBELSMAN, MD

Crisis-Proof Your Teenager: How to Recognize, Prevent,
and Deal with Risky Adolescent Behavior
WITH CHARLES WIBBELSMAN, MD

The Teenage Survival Guide: Coping with Problems in Everyday Life

The Teenage Body Book Guide to Sexuality

The Teenage Body Book Guide to Dating

For more information, visit drkathymccoy.com.

WE DON'T
TALK
ANYMORE

Healing after Parents
and Their Adult Children
Become Estranged

KATHY McCOY, PhD

Published by Sourcebooks, Inc.
P.O. Box 4410, Naperville, Illinois 60567-4410
(630) 961-3900
Fax: (630) 961-2168
www.sourcebooks.com

Library of Congress Cataloging-in-Publication Data

Names: McCoy, Kathy, author.
Title: We don't talk anymore : healing after parents and their adult children
   become estranged / Kathy McCoy, Ph.D.
Description: Naperville, Illinois : Sourcebooks, Inc., [2017] | Includes
   index.
Identifiers: LCCN 2017013758 | (pbk. : alk. paper)
Subjects: LCSH: Parent and adult child. | Interpersonal conflict. |
   Interpersonal relations. | Alienation (Social psychology) |
   Families--Psychological aspects.
Classification: LCC HQ755.86 .M399 2017 | DDC 306.874--dc23 LC record available at https://lccn.
loc.gov/2017013758

Printed and bound in the United States of America.
VP 10 9 8 7 6 5 4 3 2 1

To Tim
with love and gratitude

Contents

A Note from the Author

Dear Reader:

I can't know the exact circumstances that caused you to pick up this book, but please know that I do understand a great deal about the pain you're experiencing right now. My understanding has grown over the years in many different ways.

I was once a young adult child of troubled parents, struggling to make a decision about how close I dared be to them as I sought to build a new and independent life for myself while also maintaining loving ties and firm boundaries.

When I married my husband, Bob, I found that his family had a long history of intergenerational estrangement. His father's estrangement from his own father cut Bob's ties with his beloved grandfather, a very painful loss. Some years later, after his mother's death, Bob became estranged from his father, maintaining a stubborn silence for the last twenty years of his father's life—something he now deeply regrets.

As a psychotherapist, I have had many clients who suffered through estrangement from their parents or their adult children. I've spent countless hours listening to their tearful stories, their regrets, their anger and their fears that these painful family rifts might never heal—and working with them to find hope for reconciliation.

When my husband and I moved to an active adult community seven years ago, accounts of parent and adult child estrangement abounded: shared in the community pool as some blinked back tears behind oversized sunglasses; whispered in the gym locker room or over coffee in the local café. And then there was the new couple I recently visited to welcome to our neighborhood. Three hours and one box of tissues later, they had told me a heartbreaking tale of being blindsided with an estrangement from their adult son.

In 2010, I started my blog Living Fully in Midlife and Beyond. I have covered a number of topics in this blog over the years, but my posts about parents and adult children are by far the most popular. One in particular, written in 2012, stands out above all others. "When Parents and Adult Children Become Strangers" has been read nearly one million times by anguished parents and adult children around the world. And these readers have left hundreds of comments and pleas for advice on how to avoid or to heal estrangements.

These comments and pleas have led to this book, which covers so many of the issues that I've heard and seen among my patients, family, and friends. What I share on these pages comes from many *years of seeing and feeling the conflicts and the pain that so often divide parents and adult children.*

Your situation may be uniquely your own. But you're not alone. Let's explore together what has happened and what can be done to soothe your pain and bring hope back into your life.

Love and best wishes,

Dr. Kathy McCoy

The names of the parents and adult children whose stories are the heart of this book have been changed to protect their privacy. These patients, commenters on my blog, and interviewees have contributed so much, and I am grateful for their generosity and courage.

Preface: The Silent Epidemic

While parent and adult child estrangement is often called an epidemic, it is a silent one. Reliable statistics on the percentage of parents and their adult children who are estranged are largely absent from professional and popular literature. The reason for this shocking lack of statistical evidence for a problem that appears to be increasingly common is shame: the people involved have difficulty admitting that they are estranged from a parent or adult child.

There are celebrities whose parental estrangements have made tabloid headlines—like Jennifer Aniston, who became estranged from her mother after her mom wrote a tell-all book, and Angelina Jolie, whose feuds and estrangements from her father Jon Voight have been quite public. Most people, however, keep estrangement a painful secret, even from close friends or extended family members.

Estrangement can be a secret that is relatively easy to keep. Adult children may be living at a distance from their parents. Pictures and news about rarely (or never) seen grandchildren may be readily available on Facebook. And many busy adult children don't talk to or visit their parents on a regular basis.

But even if you keep your estrangement from the eyes and ears of friends and extended family, it is there. Others may not see it. But it's part of your daily reality—and it hurts. Some of this pain comes from feeling so very much alone.

If you're a parent who is estranged from an adult child, you never imagined this could happen.

When you think back on your years as a parent, there are so many happy memories: holding your baby in your arms for the first time; hearing your toddler's first words; cheering your little one on through Little League and dance recitals, soccer games, and school plays; comforting your child through disappointments and times of feeling awkward or unpopular; hanging on through the normal storms of adolescence; dreaming of rediscovering each other as beloved family and dear friends once they're grown.

Except that dream hasn't come true.

Maybe there was an argument, angry words, and a separation that has only deepened with time. Maybe your child left for college or is working, perhaps married, and has a home of his or her own—and suddenly doesn't seem to have much time for you. Maybe you and your adult child have become distant because of disagreements over or with his or her spouse or partner. Maybe you are divided by differences over lifestyle or religion. Maybe your feelings are hurt because your child's in-laws seem to be getting preferential treatment and more access to the grandkids.

Maybe, from the safe distance of that separate home of his own, your adult child is suddenly regaling you with angry accounts of your failings as a parent. And while you are quick to admit that, like any parent, you've made some mistakes, you can't remember anything you did, any choice you made, that wasn't made with love and wanting the best for your child. Maybe your adult child insists that nothing is wrong, from his or her perspective. She explains the unanswered emails and voicemails, the unacknowledged gifts and letters in two words: "I'm busy." But you're feeling that something is very wrong. You're feeling estranged or semiestranged from your adult son or daughter.

Estrangement—whether full or partial—is one of a parent's worst nightmares. It is a nightmare shared by an increasing number of parents, if the explosion of painful stories and comments on online chat rooms and blogs, as well as the numbers of parents seeking professional help, are any indication.

If you're feeling estranged from an adult son or daughter, you're far from alone, but you have probably been feeling very much alone. Many parents suffer in silence and shame, reluctant to discuss or even to admit the estrangement to friends and extended family.

Estrangement can mean not only angry silences between you and your adult child, but also feelings of isolation from others: solitary moments of shame and rage; times of feeling bewildered and unable to fathom the cause of this rift; lonely holidays and fictional accounts for friends of visits with grandchildren rarely seen. It can mean anguished days and nights of wondering what went wrong and how to bridge this emotional chasm.

If you're an adult child estranged or semiestranged from a parent or parents, the emotional distance within your family may be no surprise. Even if you didn't initiate the estrangement from your parents, you may have seen it coming for years as you grappled silently with your feelings and experiences, your divergent beliefs, your sexuality, your feelings of being disrespected and disregarded.

Maybe you've put distance between yourself and your parents because being close is just too painful. They have expectations that have little to do with the person you are and what you want for yourself. There are the clashes over beliefs and traditions that have diverged over the years. There is the criticism that, though your parents insist that it is given with love, threatens to undermine your confidence at close range.

You may be in a fight for your independence from parents who seem determined to keep you a perpetual child. You know that they mean well, but their hovering, their unsolicited advice, their increasingly intrusive questions are driving you into a full retreat. You're less inclined to call these days and even less likely to visit. Maybe you've even underscored your desire for independence by accepting a job hundreds or thousands of miles away from your hometown.

Maybe you've come to the painful conclusion that your parents were (and perhaps still are) abusive. Perhaps you are receiving therapy, and your therapist has suggested keeping your distance as you grapple with what has happened and what you would like to have happen in your life.

Or you may feel hurt that your parents are even uttering the word *estrangement* when, really, you're simply busy, even overwhelmed with the demands of your adult life. When you're working and commuting long hours, when you're in a new marriage, when you're combining all of the above with caring for your young children, there aren't enough hours in a day to get everything done, let alone go spend a day with the folks or an hour on the phone with your mother every day. You hear the pain in her voice when you tell her you're too busy for long talks or visits. You sift through your priorities, trying, without success, to figure out how to meet the challenges of your own independent life and how to be a loving son or daughter as well. It isn't easy, especially when your attempts to compromise are met with words that sting.

If any of the above sounds familiar to you—as the parent of an adult child or as that adult child—this book is for you.

In the pages to come, we will explore together some of the reasons that parents and adult children find themselves estranged, how to deal with the pain this causes, and what to do to help make your dream of reconciliation come true. You will also find help in living with the anguish of a relationship that can't be mended immediately—or ever.

The focus of this book is on you: how you can begin to bridge that painful distance between you and your loved one, how you can solve the mystery behind your estrangement and find clues to reconnecting, and how to rebuild a satisfying, sane life for yourself—with or without regular contact with each other.

Together, we will explore your dreams and your realities, your feelings of love and anger and grief, and the ways that, however your relationship with your adult child or your parent evolves, you can build a satisfying life filled with love, peace, and warm connection.

SECTION ONE
WHAT'S GOING ON?

CHAPTER ONE

Exploring the Mystery of Estrangement

"I just don't understand," Linda said, as she dabbed at her tears with a crumpled tissue. "I don't understand what has happened to my daughter and me. We used to be close, even when she was a teenager and always challenging my rules and opinions. We enjoyed doing things together. I thought it would be even better when she finished school, was working, and was an independent adult. I hoped we'd be best friends. But something has happened the past few years. She rarely calls me and often doesn't return my phone calls or emails. Do you know how that feels? I'm sad and angry and, most of all, confused. I don't know what could have caused her to pull away from me like this…"

Linda was one of many parents I have seen over the past decade who complained about an increasingly distant relationship with an adult child. To many, it's a painful mystery. How could a previously close and loving relationship change so dramatically? Why do some adult children drift away, both physically and emotionally, from their parents?

Many adult children who feel growing distance from their parents don't find it such a mystery. "I keep my distance from my parents because their opinions and unasked for advice just drive me up the wall," says Jillian, twenty-seven years old, single, and living one thousand miles from her hometown. "I love my parents, but being with them is tough going."

And some young adults question the idea of estrangement altogether. "My parents think we are estranged, but, really, I'm just busy and not able to call or visit as much as they'd like," says Brandon, a thirty-year-old IT professional. "And, too often, when I do go home, there's a scene with one or both of them over my supposed selfishness. But estrangement? I don't think so."

Both parents and adult children may wonder (and not always agree on) what it means to be estranged from someone you love.

There is **physical estrangement**—when parents and an adult child are cut off from each other with months or years passing without contact.

There is **emotional estrangement**—when one or all of you feel your relationship become increasingly distant, with only periodic, often perfunctory contact with each other. There may be times when hope returns, when an adult child calls or comes by or invites you over for dinner. Or when parents call a truce and invite an adult child over for a visit or a special night out. But, all too often, this respite may be followed by more silences, angry or otherwise. And the parents or the adult child are left baffled and at a loss to explain just why you are drifting apart.

For many, estrangement isn't a sudden event, but a process that takes place over time. It may be a gradual loosening of ties as a result of life choices and events. It may have started with a specific conflict that led to angry silences and, subsequently, to an emotional chasm that took on a life of its own. Or it may have evolved from an erosion of intimacy and goodwill as the adult child has struggled for independence and the parent or parents have struggled to maintain close ties. It may have started with new alliances or with divergent views of a shared past.

This phenomenon, which psychologist Joshua Coleman, an expert on parent–adult child conflict and estrangement, calls "the silent epidemic"* has captured the interest of many researchers in the fields of psychology, sociology, and gerontology. As a result, this research and some clinical observations can be distilled into the following:

TEN FACTS ABOUT PARENT– ADULT CHILD ESTRANGEMENTS

1. You Are Not Alone

When you're estranged from an adult child or from a parent, you may feel very much alone. Shame can be a part of this feeling,

---

*   Joshua Coleman, interview by Savannah Guthrie, *TODAY* show, NBC, April 1, 2013.

as estrangement from parents or grown children isn't something people talk about in casual conversations.

"Are you kidding?" Diane, estranged from her thirty-four-year-old son for five years and never having seen her toddler granddaughter, scoffs when asked if she confides in friends. "I feel so ashamed, like a failure as a mother. Since my son and his family live out of state, it's easy to make up stories about Skype conversations and plans to visit in the future. I check out what they're doing and capture photos of my granddaughter on Facebook, print them, and put them in little frames around my living room. I'm heartbroken, but I'm too embarrassed to tell my friends that I've never met my grandchild."

But as lonely as an estrangement can feel, it's not uncommon. A U.S. study of adult children found that 7 percent reported being emotionally detached from a mother and 27 percent were detached from a father.*

2. Fathers Are More Likely to Become Estranged as a Result of Divorce, Either in the Distant Past or via a Recent "Gray Divorce"

Sometimes the distance has grown from resentments over a long-ago marital split and alienation fueled by parental anger and life choices. And sometimes a "gray divorce," a split that occurs in

---

*   M. Silverstein and V. L. Bengston, "Intergenerational solidarity and the structure of adult-child-parent relationships in American families." *American Journal of Sociology* 103, no. 2 (1997): 429–460.

long-married people over the age of fifty, sparks conflicts with adult children who feel compelled to take sides or who resent the changes this brings to their own lives.

"I'm really angry at my dad for leaving my mom after thirty-six years of marriage," says Jenna, thirty-two, married and pregnant with her first child. "I know they've never been that happy together, but they made it work all those years. Why give up now? It's not like either of them had anyone else waiting on the sidelines. They had an argument, and it was like the last straw for him. My poor mom never expected this after all these years. Now my baby will never know grandparents who are together and, well, normal grandparents. I feel really hurt about that. And I think Dad is being really selfish. I have nothing to say to him anymore."

Jenna's situation is not unusual. A study of late-life divorce and its impact on relationships between the divorcing parents and adult children found that while fathers were more likely to experience a decline in contact with adult children, the divorced mothers were more likely than married mothers to report an increase in weekly contact with adult children.[†]

These differences in contact may happen for a number of reasons. Newly divorced mothers are more likely to ask adult children for help with tasks previously performed by the departed spouse. They may be more likely to talk about their feelings with

---

† Adam Shapiro, "Later-Life Divorce and Parent–Adult Child Contact and Proximity: A Longitudinal Analysis," *Journal of Family Issues* (March 2003): 264–285.

adult children. Newly divorced fathers may find it difficult to talk about their feelings, including depression, with anyone. And they are likely to remarry more quickly and in greater numbers than mothers. These remarriages can be as disruptive to father–adult children relationships as the original divorce.*

3. Mothers Are More Likely to Become Estranged as the Result of Continuing Demands for Closeness or Giving Unsolicited Advice

This kind of estrangement can spring from conflicting needs and perceptions about how much contact is too much, what advice can feel like criticism (particularly in the areas of child rearing), and what actions can feel intrusive. The mother may feel she's just being helpful. The daughter or daughter-in-law may have a very different view.

"My mother thinks she is being just so helpful and always says 'But I'm your mother. Who else is going to care enough to tell you the truth?' and I can't stand it," says Laurel, a twenty-nine-year-old financial analyst whose apartment is across town from her parents' home. "And it drove me crazy when she thought it was perfectly okay to just drop by my place! I mean, that was just one of many ways I felt she didn't respect my independence. It was so embarrassing. One Sunday morning, my boyfriend and I were

---

*   Constance R. Ahrons and Jennifer L. Tanner, "Adult Children and Their Fathers: Relationship Changes 20 Years After Parental Divorce," *Family Relations* 52 (2003): 340–351.

having coffee—me in my robe, my boyfriend in his underwear—when my mother knocked on the door, totally unexpected and uninvited. I told her later I felt this wasn't acceptable. She got mad and we haven't spoken for five months now."

Some parents, like Laurel's mother, are astounded when their adult children object to behavior they find normal and perfectly acceptable. Social policy researcher Dorothy Jerrome has observed that "the principle of an open house is one-sided. Casual visiting by children [to the parents' home] is acceptable; if done by parents, it is intrusive, and in breach of the norm of noninterference."[†]

4. An Adult Child Who Is at Odds with Mother's Core Values Is More Likely to Become Estranged than an Adult Child Who Is Arrested or Involved in Substance Abuse

This was a surprising finding in a study of estranged mothers headed by Megan Gilligan of Iowa State University.[‡] Dr. Gilligan and her colleagues interviewed 566 mothers between the ages of sixty-five and seventy-five. They found that sixty-four of these women had at least one estranged child. The mothers reported

---

† Dorothy Jerrome, "Family Estrangement: Parents and Children who 'Lose Touch,'" *Journal of Family Therapy* 16 (1994): 241–258.

‡ Megan Gilligan, J. Jill Suitor, and Karl Pillemer, "Estrangement between Mothers and Adult Children: The Role of Norms and Values," *Journal of Marriage and Family* 77, no. 4 (August 2015): 908–920.

clashing values, such as in religion or partner choice, as a major factor in their estrangement from an adult child, while at the same time being quite tolerant of other adult children showing socially deviant behavior.

For example, Ruth, a seventy-five-year-old devout Catholic who participated in the study, had two sons and one daughter. She was estranged from her middle child, Mark, because he had divorced and remarried, life choices quite at odds with the Catholic faith. However, Ruth did not appear to be bothered by the fact that her other two children both had histories of substance abuse, DUI arrests, and—in the case of the other son Paul—other problems with the law. In fact, she talked of Paul with pride because he was still in his first marriage, stating that "Paul is my success story!"

Another study participant, Beverly, who was seventy and the mother of three grown children, reported that she was estranged from her second son, Robert, who was married, a parent, and financially stable, "because he's not very truthful. I don't like it when people say things that aren't true." But she reported a warm relationship with her oldest son David, who was in prison, had a history of drug abuse, and had fathered multiple children with different women, none of whom he had married. She kept in close contact with him, sending him money despite the fact that her resources were limited. The researchers noted that she expressed some disappointment in David, but was more sympathetic than critical.

Many estranged mothers don't have such dramatic contrasts in the way they view their differences with their adult children.

But when adult children have feelings and choices that are in opposition to a mother's most fervent beliefs, estrangement is much more likely to happen.

5. Estrangements Are Less Likely to Spring from Verbal Sparring than from a Conflict of Needs

This is often the need of the adult child to be independent and in control of his or her own life and the need of a parent to remain closely connected and, ultimately, in control. When tensions arise over this conflict, the adult child may seek autonomy by making a complete break with parents.

As researchers have examined conflicts between parents and adult children, another sobering fact has emerged: that parents are more emotionally invested in their relationships with their children than their children are with them. This is called the "developmental stake hypothesis."*

This generational difference is consistent across the lifespan. As parents age, closeness with an adult child may become even more important to them, with the adult child often their primary social contact. However, the parents' needs may escalate just as the adult child's responsibilities to his or her own growing family and career are also increasing. Perhaps the parents have new limitations as they become increasingly frail. Poor eyesight may make driving

---

*   K. S. Birditt et al, "Tensions in the Parent and Adult Child Relationship: Links to Solidarity and Ambivalence," *Psychology and Aging* 24, no. 2 (2009): 287–295.

difficult or impossible. Doctor appointments suddenly dominate parental calendars. For both physical and emotional reasons, as their friends die and their social ties weaken, aging parents may become more dependent on adult children. This dependence can prompt intergenerational ambivalence—the adult child wanting to help parents while resenting or feeling overwhelmed by their increasing neediness, and parents who may be grieving their physical and social losses and may be having mixed feelings about needing their adult child so much. All of this can spark conflict and distance between parents and adult children.

Jack is a forty-five-year-old engineer and his wife Kara a forty-two-year-old nurse working the night shift so that one parent is always home with their three children, who are now young adolescents. "The old saying that teenagers need parents less is wrong," Jack says. "We both need to be there for them and keep an eye on them in these important growing-up years. Our parents need us, too, but we've learned to keep our distance. Otherwise we get overwhelmed with requests that we just can't meet. Of course, in a crisis, we'd be there in a minute. But just to keep them company or to help them feel not quite so bored...that just doesn't feel reasonable right now. My in-laws seem to understand and accept this. But my parents got very offended when I tried to explain our pressures and priorities to them. Their reaction is 'If you can't come over just because we want to be with you, don't bother to come over at all, even in a crisis.' They don't seem to understand that they can't always come first with me. And this has come between us big time."

6. Some Emotional Distance Actually Can Improve the Relationship and Make Estrangement Less Likely

The paradox of an intimate yet distant parent–adult child relationship can be a source of pain *or* a path to new intimacy, according to research by K. L. Fingerman of Pennsylvania State University.*

She has found that while some parents and adult children report close ties, this closeness nonetheless involves psychological distance. She noted that parents tended to stop trying to direct their children's lives, and their grown children, in turn, sought to protect their parents from worry, often by not discussing their problems with their parents. She noted that this distance tended to improve the relationship and can serve as a bridge to a different kind of intimacy.

"I used to see my daughter's not telling me everything as a kind of loss of closeness, but now I'm realizing that it has helped curb my unsolicited-advice-giving habit," says Wendy, a sixty-one-year-old mother of a thirty-three-year-old single businesswoman. "What I don't know won't worry me. And I don't regale her with all my aches and pains in return. When we talk, it's enjoyable. It may be an impassioned discussion of politics or some other news development. Or it may be about feelings in general. But our visits are more frequent these days. For a while, I wouldn't see

---

* K. L. Fingerman, "Sources of Tension in the Aging Mother–Adult Daughter Relationship," *Psychology and Aging* 11 (1996): 591–606.

her for weeks, sometimes months, at a time. Now that we've both stepped back and re-evaluated, our relationship feels closer and better than ever."

7. Helping an Adult Child Financially Can Actually Increase the Likelihood of Estrangement

While we often see parents and adult children become estranged when parents can't or won't offer their grown children financial help, offering such help can also lead to conflicts and estrangement.

"Financial contributions are often an expression of power relations between the generations," observes researcher Marc Szydlik. He notes that much-needed financial support may be seen by the adult child as a kind of bribery or as a way of having more of a say over an adult child's life.*

An adult child's financial neediness may also spark conflict with parents who are upset that a son or daughter is not meeting expected age-appropriate goals for financial indepen-dence and responsibility.

"Giving our son a loan to buy a new car and get into an apart-ment was a mistake," says Chris, the forty-seven-year-old father of twenty-three-year-old Tom. "We couldn't afford to just give him the money, but we wanted to help him get a start in life, and so we gave him the loan. He has been very casual about paying it

---

* M. Szydlik, "Intergenerational Solidarity and Conflict," *Journal of Comparative Family Studies* 39, no. 1 (2008): 97–118.

back. We get twenty-five dollars maybe once or twice a year. At that rate, it will never get paid back in our lifetimes. So, yes, it pisses me off when he hits Starbucks every day or buys electronics stuff or goes out partying with friends every night or goes off with friends for weekend trips. I don't think he realizes how much he's spending on frivolities and how much we need to be paid back sooner rather than later. When I mention this to him, he blows up and accuses me of trying to control his life. He hasn't spoken to us for two months now."

8. An Estrangement Isn't Just between a Parent and an Adult Child

Estrangements can impact the whole family. This is something we see in therapy all the time, especially with siblings, grandparents, aunts, and uncles who get dragged into—or insert themselves into—family conflicts. Being on the frontline of an estrangement can bring up a myriad of feelings, old conflicts, and rivalries.

"Just what I needed: old family drama on top of my current crisis," says Jean, a fifty-eight-year-old widow estranged from her thirty-five-year-old son Dan. "I cut off the financial pipeline to my son and urged him to take responsibility for himself, and my mother comes to his rescue, convinced that I'm being mean. And my sister, with whom I've never gotten along, is suddenly his new BFF. I'm convinced it's just to upset me, the kind of stuff she's been pulling all our lives. So now I'm feeling cut off from most of my family."

Sibling involvement can be especially painful and complicated. Some siblings take advantage of an estrangement between the parents and a brother or sister to enhance their own standing with parents. Some add fuel to the fire. And some feel painfully caught between parents and a sibling they love.

"Both sides have tagged me as a go-between," says Samantha, thirty-eight. "My parents try to get information about my sister from me and want me to carry a message to her, and my sister Shannon does the same. I finally said to them that they obviously need and want to talk with each other again and that they should just do that. I don't want to be put in the position of being a messenger or of not honoring confidences. That's not fair. And I think it just serves to extend their estrangement from each other."

9. Having a Good Relationship in the Growing-Up Years Is No Guarantee That You'll Never Be Estranged

No matter how close you may have felt to a son or daughter, or to your parents, in earlier years, you may still face an estrangement later on.

Sometimes this comes as the result of a later-in-life parental divorce—when an adult child feels compelled to take one side or the other or blames both parents for breaking up the family.

Sometimes it comes as an adult child tries to find a balance between independence and continuing to stay connected to parents who might be reluctant to see their relationship with their newly adult child change.

And sometimes an estrangement can happen in the wake of the mental illness of a family member. This is particularly true with personality disorders such as borderline personality disorder or narcissistic personality disorder, both of which may first become evident in late adolescence or early adulthood.

When someone has borderline personality disorder, he or she shows a pattern of unstable relationships, which can include turmoil with family, friends, and coworkers. These relationships can be intense—due to the person's deep fears of abandonment—with a pattern that often starts with idealization and ends with devaluation. The "new best friend" of yesterday becomes the "total bitch" of today. Parents may find themselves vilified. This is an important feature of borderline personality disorder: the person can't integrate the good and bad parts of another (or herself). In a process called "splitting," the person sees another as all good or all bad, with no shades of gray in between. Other conditions may also be present, such as depression or panic attacks, chronic anger, or harmful impulsive behavior that might include substance abuse, eating disorders, or self-injury, or even suicidal behavior.*

A person with narcissistic personality disorder may be, quite predictably, self-centered. But there's more to it than that. The

---

*   The descriptions above of some of the features of borderline personality disorder can be found in the *DSM-V* and is discussed in more detail in chapter 9.

person with NPD may be unable to tolerate different points of view, criticism, suggestions, or the conflicting needs of others.

All of these behaviors can cause considerable conflict with those closest to them—quite often parents.

And when an adult child has grown up in a home with a parent who has one of these disorders, he or she may have adapted as a child, being an emotional caregiver of the needy parent. But when the young adult seeks independence from the parent, this may trigger a stream of accusations from the parent who sees only betrayal in the young adult's bid for a separate life and, in the growing distance that is part of breaking away, the adult child may find the parent's behavior increasingly intolerable. And so the estrangement begins.

10. Parents and Adult Children Don't Always Agree on the Reasons for Estrangement

A recent study of estranged parents and adult children found that parents tended to blame the estrangement on sources outside of themselves, such as relationships they find objectionable. Adult children tended to attribute estrangement to the personal characteristics or behavior of their parents, such as toxic behavior or feeling unaccepted or unsupported.[*]

"My parents are so narrow minded," said Gabe, a

---

[*]   Kristen Carr et al, "Giving Voice to the Silence of Family Estrangement: Comparing Reasons of Estranged Parents and Adult Children in a Nonmatched Sample," *Journal of Family Communication* 15 (2015): 130–140.

twenty-four-year-old insurance adjuster who recently came out to his parents as gay. "I know they've always been pretty homophobic, under the disguise of religious beliefs, of course. But you'd think...well, I had hoped...that when I told them I was gay, they would find it in their hearts to be accepting out of love for me. But they're convinced that I've fallen in with a bad crowd and that my relationship with my boyfriend Ben is something shameful that will someday just go away if they pray enough. So I just don't see them anymore. It hurts too much. I just can't go there anymore."

• • •

While research into reasons for parent–adult child conflict and estrangement offers some interesting clues into the mystery of estrangement, some distressed parents have little patience with academic views of this painful, often devastating situation.

"Psychobabble!" scoffed one parent in an online chat room. "I'm so tired of hearing about these studies that have nothing to do with me! It's one thing to study this problem. It's something else to be living it!"

You may be echoing such sentiments, with a life situation that feels both puzzling and painfully unique. And yet, exploring the clues to estrangement through the eyes of researchers and therapists and—perhaps most important—the experiences of parents and adult children, you may begin to uncover the clues to your own estrangement and to ways you can begin to rebuild your relationship with your adult child, or with your parents.

Even if certain clues don't seem relevant, at least initially, it's important to keep an open mind. That isn't easy when you're hurting and your parents just don't understand. It also isn't easy when you feel that your adult child is rejecting you or ignoring you for no good reason. The fact is, there is always a reason.

Even if the possible reason for your estrangement feels outrageous, lame, inauthentic, or just plain crazy to you, if you want to have any chance at reconciliation it's important to see it from your adult child's point of view, if you're a parent, or from your parents' view if you're a grown child.

Many parents, feeling that they're on the receiving end for unearned emotional abuse or neglect, quite understandably balk at this idea. I'll never forget a woman, a beleaguered mother of seven whose kids ranged from fourteen to thirty-two and who was estranged from her twenty-eight-year-old daughter. She appeared on a television show with me in Sarasota, Florida, some years ago.

I was on a national book tour, promoting one of my books for teenagers. The topic on this particular show was parent-teen communication. This mother was asked to be on the show as an experienced, if battle-scarred, parent. As the live show went on, however, the mother became increasingly emotional about the topic of communication problems between parent and child. She deviated from the teen topic to the one causing her the most distress: the rift with her young adult daughter. My memory of her anger and grief is still vivid. She said that she and her daughter couldn't possibly reconcile because every time they spoke, which wasn't often, they ended up in a fierce argument that led to greater estrangement. I suggested that a third party—possibly a psychologist or family therapist—might help them to connect in a less contentious way.

She glared at me and snorted with derision. "Why should I humiliate myself like that just because my kid's an asshole?" she asked, sitting back, her arms tightly folded, guarding her pain.

Why indeed? Because there are times when, as a parent, you may choose to do something painful in order to reconnect with your adult child. It takes tremendous love and humility and commitment to your relationship for you to step back and look at the whole picture of what has happened between you and your grown son or daughter and to consider what role you may have played—or not—in your troubled relationship.

The same is true for adult children who feel that their parents are to blame for all that has come between them. In order to build a more satisfying relationship with your parents, it may be necessary to step back and consider what you have done to help create the chasm between you and what you might do to help it heal. Even if you're sure that you know the reasons for your estrangement, there may be factors behind these reasons that will help you to understand what's really going on and how to make a difference.

When I look at the information available, not just from academic research but also from other parents and adult children themselves, whether they are speaking in therapy sessions, in online forums, or in interviews, some common triggers for estrangement begin to emerge. They might provide valuable clues to your own unique situation.

Is it possible that you and your adult child may be experiencing a **developmental divide?**

As a parent, are you finding that your wishes for frequent contact with your son are in conflict with his need for independence or his responsibilities for a young, growing family?

Is it possible that you and your parents have **clashing expectations?** These can include differing views about what it means to be close, the roles you play or need to play in each other's lives, and feelings of entitlement that may conflict with another's willingness to give.

Is it possible that you're divided over issues related to **marriage**—either your marriage or theirs? Maybe your adult child is seeking to escape getting caught up in tensions within your marriage. Maybe he or she feels resentment over your remarriage. Or perhaps a romantic relationship or marriage is an emotional minefield causing conflict and estrangement between you.

Is it possible that your estrangement was sparked by **life paths taken or not taken**, conflicting views over life choices—to continue with school, to choose a certain career, or to convert to another religion?

Are you distant because of a discussion of sexuality that may be at odds with your personal beliefs—such as your son or daughter's coming out as gay or transgender?

Is it possible that you and your parents are at odds because of **cultural conflicts?** These can include the gulf between immigrant parents and their American-born children who may have differing views of family loyalty and emerging independence. It also can

involve vastly different perceptions between the generations—
native born or not—in terms of moral choices, emotional intimacy,
and what it means to stay in touch. For example, a young adult
may see texting as a perfectly good way to keep in touch, while a
parent may long for a visit or phone call.

Is it possible that **money issues** are dividing you? These can
include conflicts over parental financial help or well-considered
refusal to help. These can also include tensions between newly
affluent adult children and their retired parents on a fixed income,
or parents (or children) who use money to gain power or control
over the other.

Is it possible that the roots of your estrangement may lie in
the legacy of a long-ago **divorce** or in the wake of an announce-
ment that parents, married for decades, are considering or are in
the process of divorce?

Is it possible that you are split by **divergent memories?** Do
you have vastly different memories of the same past events and
experiences? These differences, if unheard and unresolved, can
drive you apart.

Is it possible that you are divided by **echoes of the past, both
yours and theirs?** These echoes may cause you to treat your adult
children as you were treated by your parents. Or you may have
tried to be a vastly different parent than your own parents were
(while expecting quite different feelings and reactions from your
adult children as a result). Or these echoes may come from a
happier, closer past as a family and may cause you (or your adult
child) to hang on and try to preserve that—trying to freeze these

familial relationships in time despite developmental changes for both of you.

It isn't easy to consider these possibilities, but it's important to think about all the factors that might be contributing to the distance you're feeling from each other.

It's important to see and try to understand the situation through each other's eyes.

It's important to accept the reality that you have no power to change each other's perceptions, attitudes, and behaviors directly, but you can change your own and, in so doing, may forge new bonds with your son or daughter.

It's important to realize that delving into the underlying cause of your estrangement isn't about blame or who is right and who is wrong, but about mutual understanding and forgiveness and finding new ways to be together.

It's important to keep your heart and mind open as you explore the painful mystery of your estrangement from the child or the parents you have loved so much.

The chapters that follow will look at each of these causes, which we'll call *estrangement triggers*, to see how each can build a painful distance between you; how distance, anger, and hopelessness grow; and what you can do to bridge this emotional chasm. You will also discover how to heal your broken heart, how to deal with your anger and grief, and how to feel less alone—whether or not reconciliation ever happens.

SECTION TWO

WHAT CAN WE DO?

CHAPTER TWO

Developmental Divides and Clashing Expectations

Whether you're a parent or an adult child, there are times when you just can't win. In the eyes of your parent or your grown child, you're viewed as:

+ Too independent—or not independent enough
+ Too intrusive—or totally uncaring
+ Hopelessly immature—or so dedicated to achievement that you are forgetting where you came from
+ A constant on-call babysitter for your grandkids—or a burden, if you need more help than you can give right now

Developmental divides and clashing expectations loom large as triggers for parent–adult child estrangement as the generations grow, change, and inevitably disappoint each other in their often-conflicting goals and needs.

Once upon a time, growing into independent adulthood followed a predictable course: a person finished high school or college, got a job, got married, and started a family—all by their early twenties.

The scenario can be quite different today as young adults take longer to find and begin a lifelong career, and are more likely to live with their parents for longer periods and to postpone marriage and parenthood.

According to a census analysis by Pew Research, 62 percent of young adults ages eighteen to thirty-four lived with a spouse or romantic partner in their own home in 1960. The average age of marriage was twenty for women and twenty-two for men. According to a 2014 census analysis, it's now twenty-seven for women and twenty-nine for men. So living arrangements have changed considerably. By 2014, the percentage of young adults living with a spouse or romantic partner in their own home had fallen to 31 percent, with 32 percent of young adults living with their parents. This was the highest percentage of young adults living with parents since the peak in 1940. Then, the country was just emerging from the Great Depression, and it was often the norm for young adults to live with parents until they married, but the 2014 numbers had a story to tell, too: one of young adults struggling to get an economic foothold in times of crushing college-loan debt and fewer job opportunities.

The study also found gender differences in those young adults who, in 2014, were choosing to live with parents: while

35 percent of young men were still living in the home of their parents, only 29 percent of young women were still at home.*

In analyzing the census data, Pew researchers noted that young men's prospects have been declining significantly in recent years. In 2014, only 71 percent of eighteen-to-thirty-four-year-old men were employed, and young men's wages fell significantly between 2000 and 2010. With these economic realities, the number of young men living with their parents has risen.

Young women, on the other hand, have accounted for an increasing number of college graduates and have had growing success in the paid labor market in recent years. They are also more likely to be married—often to men somewhat older and more established—or to be heading a household as a single parent.

A number of the parents and young adults I've talked with concur, attributing these changes to the economy: the difficulty in launching a meaningful career; the proliferation of unpaid or low-paid internships as starting points to desirable career paths; and the crushing burden of student loans for many new college graduates. However, some researchers see other factors in the ways that young adults evolve these days. For example, among the primary factors in the phenomenon of "emerging adulthood" were, first, the change from an industrial to an information-based economy, requiring more education, a factor in delaying marriage and parenthood; second, new opportunities for women who are

---

* Richard Fry, *For First Time in Modern Era, Living with Parents Edges Out Other Living Arrangements for 18- to-34-Year-Olds* (Washington, DC: Pew Research Center, 2016).

attending college and launching careers in ever greater numbers instead of marrying and having children in their early twenties; and, third, greater societal tolerance of premarital sex.*

There can be considerable disagreement between parents and their children on what it means to be an adult. While parents often cite as markers of adulthood the familiar milestones of their own youth, such as marriage, a full-time job, and parenthood, young adults are more likely to cite learning to stand alone, taking responsibility for one's actions, establishing a relationship with parents as an equal adult, and financial independence.†

These different views can spark conflict between parents and their adult children. Parents who feel that their children are behind the expected timetable for marriage, children, and full-time employment tend to express greater ambivalence.‡

"I get angry at my son Jonathan and, at the same time, feel bad for him," says Marta, a forty-nine-year-old single mother. "He's twenty-six, still working stopgap, noncareer jobs, living at home in his old room and trying to pay down his college loans— which is tough considering how little he earns at these jobs of his. I wonder if he will ever get to the point where he can be

*   Jennifer L. Tanner and Jeffrey J. Arnett, "The Emergence of 'Emerging Adulthood': The New Life Stage between Adolescence and Young Adulthood," in *Handbook of Youth and Young Adulthood: New Perspectives and Agencies*, ed. Andy Furlong (New York: Routledge, 2009), 39–45.

†   Jeffrey J. Arnett, "Conceptions of the Transition to Adulthood: Perspectives from Adolescence through Midlife," *Journal of Adult Development* 8, no. 2 (2001): 133–143.

‡   K. L. Fingerman et al, "Ambivalent Reactions in the Parent and Adult-Child Relationship," *Journals of Gerontology: Psychological Sciences* 61B (2006): 153–160.

independent. Most of our arguments are about this, and I've set a deadline of six months, at which point I want him to have a real job and move out of the house. He sees this as me being mean and unsupportive. We're barely speaking, and I think we're in real danger of becoming estranged even though we're still, at this point, under the same roof."

There are many parents who feel as Marta does—and adult children who feel like Jonathan.

In an article for the *Atlantic* titled "When Are You Really an Adult?" Julie Beck described a boomerang adult child named Henry who moved back with his parents after his graduation from Harvard.[§] The parents were delighted when, despite the recession, Henry managed to get a teaching job and furious when, after two weeks, he quit the job because it wasn't for him. He worked odd jobs for a while before focusing on his true passion: writing. He was thirty-one before he published his first book, and during the years in between his college graduation and his emergence as a published author, he had alternately lived with his parents and crashed at the home of a buddy, who encouraged his dreams.

Sound familiar? But this boomerang kid was Henry David Thoreau and his buddy was Ralph Waldo Emerson.

The article, citing a number of studies, suggested that young adults who married, had children, and got lifetime jobs in the fifties and early sixties were the exception to the historical rule

---

§   Julie Beck, "When Are You Really an Adult?" *Atlantic*, January 5, 2016, https://www.the atlantic.com/health/archive/2016/01/when-are-you-really-an-adult/422487/.

of young people taking most of their twenties to become full adults. This anomaly was due, at least in part, to the booming post–World War II economy, when a person with a high school education could get a job that could support a family and when societal mores frowned on premarital sex and strongly encouraged marriage.

Intrigued by different perceptions of and trajectories toward adulthood in recent decades, Dr. Jeffrey Arnett, professor of psychology at Clark University and a prominent researcher in the area of young adult development, has spent years exploring "emerging adulthood," a life stage he sees as quite distinct from both adolescence and adulthood, where young people, typically between eighteen and the late twenties, discover who they are and what they want and develop independent living skills before taking on adult roles. Some other researchers disagree about "emerging adulthood" as a distinct life stage, seeing it either as prolonged adolescence or long-developing adulthood.

However researchers choose to see these times of transition, countless parents and adult children are living through them—and they can lead to considerable conflict, sometimes leading to estrangement.

While some young adults today feel close to their parents and don't see daily parental involvement in their lives as intrusive, others chafe at parental helicoptering and are increasingly anxious to make their own choices and pursue their own life paths.

"I feel like I've had to battle my parents all the way to independent adulthood," says Robyn, who recently turned twenty-six. "I don't know what it is. Maybe parents are just more reluctant to let daughters go. But I had a very hard time convincing them that my best college choice was one thousand miles away. They wanted me to attend the local college. It wasn't a matter of finances. They just wanted me close by. And after I graduated, they begged me to come back here, at least for a few years. I came back, lived at home until I found a job, and then moved out to my own small apartment. My God! You'd think I had committed a major crime. They cried and railed. My dad dumped my childhood belongings on my apartment doorstep. They wouldn't speak to me for months. Now I'd describe us as semiestranged, speaking only occasionally at larger family gatherings. They want more contact. But I feel trapped by their expectations whenever we do spend time together. Whatever I do, it's never enough."

Many parents have a different view of the gulf between them and their newly independent children.

"We used to be so close," says Karen, the sixty-seven-year-old mother of a twenty-nine-year-old son who is living with a longtime girlfriend, and a thirty-five-year-old daughter who is married and has two school-age children and a new baby on the way. "Then they left home, started working and it was 'Hasta la vista, Mom!' They're too busy to get together most of the time. Everyone else comes first. I don't understand this kind of reasoning. I saw my own parents all the time. I included them in my life. But my kids just don't. It makes me angry—and very sad."

As we saw in the previous chapter, much conflict and estrangement between parents and adult children springs from clashing expectations and different levels of desired closeness as the years go on. Researchers call the latter "the developmental schism hypothesis," and it may be especially noticeable among middle-aged children and their aging parents. Middle-aged adult children sometimes struggle with expectations rooted in the past, when fewer women worked outside the home and were readily available as caregivers for their parents.

At this stage of life today, however, middle-aged adults have multiple demands on their time—marriage, children of their own, busy work lives—and may be less invested in their relationship with their parents, while the parents desire increased closeness with their children as they age.*

Some parents feel estranged, while their middle-aged children describe themselves as simply busy. Those at greatest risk for estrangement are parents who don't accept the need for their relationships with their children to change as life changes for their sons and daughters.

While some parents are relieved to be finished with active, daily parenting responsibilities, others struggle with the transition to a different role. It can be emotionally difficult to step from the center of a child's life to the periphery. While some see this as a natural, albeit sometimes wrenching, progression, others see themselves, as one mother described it, as "cast out on an emotional ice floe."

---

*   K. S. Birditt et al., "Tensions in the Parent and Adult Child Relationship: Links to Solidarity and Ambivalence," *Psychology and Aging* 24, no. 2 (2009): 287–295.

Clashes sparked by a family member wanting to freeze time can involve not only parents expecting to continue to occupy central roles in their grown children's lives and decision-making, but also adult children who may expect more support, both emotionally and financially, and for a longer time, than their parents feel comfortable giving.

The father of one twenty-seven-year-old son confided during a therapy session, "I'm afraid he'll never leave, the more time passes. I don't see a lot of progress. He has a retail job and spends whatever he makes. We insist that he pay his own car expenses, cell phone, and the like, but he doesn't pay us rent or for food, and I think he should. He has no sense of what it costs to live in the real world. This is beginning to feel like endless adolescence, and I'm wondering how long this is going to go on…or how long we should allow it to go on. His brother was the same—lived with us until he was almost twenty-nine and then split and hasn't spoken to us since. I don't want to be estranged from my sons. I just want them to grow up and move on."

As this distressed father illustrates, estrangements can happen over differing views of what it means to be grown up.

Jack, forty-two and estranged from his parents for more than two decades, remembers a traumatic coming of age that led to his not wanting his parents to be part of his life. "My dad had this notion that once you turned eighteen, that was it: you were out of the house, totally on your own. But he didn't share this philosophy with me until I was eighteen and ready to start college. No one in my family had ever gone to college. To be fair, they didn't know squat about how to be supportive by helping me get into a dorm (my college was more than five hundred miles from home). My dad gave me twenty-five dollars and a one-way bus ticket to Berkeley. That was it. I arrived in this unfamiliar place with nowhere to live, knowing no one, and with very little money. I ended up living in a transient hotel, washing dishes at a restaurant and, oh yeah, going to classes. I didn't know any other students. I was so totally alone. My loneliness and depression took a toll. I only made it two years. Not getting a degree, not achieving up to my potential has led to such deep regrets. There were a lot of factors in my not making it through college—including my own immaturity and some poor choices. But the major factor was the bad start I got thanks to my dad. I wasn't ready to be so totally on my own. I was willing to work my way through school. But some emotional support and, yes, a little more financial help— which they could easily have given—would have made such a difference. There are a lot of reasons why I don't want to be in touch with my dad (my mother passed away many years ago), but that shocking introduction to adult life is right up there."

So what can you do when development issues have divided you and are threatening to cause or have caused an estrangement?

If You're a Parent, Upset over Your Adult Child's Progression toward Full Adulthood

Realize that the rules have changed: The traditional markers of marriage, parenthood, and a full-time career position—which all hit in one's early twenties back in the day—commonly happen in the later twenties or early thirties these days. And young adults have different measurements of adult development, considering more individualistic characteristics such as the ability to make one's own decisions, to stand on one's own, and to be financially independent as signs of adulthood.

"There is this tendency to do comparisons," says Mary, fifty-six, the mother of three unmarried adult children in their thirties. "I hear myself saying 'But your father and I were married and parents when we were ten years younger than you are now!' And my daughter will say 'Yes, and you were trapped. You didn't finish college. Dad took the first job he could get and has never been happy with it. I want to reach all my personal goals before settling down—so I don't have to settle for a life that isn't what I really want.' And I find it hard to argue with that…though I do wonder if I'll ever have grandchildren…"

Consider the advantages of these changed markers of adulthood: Young people aren't rushing into marriage these days, either for sex or for validation as an adult. It's possible that the tendency of young people to wait for marriage until their late twenties or beyond will lead to more marriage stability and relationships built on love and true partnership rather than the desire to get out of the parental house, making the "starter marriages" of yesteryear obsolete.

Encourage rather than criticize as your young adult child struggles toward full adulthood. Applaud progress rather than noting setbacks. Building a strong new relationship with your adult child means cheering him or her on rather than trying to control the progress and the outcome of their life choices.

"This was a hard lesson to learn," says Ray, fifty-two, the father of two sons in their late twenties. "My older son took several years of temp jobs and failed jobs to find his real career in marketing. When he would quit or lose a job, my first impulse was always 'What? You quit? You got fired? What's the matter with you?' But when I would ask 'Well, what did you learn from this experience?' or 'What do you think you'd like to try next?' we would have some productive discussions. I have learned not to give advice or opinions unless asked. I'll admit, that's still a hard one for me."

Jessica, the mother of a young singer whose career has hit a snag, admits that she, too, struggles to keep unsolicited advice to a minimum. "It's hard to see my bright, talented, college-educated daughter waiting tables to keep solvent while not working, I think, as strategically and aggressively as she could at her singing career. But she hasn't asked what I think, and I'm not opening my mouth with an opinion. She's an adult. I've learned to take a deep breath and hope for the best—trying to see the best outcome as *she* sees it!"

In a nonpunitive way, be clear with your adult child about the limits of your ability to help. While your adult child may take longer to reach the markers of adulthood, whether those expectations are yours or his, you may well have your limits about how and for how long you will fund what looks like a prolonged adolescence. If, for example, your adult child has settled back into his childhood room and shows scant evidence of progress toward goals for independent adult living, it's time to set some limits.

Josh, a twenty-year-old college student who left school to return to his parents' home to write a novel, quickly settled into a pattern of playing video games well into the night and sleeping until noon each day. In five months, he produced only a few pages of a young adult novel. "I know my parents, especially my dad, are upset about my dropping out of college," he says. "But you don't need a degree to be a novelist. I'm working at it. But you can't rush inspiration. I figure that this is a perfect time to give writing a shot. Both of my parents are working and making good money. I don't have any obligations. There will never be a time in my life when I'm as free to experiment as now."

His parents agree that this is a good time for Josh to take risks, but they're growing impatient with what they see as a lack of motivation or sincere effort.

"If I could see any measurable progress on the novel, I would be fine with this," says his father Steve. "But we're working our butts off and he's sleeping and playing video games and then calling to ask us to pick up a pizza for him on the way home from work? Uh-uh. Not what we agreed to. I told him that we won't always be around to work and support him while he waits for inspiration. Thus, he has thirty days to either get a part-time job to keep him in pizzas or return to school. I support his dreams of being a writer—though secretly I wish he'd go for a more financially stable profession—but I don't support laziness and wasting time."

As this book goes to press, there is a postscript to this story: Josh found a part-time clerical job, which he kept for about six months before he decided that being a novelist might not be for him. He returned to college to prepare for an IT career. "The writing thing was harder than I thought," he wrote recently. "And I hated working for so little in that boring clerical job. I want a job in an area of interest to me, and I also want to make decent money so I can have cool stuff and just not have to worry. So I'm going to work with computers. Maybe I'll try some writing on the side again someday. Or maybe not."

For Josh and his family, setting limits enabled him to get a sense of what life could be like with financial uncertainty or feeling trapped in a boring job.

Another family set limits around a parent's timetable.

Alan, a doctor who essentially lost his first family in an acrimonious divorce, treasured his second family of two children, who were born when he was well into his forties. Now he is seventy and hoping to retire in two to three years. But his twenty-eight-year-old son Kevin is still at home, having dropped out of college and made the decision that his future lies in filmmaking. He has taken a few courses in film, but mostly sits in his boyhood room, smoking pot, listening to music, and waiting for his dreams of being the next Quentin Tarantino to materialize into fame and fortune.

Alan finally sat down with his son to talk about the future. "I told him that I believe in his talent and imagination," he says. "But I also said that I am planning to retire in three years and will be unable to support him beyond that time. I said that, in the meantime, I would pay his tuition at film school, fund a student film, help him in whatever way I could. But that he could not continue to sit in his room doing nothing toward his goal. I suggested that he get a low-level job in the industry just to get his foot in the door. He got surly, as he always does, asking why he should have to get a shit gofer job when he is a genius. I was ready for him this time, telling him that I had read that Quentin Tarantino started out in retail, working at a movie memorabilia and video store, his love for movies so apparent that it caught the attention of some people in the industry. He's looking into that story—doesn't quite believe it—but is also looking seriously at film schools. So we make progress."

If You're an Adult Child Caught up in Conflict over Your Adult Development Timetable

Recognize that your parents' reality of what it means to be an adult is no less valid than yours, though rooted in a different time. It's important to honor their point of view. It made sense when they were younger. Times were different. It was possible to support a family on one salary, even if one had only a high school education. Premarital sex was frowned upon and logistically difficult with both young people still living with their parents. So marriage was liberating then in a way it isn't necessarily today.

Now there are many paths toward independence, and what it means to be an adult to this generation is more individualistic—attainable through your own efforts, with no potential partner required. So you can find your passion, make your own choices (and mistakes), and achieve varying measures of financial independence often before even considering marriage. Consider yourself fortunate to be coming of age now rather at the time your parents were young. Despite tough economic times and the burden of student loans, you're lucky to be in the resourceful and intelligent Gen-Xer or Millennial generations.

Coming from that sense of strength and confidence, try talking with your parents about your own sense of what it means to be an adult while letting them know that you also value and hope to attain their markers of adulthood—marriage, parenthood, a career position—but in your own way and in your own time.

When asking for parental help, don't make assumptions about their ability or willingness to help and equate it with their love for you. Your parents may love you very much, but may not be able or willing to support you financially for years to come as you struggle to find your true calling in life. If you would like to move home for a time or go back to school or take the risk of trying for a career that pays too little to support you in its beginning stages, let your parents know what you would like and then listen to their take on what's possible for them.

Perhaps, like Josh's family, they can keep a roof over your head while you work part-time to earn money to cover basic expenses while pursuing your dream. If you can agree on a partnership toward your goal—rather than assuming that if they loved you, they'd offer a free ride—your chances of meeting your goals and of preserving your relationship with your parents are greater.

Make steady (even if slow) progress toward full adulthood, both for your own positive sense of self and to reassure your parents (and keep them off your back). Becoming a full adult is a process, and part of that process is learning to take responsibility for your own choices and your own mistakes. That can mean taking the initiative in finding a career path, or at least a transition job to keep you solvent in the meantime. It can mean admitting when you've made a mistake, not blaming others for it, and reflecting on how things might be different the next time around. It can mean asking for advice from others, but not running to your parents to be bailed out of a difficult situation. It can mean taking increasing financial responsibility for yourself and then, someday, finding that you're totally financially independent and fully adult.

If You're an Adult Child Caught in a Conflict over Clashing Developmental Stages

Be assured that your wishes and your priorities are valid. It's normal and natural, as an increasingly independent young adult, to give time and importance to your own education, career development, friends, romantic relationships, and time just to be, to explore the intricacies of the adult person you're growing to be. You love your parents. You don't want to hurt or disappoint them. But the key to a healthy relationship is not invariably to put their wishes above your own. There are certain developmental tasks you face right now that are critical to your future well-being. You need to create your own individual life, develop your career, spend time with or search for that special person to love, and create a strong and loving circle of friends, some of whom may be with you for the rest of your life. This all takes time and energy. It doesn't mean shutting your parents out of your life, to be sure. But it does mean that they may no longer be at the center of your new adult life.

Establish a routine for keeping in touch with your parents and stick to it as much as possible. This may mean a phone call at regular intervals and texting in between. It may mean showing up for a family dinner or special celebrations. It may also mean setting limits with your parents, letting them know what feels reasonable for you. This may mean being in touch but not necessarily visiting every week. It may mean asking your mother to please not call you at work, where personal phone calls are discouraged and time doesn't permit a prolonged conversation. It may mean asking your parents to call before showing up at your apartment, emphasizing that you want to be sure to be home and/or able to devote your full attention to them. (It may not be quite so productive to add that it's so frustrating and embarrassing when you're there with your boyfriend, anticipating an evening of passion, and your parents show up unexpectedly!)

Change your behavior and patterns of relating to your parents to avoid sliding into patterns of the past. One of the markers of being an adult is establishing an adult relationship with your parents. Talk to them as you would another adult. Continuing to see your parents only in the parental role relegates you to the child role. If it seems they always treat you like a kid, ask yourself if, once you walk in the door of the family home, you revert to childish or adolescent behavior. Think of how you talk to friends and colleagues. Use that tone and that sense of respect with your parents, too. You may find that they begin to treat you like an adult as well.

Surprise your parents with evidence that you're thinking of them in ways that are meaningful to them. Write notes, letters, and cards that express love or humor or sweet "just thinking of you" sentiments. These don't have to be long or elaborate. A few lines can do wonders. Never underestimate the power of snail mail in reassuring your parents that all is well and that you love them, are thinking of them, and want them to be a part of your new life. Text, email, send fun attachments and photos. Don't assume they can just follow your life and adventures via Facebook. Do something special to help them to feel included. This can be especially important when you sense that they want much more time with you than you are able to give at the moment. Never underestimate what making a little effort to stay connected can mean to them.

I remember, during my own busy youth, realizing that my favorite aunt, who had never married or had children of her own—and who had lost her best friend and only sibling when my mother and father both died at young ages—was becoming wistful about being very much in touch with my siblings and me. She was an intelligent, independent woman with her own interests and a great circle of friends. And yet, as she grew older, she yearned for more time with us, wanting to stay a part of our changing lives. I called her regularly, and we got together as often as possible, which was probably never enough as far as she was concerned, though she never complained. In the times in between, I sent her notes, letters, and cards, letting her know I was thinking of her and how much I loved her.

After she died at the age of eighty-six, and my husband and I were cleaning out her house, I opened the drawer of the end table by her bed. There, tied up with ribbons, were bundles of those notes and letters and cards I had sent—treasured more than I had ever realized at the time.

So these little gestures that say "I'm thinking of you and I love you!" can mean so very much to parents and other loved ones who need your love and reassurance ever more as time passes.

If You're a Parent Caught in Conflict over Clashing Life Stages and Expectations

Accept the fact that your life and your children's lives are changing and that these changes are necessary. In growing toward independence, our children leave us in stages. Think back in time to how life changed when your baby became a toddler, when your child started school, when friends became newly important in his or her sometimes distant and sullen adolescence. This need for distance grows in young adulthood as the adult child begins to make more and more decisions without our input, have friends we may or may not ever meet, and have life experiences and adventures that we never share, except in their recounting.

In building their independent young adult lives, they are learning to live without us, preparing for that distinct possibility that a major portion of their lives will, indeed, be lived without us. Their ability to stand on their own, now and in the future, is critical to their continuing well-being. And as their lives change, ours do too, as we step back from daily parenting to a more hands-off, but no less loving relationship.

Think back and remember how it felt to be caught in between parents' or in-laws' needs and expectations. You may feel hurt, frustrated, and sometimes very much alone as your adult children move on with their lives. Think back for a moment to your own young adulthood.

Your first thoughts might be "Yes! I was totally different. I spent a lot of time with my mother. I never missed going for Sunday dinner or including her in our plans." But think back to your feelings at the time. Did you always go willingly, or did you feel coerced? Did you have more time to offer attention to your parents as well as to your own growing family? Did you make your decisions with joy or with a sense of dread and obligation? And, looking back, would you make the same choices again?

Betsy, for one, says she wouldn't. Now sixty-two and a grandmother of five, Betsy looks back wistfully on all the family adventures she, her husband, and their four children might have had, if only they hadn't felt obligated to spend every bit of vacation time they had visiting with both sets of parents. "Mostly, it was a pleasure to spend time with our parents and to have our children really know and love their grandparents," she says. "But I wish— maybe just once or twice when the children were young—that we had taken a trip, just the six of us, to someplace else, someplace like Disney World or a national park or a beach resort. It would have meant so much to build our own memories like that as a family. I felt bad when my daughter skipped her visit with me this spring to take the kids to Washington, DC, to spend a week at museums. But, oh, to hear their stories about this adventure together! I understand. I wish I had had the courage to say 'No, not this time' to my own parents and in-laws. Even though I wasn't happy when the trip precluded *my* time with my daughter and her family, I do understand the importance of their choice."

Speak to your adult child as an adult, not a child. Now that your son or daughter is an adult, the parental voice of authority needs to soften into that of a friend. Give advice when asked. Make requests, not demands. Share observations tactfully. Don't rush in to correct or criticize. Let your adult child know that you care, that you will always be there for him or her. Then step back and give him or her space to make choices and decisions with or without your help. This sends the message that you have increasing faith and confidence in him as an emerging adult.

Don't equate time spent with love. Time an adult child spends with you is not always the measure of his or her love for you. An adult child can be living across the country, busy with his or her own growing family, frantically involved with building a career, and yet love you deeply and forever. Be aware of signs of that love in stories shared, phone calls or letters, or the simple knowledge that they're raising their children with the same loving attention that you once gave them.

Keep in mind, too, that feeling that love from a distance and freeing your adult children to live their lives can cause love to grow in new ways. It can be critical to forging a lasting and loving bond with your grown son or daughter.

I found this to be true many years ago after a relative scolded me harshly for not spending more time with my mother, whose initially subtle physical decline coincided with the busy, heady days of my young adulthood. Chastened and ashamed, I went to my mother and apologized for not spending more time with her. She touched my cheek gently. "The most wonderful way you can show your love is to live your life fully and joyfully," she said. "Of course I love hearing from you. I'm always eager to hear about your latest adventure. But most of all, I just want you to enjoy your life and being young and looking forward to so much in the future."

I embraced her tearfully and with an immense sense of relief. In freeing me to live my life, she made me more willing and likely to make her a larger part of it and, in the many years I have lived without her, I remember her with immense love and gratitude.

Reframe your perceptions. If you're like most parents, you're not at the center of your adult child's life these days. It may seem that, as far as your adult children are concerned, everything and everybody else comes first. You may find yourself calling and leaving a message that starts "It's just your mother…" You may feel hurt when an adult child makes plans that don't include you. Or you may simply have the feeling that your grown son or daughter is moving on and leaving you behind. And you may be feeling sad and increasingly angry.

But instead of ruminating about how you're being relegated to the sidelines, think about it as having a front-row seat to cheer them on.

It's their time to shine, to savor new experiences, to explore a world of opportunities. There may well be times when you watch anxiously, often wistfully, from the sidelines. But as their lives change, so must yours.

To resist change, to hang on desperately to what was, is to risk conflict and estrangement. In letting go, setting them free and cheering them on, you may find that you're growing even closer in new ways to your adult children.

CHAPTER THREE
Life Paths Taken or Not Taken

Family conflicts and estrangements can arise suddenly—in the wake of startling revelations. Or they can come over time with the erosion of long-held plans and dreams.

Are the life paths of adult children—or of parents—diverging from your fondest hopes?

Divergent life paths and values may be an estrangement trigger for you if:

+ Your son or daughter has decided against college or dropped out and has a dream for the future that is at odds with what you had so hoped for him or her.
+ Your son or daughter has come out to you as gay, lesbian, or transgender, and you're still in shock or denial, furious, or just immensely sad.

+ Your adult child has converted to another religion or become a non-believer, agnostic, or even an atheist, after being raised in the faith that has been a vital part of your family's life for generations.

+ Your parents are putting pressure on you to follow a certain career path—and you're just not feeling it.

+ It has taken you years to be honest with your parents about who you are, and their reaction to your truth has been devastating.

+ You've decided that marriage may not be for you, but parenthood might be, and your parents just can't deal.

+ You and your spouse have decided against having children, and your parents are piling on the guilt and grief about not being grandparents.

+ Your semiestrangement is rooted in your heated arguments during the last presidential election, which continue to this day with such vehemence that it's becoming too painful to spend much time together.

+ Your split has become more than geographic as you feel deep hurt that your child would even think of taking a job in another state…or that your parents would dream of retiring too far away to be part of your children's lives on a daily basis.

It is hard to let go of a dream: the dream of a specific achievement you've had for your child for years; the dream of acceptance despite differing lifestyles; the dream of values shared, thoughts aligned. It is painful when your life paths veer apart, whether you're a parent or an adult child.

When Goals and Dreams Diverge

It can be hard to separate your own needs, goals, and dreams from those your parents have for you or, if you're a parent, to recognize that your fervent hopes for your adult child may not be shared. Sometimes it's a matter of differing interests and inclinations or differing long-term goals.

"I was an English major in my two years of college, and that ended up being pretty much useless in terms of a job," says Shana, the forty-five-year-old mother of eighteen-year-old college freshman Kayleigh. "I want my daughter to be able to get a degree that means something, like something that will translate into a well-paying job. I want her to major in engineering or to do pre-med or pre-law. I want her to be financially independent, free to make choices in other areas of her life that aren't motivated by financial necessity."

Kayleigh, who has barely spoken to her mother in the month since she registered for her school's liberal arts curriculum, has a different view. "I wouldn't major in something I don't like just so I can make more money," she says. "Money isn't my motivation in life. I want to find a career that fits me. I want to be able to look forward to work every day instead of dreading it. And if I were an engineer or a lawyer, I'd be dreading it. I don't think that's how I want to live my life."

In this instance, the differences of goals and dreams are clear. But sometimes, the disconnect and disenchantment don't come for years.

"I went into advertising because that's what my dad did and what he thought I should do, too," says Marty, thirty-eight, who describes himself as "a recovering ad man."

"It wasn't that I always said 'Yes!' to my dad," he adds. "It was just that I didn't know what else I might want to do and what might be available to me. But I wasn't living the life I wanted to live. I wasn't taking care of myself physically. I wasn't a treat to live with, as my former girlfriend let me know very clearly before she left. I went into therapy and over time decided that I wanted to become a psychotherapist. I went back to school at night while continuing to work in advertising. It was a tough time, managing school and work and internships. But it's a whole new life for me now. I love what I do. I feel that my life has meaning. The only problem now is that my parents aren't on board, and we're sort of on the outs as a result. They don't believe in therapy and think this is all bogus. And, of course, I'm not earning big bucks—which doesn't bother me. But it does upset them. My mom says that she just wants me to be happy. But she doesn't see how I could be happy living very simply. And I think she's afraid that I'll never get married now that I'm not making lots of money. But I don't want to be with the kind of woman who would be attracted to me because of a high income."

Some parents—whose adult children are drifting aimlessly without job skills or career directions, or have dropped out of school to hit the rodeo circuit or seek rock stardom—would be less likely than Marty's parents to object to a graduate degree and profession, even though it might veer somewhat from their original dreams. But some parents are devastated when very specific and inflexible expectations aren't met.

One mother in particular comes to mind. She wrote to me recently to complain: "I had always dreamed that my son would become a doctor or lawyer, but he has chosen to become an architect! I'm so upset, I find it difficult to talk to him lately."

But most often estrangement triggers come from less specific, but nonetheless heartfelt dreams unfulfilled: a child who chooses, for reasons hard to understand, to forgo higher education; parents who refuse to help or support a young adult child in seeking a college education or job training; parents who scoff at and dismiss youthful dreams; adult children who insist on making their own mistakes—over and over again.

If You're a Frustrated Parent

Accept the fact that you can't revisit or relive your own dreams through your children. It's tempting, especially if you spot talent and special abilities in your child that match your own untapped potential, to try to steer him or her in that direction. It's also tempting to want your children to benefit from your own hard-won wisdom or to follow a dream you've long regretted letting go. But their dreams may not be the same as yours.

From an early age, Nicole, now nineteen, was a regular in beauty pageants and, urged on by her ambitious mother, pursued acting and modeling careers. "It was what she had always wanted to do," Nicole says. "I hated every bit of it, especially being judged [for my looks] by everyone I encountered. I worked some in commercials and on television but mostly I experienced criticism, rejection, and the awful sight of disappointment in my mother's eyes. I don't know exactly what I want to do with my life, but I'm very clear about what I *don't* want!"

You may find yourself frustrated when an adult child pursues a way of life that you worked hard to avoid. "I saw my mother suffer so much as a 1950s housewife," says Jana, a successful attorney and mother of Amy, a twenty-eight-year-old stay-at-home mother of two young children. "I saw my mother's economic dependence, her lack of options in an unhappy marriage, and I didn't want any part of it. I worked during my marriage and after the divorce. I feel I'm in control of my life and frustrated that Amy has been so quick and so happy to relinquish control over her own destiny."

Amy's take on the situation is quite different. "I have an education and skills," she says. "Staying home with my children is a choice for now. My grandmother didn't really have a similar choice. She married at eighteen. She had no outside job ever. She was in an unhappy marriage. I'm happy. I chose this freely. My marriage is loving and solid. My children are doing wonderfully. I'm exactly where I want and need to be at this point in my life. In ten or twenty years, things could change. I probably will go back to work at some point. I don't know why my mother can't see that I'm doing what makes sense to me right now."

Ask, don't tell. Encourage your young adult children to share their hopes, dreams, and goals with you, and listen without challenging them, even if they seem unattainable or impossibly far-fetched. If your son aspires to rock stardom, ask if he has a plan for getting there, what needs to happen between dreaming and actual work toward his goal, and how you might help, within reason. Particularly if your young adult aspires to a highly competitive career in the entertainment industry, ask which steps come soon, which come later, and about any contingency plans for self-support in the meantime. Ask about a Plan B or Plan C if, despite his best efforts, his dreams hit a snag. But don't tell him what to do. Ask what his plan is and express your support. Offer opinions only if asked, and even then, preface them with "Have you thought about…?" or "I'm wondering if…"

Don't allow fears about what others will think to dictate your reactions to an adult child's life plans. This is especially important to remember when your young adult is following a career path quite different from the plans of other young family members or the children of friends.

Jason's parents are high school sweethearts who married right after graduation and have spent their working lives in local factories. They had hoped for a different future for their son: that he would go to college and follow a profession like his two cousins. "I found in high school that I totally love woodworking," Jason says. "I want to be involved in making furniture and eventually have my own custom-furniture and wall-unit business. I love working with my hands and having something to show for it. And I'm really good at this. I would be so happy to do this my whole life. I'm not a good student. I don't think I'm meant for college. I don't understand why my parents are so disappointed. Their wish to be able to brag to their friends about my college degree or whatever should be much less important to them, I think, than whether or not I'm happy in my work and in my life."

Let your adult child feel your support and your faith in him or her. It can be a delicate balance—having your concerns about an adult child's career directions and yet expressing faith in him whatever happens.

Mark's parents discovered how difficult this balance could be when they were listening to their twenty-two-year-old son's plans to pursue an acting career. "When I heard my mother's sharp intake of breath as I talked about being an actor, I felt like she was saying that I had no talent, that I didn't have a chance. I mean, she did a little acting herself back in the day. So just the way she reacted, without saying anything, upset me."

Mark's mother Erin was finally able to explain her feelings of both concern and faith in her son. "My first reaction was negative, but not because I don't think that he has talent. He does—and I truly believe in his talent. It's just that I know how hard it can be to try to make it in the acting business. I know a lot of very talented people who are still waiting tables, driving taxis, and parking cars in middle age, still waiting for the big break that they so deserve but probably never will have," she says. "I hate to see my son go through that kind of pain—having the talent, working so hard, and yet having so much of one's destiny be a matter of luck or who you know or having a certain look that's all the rage. Of course, I believe in him. He's talented and disciplined. He has a good chance. I want to encourage him and see him succeed. I just hope this business doesn't break his spirit—or his heart."

If You're a Frustrated, Perhaps Estranged, Adult Child

Don't immediately assume that a parent's concern about your goals and plans signals a lack of confidence in you and your abilities. It's important to understand that their caution, concern, and seeming lack of enthusiasm may be coming from love and fear for you rather than from a lack of faith in you. Give them the benefit of the doubt, and don't lash back. Try to clarify what they mean when they express concern and ask their opinions about your plans, even if you disagree. Hearing them out may give you some ideas or a reality check that can help you make even more solid plans and goals for the future. Or not. But your willingness to listen to their views may make them more willing to listen to yours.

Show your maturity and determination to succeed by having a detailed plan and sharing this with your parents. It isn't enough for them—or for you—to simply say "I want to be a filmmaker (or actor, writer, musician, etc.)." If you can show your parents that you have thought this out, that you have a solid, reasonable plan for training, for breaking into the business, and for building a career, they will be more likely to be supportive.

They may never understand why you'd want to do this rather than to stay in your hometown and work in the family business, but they may be somewhat reassured that you're not simply headed to New York or Los Angeles with your guitar and a dream. And having a Plan B in mind if that big break is delayed or never comes can help ease their minds (and possibly your own).

Realize that as a young adult, you're responsible for your own choices. If your parents aren't supportive of your dreams for the future, that may be disappointing. It may even change how you approach your goals if you had hoped for their financial support. But their lack of support doesn't have to change what you feel is right for you.

"My falling-out with my parents has been due to a long history of feeling dismissed because I'm female," says forty-one-year-old Jody. "They weren't being mean. They were just locked into a very different time and mindset. They happily sent my brother to college but told me they wouldn't do the same for me, that my option was to take a secretarial course and get really good at typing. I realized that if I wanted to go to college, I would have to do it on my own. So I worked and went to the local community college. Still working, I transferred to our state college. It took me eight years to get my BA degree, but I got it and a master's degree as well. I'm a high school English teacher and love it. I reached my goal my way. I'd say 'No thanks to my parents!' But they unwittingly helped propel me forward by making me so mad, I was just determined to make my dream happen."

Allow your parents the same freedom of choice that you'd like them to show you. Particularly if they're nearing retirement, your parents may have their own dreams and goals that are divergent from your visions of their parenting and grandparenthood.

"When my parents told me that they're planning to sell the house I grew up in and move to Arizona, I was in shock," says Jennifer, the mother of three young sons. "I had this dream that my boys would grow up with grandparents they saw every day. I imagined them having overnights at the old house and making cookies with their grandma and celebrating birthdays and holidays together. Every time I think of their moving more than a thousand miles away, I feel like crying."

It's important to keep in mind that dreams and visions aren't always in sync. Many older couples want to travel or live in warm-weather resort-like settings or have more time just with each other.

"We were living our lives as Grandma and Grandpa, babysitting our various grandkids on a daily basis," says Arvilla, seventy-two, who moved from Washington state to Arizona eight years ago. "On one level, it was great. We love our grandchildren so much! But we looked at each other one day, and my husband, who married me when I was a young, divorced, single parent, said 'You know, we've never had a chance to just be a couple, to build a daily life that was truly ours.' As it turns out, we had to move in order to make that happen. We see the children and the grands at least three or four times a year, visiting back and forth. But I think this move has been advantageous to all, though it took a while for our kids to realize that."

WHEN YOUR VALUES CLASH

The Trump/Clinton presidential race was the final straw for Jessica Anderson's difficult relationship with her parents.

"Our problems go back a long time," the thirty-two-year-old administrative assistant admits. "I've always found their worldview problematic: mean-spirited, racist, narrow-minded. But their vociferous support of Trump and all his verbal garbage was just too much for me. I can't bear to hear what they have to say. They can't tolerate my views. It's sad. They're my parents and, on one level, I love them. But I can't stand to be around them!"

Quite often, political dissension between parents and adult children reveals a divide in a number of values and beliefs about what we owe each other and what we don't, the role the government should or shouldn't play in our lives, the rights of both generations to have and voice opinions, and how central—or not—the role of parents may be in influencing values and worldviews now that children are grown.

While such disagreements over politics and generational power can be quite divisive, threatened or existing parent and adult child estrangements are more often the result of clashing values over religion.

Religious beliefs loom large in estrangements. As we saw in the first chapter, a study by Dr. Megan Gilligan of Iowa State University and her colleagues revealed that clashes of values—religious differences significantly among these—were a frequent factor in parent–adult child estrangement. Mothers especially tended to be much more tolerant of adult children with police records or drug problems than they were of sons or daughters who violated or rejected major tenets of their faith.*

The generational shift in religious beliefs and affiliations is a major factor in these value clashes. According to findings by Pew Research Center's second U.S. Religious Landscape Study, the percentage of adults over eighteen who describe themselves as Christian declined 8 percentage points—from 78.4 percent to 70.6 percent—in the seven years between Pew's first religious study in 2007 and its second survey in 2014. At the same time, the percentage of adults describing themselves as religiously unaffiliated, atheist, or agnostic increased more than six points—from 16.1 percent to 22.8 percent. Some age groups showed higher levels of non-affiliation: 36 percent of those between the ages of eighteen and twenty-four; 34 percent of those between the ages of twenty-five and thirty-three. The median age of mainstream Protestant adults is fifty-two, and the median age of Catholic adults is forty-nine.†

The 2014 Pew Research Center Study also found that, among those adults who identified as Christian, many had switched from their childhood faith. For example, if all Protestants were considered to be a single religious group, then 34 percent of American

---

*   Megan Gilligan, J. Jill Suitor, Karl Pillemer, "Estrangement between Mothers and Adult Children: The Role of Norms and Values," *Journal of Marriage and Family* 77, no. 4 (August 2015): 908–920.

†   Pew Research Center, *U.S. Religious Landscape Study 2014* (May 12, 2015).

adults currently have a religious identity different from the faith of their childhood. That is up six points since the 2007 survey.

The researchers found that religious intermarriage was also on the rise. Of those marrying between 2010 and 2014, 39 percent reported that they were in religiously mixed marriages, compared with 19 percent who got married before 1960. Many of the most recent intermarriages are between Christian and religiously unaffiliated spouses. Only 5 percent of people marrying before 1960 fit that profile.

While these figures are interesting, what matters here most are the stories and feelings behind these statistics: the shock, the tears, the anger, and the broken hearts.

"It isn't just a difference of opinion to me," says Anne, the mother of a twenty-two-year-old daughter who recently told her parents that she was disavowing their evangelical faith and considered herself agnostic. "I really believe in the Rapture and want our whole family being taken up and no one left behind. It terrifies me that Marianne is walking away from our faith, from everything that really matters to us. In our family, we can tolerate a lot of differences and disagreements, but when my daughter is jeopardizing her eternal life, I'm shocked and…just devastated."

Therese's reaction to her son's departure from the Catholic faith is similar. "We've built our family life around the Church," she says, her eyes filling with tears. "His turning his back on the Church is turning his back on us."

Her son Jason, twenty-six, is sad about his parents' reaction to his decision to leave his childhood religion. "I'm not rejecting

God or faith," he says. "I'm just fed up with the corruption, hypocrisy, and the politics of the Catholic Church. I'm sick of their social policies. I'm angry about all those priests abusing children and then being protected from prosecution. I'm upset about the Church's treatment of women. I just joined a wonderful Episcopalian church. There is a female pastor who is a real social activist, and so is her community. I really like that. To me, that's what religion should be all about: standing up for what's right and sharing and giving joyously."

Not all religious differences are between devout parents and adult children who have differing views. Sometimes religiously unaffiliated parents can be blindsided by conflict with an adult child who has converted to an unfamiliar religious domination, such as an evangelical or Jehovah's Witness congregation.

"We always believed that it was each person's right to choose a religion for themselves," says Juanita, sixty-two, who is currently facing an intermittent estrangement from her eldest daughter Alicia, thirty-seven, who is married to an evangelical Christian. "We aren't antireligious. But our son-in-law thinks we're heathens, is quite controlling, and this has kept us mostly estranged for years. It isn't that we disagree with their faith. We're fine with whatever they choose to believe. We would embrace them—both of them—if they came to visit. But he doesn't want her to be mingling with nonbelievers. It breaks my heart."

What can you do if a clash of values—most likely religious differences—is keeping you apart?

Ideas for Parents and Adult Children

Don't try to convert your religious parents (or adult child) to your way of thinking…or to minimize the impact that leaving the religion of your childhood for another may have on your parents. Deeply held beliefs and lives built around a church community are precious to many. These are part of their identity and often a vital support. You may have decided this isn't for you, but that doesn't mean that others in your family must follow suit in order to have a relationship with you. Tread gently when you announce that you're switching from the Catholic to the Methodist church or converting to Judaism. You have your own good reasons for doing so and may be converting with a joyous heart. But, particularly if your parents' lives revolve to a large extent around the faith of your childhood, your conversion isn't easy news to absorb. Don't expect that they will greet this happily. Don't assume that their reserve or their grief is a rejection. It may take some time for them to absorb this change in your life.

Show curiosity, not contempt. If your adult child is rejecting your faith, either as an atheist or agnostic or having joined another church, don't yell, scream, or berate him or her. Express curiosity about how your adult child arrived at this decision. How has he come to his set of beliefs? What troubled her about the faith of her childhood? Listen without interrupting or arguing. To understand what's going on with your adult child, you do need to listen. You do need to avoid putting barriers of anger and rejection between you if you want to continue to have a relationship.

Don't engage in preaching or threats of hellfire and damnation. If you're frightened for your nonbelieving adult child's spiritual and eternal future, it can be tempting to haul out the major threats. But the problem is that your agnostic or atheist child no longer believes in the Rapture or in hell or in any possibility of eternal damnation. All of your concerns will go in one ear and out the other as the adult child simply shuts you out, hearing your words not as fear and genuine concern but as mindless ranting. Take a deep breath and leave your Bible where it is. Your adult child grew up reading the Bible and hearing the tenets of your faith. His departure may not be forever. And even if he or she never comes back to your family's faith, some of what you taught and what your adult child embraced years ago will always be part of him or her.

Share your feelings in a loving way. You may certainly express feelings of shock or sadness or disappointment, but it's also important to express your love for your adult child, however far apart your values and beliefs may be.

"What I said to my daughter, who left the Catholic Church three years ago, is 'I feel so sad because this is something we've always shared as a family,'" says Lisa. "I told her that I loved her and would always love her even when I don't understand. And that seemed to help heal or begin to heal the growing rift between us."

Avoid ultimatums. This is an especially important piece of advice for parents. Remember the research cited in chapter 1 that found that parents have a greater emotional stake in maintaining their relationships with their adult children than the young adults do with their parents?* If you issue ultimatums, insisting that in order to have a relationship with you, your adult children need to think and feel and believe as you do, you may find that your adult child no longer wants or chooses to have a relationship with you.

WHEN YOU'RE AT ODDS OVER SEXUALITY

The day that Carla's nineteen-year-old son told her that he was gay "was the loneliest day of my life," she remembers. "He told me and then, when I didn't react the way he had hoped, he stormed out of the house. I was sitting there in shock. I hadn't said anything. I just started crying. There wasn't anyone I knew that I felt I could share this information with and talk it over. I just sat there and cried, afraid for my son and afraid that this would come between us."

Despite Carla's sense of being alone, many parents have shared her experience and her feelings. An estimated 9 million Americans, representing 3.5 percent of adults in the U.S., a figure roughly equivalent to the population of New Jersey, identify as gay, lesbian, bisexual, or transgender.[†]

---

*   K. S. Birditt et al,. "Tensions in the Parent and Adult Child Relationship: Links to Solidarity and Ambivalence," *Psychology and Aging* 24, no. 2 (2009): 287–295.

†   Gary J. Gates, "How Many People Are Lesbian, Gay, Bisexual, and Transgender?" Williams Institute on Sexual Orientation and Gender Identity Law, UCLA School of Law (April 2011), https://williamsinstitute.law.ucla.edu/wp-content/uploads/Gates-How-Many-People -LGBT-Apr-2011.pdf.

That's a lot of families and parents who have had a beloved child come out. A significant number, however, have yet to hear the news. A Pew Research Center survey of LGBT American adults found that 56 percent of those surveyed had told their mothers about their sexual orientation, and only 39 percent had told their fathers. The researchers noted that those who had told their parents said that it was difficult, but relatively few reported that this disclosure had damaged their relationship with a parent.

Most of those surveyed had spent a lot of time living with their feelings and emerging identity before sharing this information with parents. The findings: twelve was the median age when gay, lesbian, or bisexual adults had the first inkling that they might not be heterosexual; seventeen was the median age when they knew for sure what their sexual orientation was. And those who had come out to a family member or close friend did not do so until the median age of twenty.[‡] So, by the time a young adult shares this information with a parent, the answer to the often-asked question "Are you sure?" is "Yes!" They know, by that time, that their sexuality is not just a passing phase but part of their identity.

How parents react to this news can have a major impact on a young adult's health and safety as well as the future of the parent–adult child relationship. In a 2013 study, the Pew Research Center surveyed gays and lesbians regarding their difficulty with coming out to parents. The findings: 74 percent of gay men reported that

---

‡   George Gao, "Most Americans Now Say Learning Their Child Is Gay Wouldn't Upset Them," Pew Research Center, June 29, 2015, http://www.pewresearch.org/fact-tank/2015/06/29/most-americans-now-say-learning-their-child-is-gay-wouldnt-upset-them/.

it was tough to come out to their fathers, and 64 percent said that it was difficult to come out to their mothers. Coming out to fathers was difficult for 63 percent of lesbians polled, while 64 percent said that it was tough to come out to their mothers.*

So what is a parent—or a young adult—to do when hearing or delivering this news?

If You're the Parent of a Gay, Lesbian, Bisexual, or Transgender Adult Child

Accept the fact that change is off the table. Many parents go through a period of denial, thinking that this is just a phase, an attempt to be trendy, or the result of falling in with the wrong crowd. Some urge their adult children to seek help from counseling services purporting to change homosexual adults to heterosexual adults. The problem with this way of thinking is that, while a very highly motivated person might be able to change his or her sexual *behavior*, no amount of counseling or preaching can change what a person feels inside. Sexual orientation is an intrinsic part of a person's identity. And by the time your adult child comes out to you, this is most likely to be a fact of his or her life, not a theory or a passing phase.

Know that taking this information in and finding a way to be accepting and supportive of your adult child may take time. Many parents are in shock when they first hear the news. Some

---

*   Gao, "Most Americans Now Say Learning Their Child Is Gay Wouldn't Upset Them."

need time to grieve the loss of the vision they had for their adult child and themselves: a heterosexual marriage, biological grandchildren. Keep in mind that times are changing, and gays and lesbians are able to marry and, in many cases, have families. But if you're sitting there grief-stricken and shocked, try to express love for your adult child while asking for time to pull your thoughts together. It's better to ask for time than to blurt out comments or questions that are hurtful. Those can cause a rift between you even as you struggle to reconnect.

Evan's mother found out by accident that her twenty-seven-year-old son was gay: when she was helping him unpack after a move, she came across naked pictures of him and his college roommate, supposedly "just a good friend." She reeled with shock and ruminated all day about this horrifying discovery. When Evan came home from work, she met him at the door, screaming "I wish you were dead! I'd rather see you dead than homosexual! I wish we had never adopted you!"

Although Evan and his mother eventually reconciled and she became quite accepting of his sexual orientation and his eventual life partner, the memory of that raw moment lingered for years between them.

For many parents, fear of the special challenges their gay son or daughter may face in this society, rather than disapproval, may prompt initial negative reactions when their adult children come out to them.

Rachel Wahba, a psychotherapist and writer noted for her blog posts and articles about Iraqi Jewish history, has known the pain of difference and dislocation on a very personal level. She has both a traumatic family history of fleeing murderous oppression and, later on, her own experience of coming out as a lesbian to parents who were from the Middle East.

Her mother was sixteen during the infamous Baghdad Farhud in June 1941. In rampages sparked by the collapse of the pro-Nazi government of Rasid Ali, violent mobs swept through the city's Jewish quarter, murdering hundreds of Jews and destroying thousands of Jewish homes and businesses. After several days of hiding on their rooftop to avoid the violent mobs, Rachel's mother and her family fled for their lives to India, where, some years later, Rachel was born. After World War II, the family fled once again, this time to Japan, where they lived stateless for twenty years until finally being allowed to emigrate to the United States.

When, as a young adult, Rachel came out to her parents as a lesbian, her mother declared that this revelation was "worse than the Farhud." Rachel was stunned, disbelieving. How could anything be worse than the Farhud? In time, her mother was able to explain what seemed to be an extreme reaction: that she had feared her beloved daughter being hurt, marginalized, or worse— much as she had been as a Jew in Iraq.

"My parents had fled dhimmitude in Muslim lands and here I was going gay in a straight world!" Rachel says. "My parents were traumatized for the first few years. They had so many fears for me. But with time came change. My parents supported me enthusiastically in my studies and my work. They loved my partner. And, as time went by, I was better able to understand and to accept that for my mother, my initial coming out sparked so many fears for me that it was, indeed, her own personal Farhud."

Concerns about a gay, lesbian, bisexual, or transgender adult child's safety in a society where homophobia lingers are not unrealistic. In a 2013 Pew Research survey of gay, lesbian, bisexual, and transgender adults, 58 percent reported that they had been the target of slurs or jokes, 21 percent reported being treated unfairly by an employer, 30 percent said they had been physically attacked or threatened, and 39 percent said that, at some point in their lives, they had been rejected by a family member or close friend because of their sexual orientation or gender identity.*

So keep in mind that it may take time for your adult child to come out to you, as well as for you to work through your fears and concerns to arrive at a loving acceptance.

As you struggle to understand, seek help and support. Check with your local chapter of PFLAG (pflag.org) or check out the information available from PFLAG of New York City (pflagnyc.org).

Reflect on the person you've always known your adult child to be. How would you have described your son or daughter to another before hearing this news? Consider that his or her wonderful qualities, talents, and other things that have delighted you over the years are still very much there. You just know another aspect of his or her life now. While it can be difficult, at

---

* Gao, "Most Americans Now Say Learning Their Child Is Gay Wouldn't Upset Them."

least initially, to reconcile this new information with everything you know—or thought you knew—about your adult child, sexual orientation is simply a part of the person he or she is. The adult child you knew and loved is still there—unless you drive him away.

Know that rejecting your child at this juncture is a major estrangement trigger. Your adult child is in a highly vulnerable position when coming out to the people he or she loves most. Meeting this vulnerability with anger and rejection can cause pain that endures through time.

When a college student named Whitney came out to her mother, her mother screamed at her and told her that if she were gay, she would no longer pay her college tuition. Whitney recanted her confession and told her mother that she was straight so that she could continue her education. But, in time, the truth came out, and Whitney is now estranged from her parents.

Writing in the online publication *Autostraddle*, Whitney said, "When I came out to my parents, the rejection hit me so badly I could barely get out of bed most mornings in college… There is such hurt and devastation in being disowned or estranged. Estranged. It's taken me five years to use the word."*

Writer David Michael McFarlane recently blogged about his estrangement from his fundamentalist Christian mother after coming out to her: "I came out as an environmentalist, then an

---

* Whitney, "Estranged: How I Fell in Love with a Girl and Lost My Family," *Autostraddle*, July 3, 2012, https://www.autostraddle.com/letting-go-on-being-gay-and-estranged-from -my-parents-14066/.

English major, and inevitably a full-blown liberal. Being gay was the coup de grâce of our defeated relationship… It is still painful, still feels like a divorce, or on the worst days like a death…"[†]

Focus your attention on your love for your adult child. Even if you're shocked or sad or confused about what you're hearing, keep the focus on your son or daughter and your love as a parent.

"I can't really say I was shocked when my fourteen-year-old son told his mother and me that he was gay," says Dale, who was fifty-two when he got the news. "My first reaction was fear: 'Oh, my God, please! Please don't let him be hurt! Please, no one hurt him!' Then I took a deep breath and looked at this marvelous son I love so much. And I thought, 'I hope someday he finds someone wonderful to love.' And he has. I am so thankful and so proud of the man he has grown up to be."

If You're a Gay, Lesbian, Bisexual, or Transgender Adult

Limit your initial expectations. When you first come out to your parents, don't expect them to be instantly on board with you. If they are, that's great. If they're less supportive than you had hoped, have patience. You've had years to figure this out. Your parents may need time too. While some parents never do reach a point of acceptance, most come around, given time. Most

---

† David Michael McFarlane, "How to Be a Good Son When You're Gay," Huffington Post, last modified February 2, 2016, www.huffingtonpost.com/david…/how-to-be-a-good-son-when_b_3237740.html.

eventually put their love for you above any religious beliefs, social anxieties, or shock and disappointment. What you see—in an initially shocked and sad reaction—might be rejection. To your parent, it may be a process of grieving the loss of dreams of your duplicating their lifestyle and life trajectory. In time, they may well embrace you, along with new hopes and dreams for your future. So don't let disappointment at their initial lack of enthusiasm discourage you or lead you to a conflict that drives you even further apart.

Avoid "in your face" moments with the folks. Don't make a coming-out revelation concurrent with introducing them to your lover. Don't share your news about being transgender and then make an immediate request for financial help with sex change surgery. Take this step by step. Work out feelings with your parent before bringing another person into the mix.

"I wasn't seeing bringing my partner home from college as especially being in their face," says Lesley, now twenty-five and married to her life partner, Cindy. "I thought that maybe the shock of my being a lesbian would be softened by the fact that I am with a really good and loving partner. But it was too much. They said things that hurt me and, even worse, hurt Cindy, which made me react even more negatively to their reaction. It all worked out eventually. They're very accepting now and were celebrating right along with us at our wedding last summer. But it wasn't easy at first. All of us said things we wished we hadn't."

Give your parents resources to help them understand: A good start might be literature, either paper or online, from

PFLAG and encouragement to attend some meetings. You might suggest attending family therapy together—not with the goal of getting you to change, but with hope of rediscovering the love you share and communicating that to each other.

"I found a sympathetic priest to talk with my parents, and that helped a lot," says Matt, twenty-six, whose coming out to his parents three years ago was initially tumultuous. "When they could start to make sense of what I was telling them within the context of their religious beliefs, that made a huge difference."

Appreciate incremental progress. Many parents are not going to segue from initial shock and dismay to joyous acceptance. This is likely to be a process, perhaps somewhat similar to your own process of discovering and accepting your sexual orientation. If you react positively to small victories, it will keep the process toward acceptance going.

Evan, whose mother initially screamed that she wished him dead and that she regretted adopting him, is now forty-eight and, thinking back, recalls that he saw the initial sign of major progress the first Christmas after her discovery that he was gay.

"She actually sent a gift for my partner that Christmas," he remembers. "Okay, so the present was socks…deodorant socks. But we chose to see this as an olive branch. We expressed appreciation and sent her a nice gift from both of us. And things grew from there. Before I knew it, she was knitting him an afghan, which she had done for my college girlfriend whom she had assumed I would marry. *That* was major. And she used to talk about how she wished we could marry. Unfortunately, she died of a heart attack several years before that was possible. But we remembered her with a special prayer on our wedding day two years ago. We both loved her so much."

When You're at Odds over Lifestyle Differences

Some lifestyle clashes involve children—or lack of them.

For Sally and her thirty-two-year-old daughter Brittney, the trouble started when Brittney experienced a planned out-of-wedlock pregnancy two years ago and presented her deeply religious mother with a racially mixed grandson. For Sally, who grew up in the Deep South, this was a double shock, and she initially didn't want to have anything to do with either of them.

"I wish I could say that we're out of the woods with this and everything is just dandy," says Brittney. "She was angry and reject-ing when I needed her most, and she didn't want anything to do with my child. That cut deep. The hurt, to some extent, will never go away. But things are better between us. Couldn't have been much worse. She talks to me on the phone. She visits occasionally and brings little presents for the baby. She's warming up to Jake, and he has reacted very well to her. I have hope that things will continue to get better with us."

The difficulties Kimberly has been experiencing with her parents are different but no less distressing.

Kimberly, a thirty-five-year-old attorney, married Jack, another attorney in her law firm, last year. When her parents started asking about grandchildren shortly before their first anniversary, Kimberly told them that she and Jack had decided— well before their wedding—not to have children. There were some heated exchanges with her parents, followed by two months of total silence.

"We have good reasons for not wanting children," Kimberly says. "It's a critical and very private decision that we alone can make. I know my parents want more grandchildren. But they already have four from my two sisters. I don't think we should have to explain ourselves to anybody or apologize. We're both working a lot of hours and both seeking to become partners in the firm. The timing wouldn't work. Of course, if I really wanted children, I could make career sacrifices, as so many women do. But I don't want to. I may be missing that maternal gene. I don't enjoy children especially. That may make me seem selfish or an awful person in my parents' eyes. But I think it would be much more selfish, given how I feel and what I want out of life, to bring a child into the world just to please them."

If You're a Parent at Odds with an Adult Child Who Is a Single Parent or Deciding to Be Childless

There is no decision more life-changing than the one to have a child. As a parent, you know that well. What has changed over the years has been how younger generations have approached this adult milestone. Because it is taking the current generation of younger adults longer to get established financially, they are marrying later. And sometimes a daughter in her thirties may not be married and yet yearn for a child. When she happens, by accident or design, to become a single parent, support from family can mean much. At the same time, knowing as you do the considerable demands and responsibilities as well as the incredible joys of parenthood, would you wish an adult child who is reluctant—or at best, conflicted—to take this on just because you want a grandchild?

Don't focus your anger or disappointment on the child. So the grandchild's parents aren't married. So the grandchild is racially mixed. So the grandchild has been adopted by a gay son. The grandchild had no control over any of these aspects of his or her life—none of them negatives, by the way, unless you choose to make them so. This grandchild may not have been born under the circumstances that you would prefer, but this *is* your grandchild. He or she needs your love and encouragement just as much as your own children did—and as much as any grandchildren born under what you might consider more favorable circumstances. In fact, maybe this grandchild needs your love a little more. Think about it. Perhaps pray about it. And open your arms and your heart.

Accept the fact that the decision to have a child—or not—is a deeply personal one. It may be made by your adult child alone. Or it may be made between an adult child and his or her spouse. But this is their decision to make. You may have an opinion, but they cast the deciding vote. And the less vociferous your opinion, the better.

"My mother's nagging us to have a child every time we saw her during our first several years of marriage felt so intrusive," says Danielle, thirty-three and the mother of an eight-month-old son. "It was also divisive. My husband would get angry and offended and say to me later, 'What *is* it with your mother? Why can't she stop butting into our life like that?' I would get defensive. But, in fact, my husband and I were very much in agreement about waiting five years to have a child. We wanted to experience life as a couple first and make sure our marriage was solid. We wanted to do some traveling and work and save money for the future. We had very good reasons for waiting and felt it was no one else's business. The fact that she kept on us about this jeopardized our relationship with her. In fact, I still feel some resentment when she'll say, 'See? Didn't I tell you what a joy parenthood is?' Like she finally wore us down and we had a child, not giving us credit for making a mature decision that was right for us. I'm not at all confident that our struggles are over. If she keeps telling me how I ought to raise Noah...I might find it unbearable."

If you're sad about not having grandchildren, remember that there are many ways to show your love. There are ways of channeling the love, the wisdom, and the tenderness you yearn to share with a grandchild with children who need you so much. Sign up to be a foster grandparent to a child in need. Volunteer to help with children's charities or cuddling newborn infants who need a loving touch during prolonged hospital stays. Embrace grandnieces and grandnephews or close friends' grandchildren. Get involved in animal rescue. Channel your love to children—or other living creatures—in need. There may always be an ache, a longing, to be a grandparent. But not all of us are so blessed, for a variety of reasons. Find your own best ways to share your love with others in ways that can make a difference to one life—or to many.

If You're an Adult Child at Odds with Your Parents over Having a Child—Or Not

If you're having a baby on your own and your parents are not supportive, seek support from others. This won't take away the pain of rejection but will give you some needed support during a vulnerable time in your life, and it may also give your parents time to come around. Reach out to other family members and to friends.

"Seeking help and support from my aunt and my cousin, who is married and has a baby a year older than mine, turned out to be such a blessing and so important in many ways," says Janae, twenty-six. "It gave me help and time to calm down and feel comfortable being a single mom. And it bought time, time for my mother to stop judging me and start loving me all over again. And she ended up warmly welcoming a grandchild she treasures."

If you want to avoid estrangement, avoid lashing out in anger. This can be a tall order, especially when you feel that your parents are rejecting your child, which can be a very hurtful, enraging situation. Talk with a friend, other family members, or a therapist. Write your feelings down in a journal. And when—or if—you discuss this with your parent or parents, stay as calm as possible and concentrate on how their actions or inactions make you feel. For example: "When you refuse to visit us or to hold my baby, I feel rejected and angry." Reporting how you feel, instead of screaming out raw feelings in a verbal brawl, is more likely to lead to an emotional reconciliation in time.

Have confidence that you know what is right for you. This may be single parenthood—or nonparenthood. Whatever the choice that is dividing you and your parents, it isn't likely to be a whim on your part. You've already given this a lot of thought. Over time, you may have changed your mind about a lot of things, including parenthood. Your feelings may change again if other circumstances in your life change. You may decide to marry. You may meet someone special and decide that parenthood is the right choice for you after all. Or you may be quite certain that you're not destined to be a parent. Whatever you ultimately decide, this is a decision only you—or only you and a spouse—can make. No one else can—or should—try to make it for you.

Accept the fact that you and your parents may need to agree to disagree. They may never understand your decision not to have children. For people whose lives have been so enriched by their children, to live without having experienced parenthood is unthinkable. When they urge you to rethink your decision, it may be less out of a desire for grandchildren than it is about not wanting you to miss the joy they have experienced.

And so you may have come to this point: they can't imagine how you could live without children, while you can't imagine living with them. Perhaps the best alternative is to agree to disagree. They think that you're missing out in a major way on one of the greatest joys in life, but admit that your life as it is appears to be full and rewarding. You feel happy and content with your life as it is, but admit that having and nurturing a child is a major part of life that you're choosing to forgo—while not discounting warm relationships with nieces, nephews, or children of friends.

It can be a delicate balance when both sides have such strong feelings. How you handle this, however, can have a major impact on your relationship for years to come.

CHAPTER FOUR
Cultural Clashes

When worlds and cultures collide within a family, life can feel tumultuous. This is especially true for adult children, seeking to live their own lives in a different land from the one their parents know best. Conflicts between immigrant parents and their American-born (or more acculturated) adult children can trigger estrangements.

Could this be a problem in your family? If you are first- or second-generation Americans:

+ Are you upset because your adult children haven't met your academic or educational expectations—after all you've sacrificed to give them opportunities not available in your homeland?
+ Are your concept and your parents' concept of what it means to be a close family at seemingly impossible odds?

+ Are your young adult children not following, or even disrespecting, the values that your culture holds dear?

+ Do your parents appear to inhabit a whole different world when it comes to recognizing your adult status?

+ After immigration-related separations, do you feel unfairly blamed, like strangers to each other, and not sure how you fit into each other's lives?

+ Are you so frightened by some aspects of your family's culture and the collision with choices that you've come to value as an American that you feel the need to put distance between you?

WHEN VALUES, BELIEFS, AND EXPECTATIONS CLASH

The conflicts between Gladys ("Gladdy") Nguyen and her parents go back to adolescence. Now twenty-five, Gladdy remembers that it was her father's parenting style, setting her apart from her peers, that first sparked the arguments.

"In Vietnam, the father makes all the decisions in the family, even for grown children, and women are subservient," she says. "It's a bad combination for here. And I was born and grew up here, so no one else I know has a father who orders her around, expects her to obey, is angry that I'm not still living at home, and expects that I should drop everything and come help with my younger brother and sister whenever he demands it. He also expects that I will support him and my mom in their old age. I'm still wondering if I'll ever pay off my student loans and be able to support myself in some sort of good lifestyle, let alone support the whole family. But in Vietnam, the family comes before anything else. The individual isn't important."

The concept of adolescence is a mystery to many immigrant parents, especially those from Southeast Asia, where children as young as five start assuming responsibility for younger siblings and participating in the work of the family.*

At the same time, independent young adulthood can be a point of contention between immigrant parents and their U.S.-raised children. Authoritarian parenting—whatever the age of the child—that demands respect, deference, and obedience can grate on second-generation children who have grown up in a new culture in which early independence is encouraged and child-rearing is more permissive.[†]

Young adult daughters can also chafe under culture-based parental restrictions about clothing, dating, and socializing that not only give them much less freedom than their peers, but also restrict them more than their brothers.

Many of the issues between parents and adult children in immigrant families come from acculturation gaps that make family communication difficult.[‡] Most commonly, these gaps occur

---

* Daniel Detzner, Xiong Blong, and P. A. Elliason, University of Minnesota Extension, "Helping Youth Succeed: Bicultural Parenting for Southeast Asian Families," Facilitator Manual, out of print (1999), adapted by author for paper (2010), 1–7.

† Nancy Foner and Joanna Dreby, "Relations between the Generations in Immigrant Families," *Annual Review of Sociology* 37 (2011): 545–64.

‡ Dina Bermin and Meredith Poff, "Intergenerational Differences in Acculturation,"

when parents and children come to this country together and the children quickly pick up the language, behavior, and attitudes of the host country while the parents lag behind. But these gaps can also occur when a parent or parents have immigrated first and, perhaps years later, send for their children to join them after a long separation.

In the first instance, children—from teens to young adults— take care of the family by acting as translators for their parents and by getting jobs that contribute to the family income.

"I felt that I had to grow up too soon and still have some resentment," says Maria, a twenty-six-year-old supermarket cashier whose family came from El Salvador. "My family needed my income so much that I never even thought of going to school beyond high school. My parents still need me to act as an interpreter and translator for them. Don't get me wrong: I love my parents so much! I respect their sacrifices to give my sister and me a better life. But I get upset sometimes because I don't think they've bothered to learn English at all. I can't always be there for them. I have to work. I'm getting married soon and will have my own family. I can't always just drop everything for them. Sometimes that causes hard feelings. Once, my mother wouldn't speak to me for a month!"

In the second instance, children—often adolescents or young adults—join their parents who have been working in the U.S.

Encyclopedia of Early Childhood Development: Immigration, University of Illinois at Chicago, April 2011, http://www.child-encyclopedia.com/sites/default/files/textes-experts/en/664/intergenerational-differences-in-acculturation.pdf.

for some time and face not only acculturation gaps but also the stresses of reuniting after a long separation. Researchers have found that young people who were separated from their parents before they came to this country had more academic problems than those who had migrated with their parents. Feelings of estrangement from parents can have a long-term impact on the relationship between parent and child well into the child's adulthood, even after they are reunited.*

"I remember crying myself to sleep every night after my parents went to work in the United States and left me in Mexico with my grandmother," says Sylvia, twenty-two, a community college student. "They finally sent for me five years ago. We had all lived a lot of years without each other. They had three other kids born in the U.S. [who] I had never met. Suddenly, I'm supposed to be part of their family and take care of the younger kids. It made me mad. Why didn't they take care of *me*? Why didn't they take me with them? I still don't understand, and I still don't exactly feel like I'm part of the family."

There can also be conflict when parents choose to send an adolescent child to the U.S. alone as a "parachute child." This happens most commonly when wealthy Asian parents send their child or children to the U.S. to attend high school in areas with excellent schools to better their chances of admission to U.S. colleges. The result can be the realization of parental

---

*   Nancy Foner and Joanna Dreby, "Relations between the Generations in Immigrant Families," *Annual Review of Sociology* 37 (2011): 545–64.

hopes—or a family rift after the parachute child, sometimes simply overwhelmed by the burden of parental expectations and adjustment to a new country, language, and culture, fails academically—or even worse, left on his or her own, falls into drinking, drug use, or criminal activities.

Academic expectations can loom large in immigrant Asian families. There is considerable pressure on adolescents and young adults to excel in their studies and also to pursue successful careers in medicine, engineering, or law.* The pressure on the second generation to succeed in highly specific ways can be extreme and can lead to conflict and possible estrangement.

There are times, too, when conflicts can occur over differing views of parental roles. A recent study described how Chinese immigrant parents seek to show their love and devotion to their children by being good providers, while the children hope for parents as a source of emotional support. This, the study observed, can lead to parent-child alienation in immigrant families.†

Even when parents and adult children are in agreement over values and cultural traditions, conflicts and resentments can grow.

"I value our cultural and family traditions and beliefs greatly," says Ari, whose Jewish family fled Iraq some years ago. "But, at

---

* Y. L. Espiritu, "Emotions, Sex, and Money: The Lives of Filipino Children of Immigrants., in Nancy Foner, *Across Generations: Immigrant Families in America* (New York: University Press, 2009), 47–71.

† Desiree B. Qin, "Gendered Processes of Adaptation: Understanding Parent-Child Relations in Chinese Immigrant Families," *Sex Roles* 60 (April 2009): 467.

times, I've felt torn between what I wanted and what my family expected. That caused some hard feelings between my mother and me especially. We were never estranged—but we could have been if I had made different choices. Maybe choices more advantageous to me."

Ari's father died of diabetic complications at the age of fifty-four. Before he died, he made Ari promise to take care of his mother for the rest of her life. He took off his wedding ring and handed it to his son, who sometimes wears the ring on a chain around his neck. Although Ari's sister, with a husband and children, urged the mother to move in with her family rather than live with Ari, then a young, single adult, the mother insisted: "My place is with my son. That's the agreement."

The agreement exacted a toll as time went on. Mom expertly fended off Ari's girlfriends. Ari and his mother sparred verbally and went days without speaking to each other.

Disgruntled girlfriends have asked, "Why don't you put your mother in an apartment or encourage her to move to a retirement community?" And Ari has always replied that asking his mother to move out would violate the promise he made to his father, adding, "In our culture, we don't just discard our older people for others to take care of. We take care of our parents."

Reflecting on his mother's robust good health and his continuing single status, Ari is resigned and sure about one thing: "I would never ask or expect a younger relative of mine to take on the responsibility I have. Maybe I'm getting more American as I get older!"

There may be differences in adaptation within the same family and the same generation. The Morelli family has three living generations: grandparents, born in this country of Italian immigrant parents; their children—fraternal twins Francis and Francine—who are in their thirties and married with children; and their four grandchildren. The grandparents still identify strongly with their Italian heritage. The grandmother is the family matriarch, highly directive with her adult children and involved in a thriving business venture with her daughter, who is also a kindergarten teacher. Whether making Italian sausage and ravioli to sell to local restaurants in Francine's spacious kitchen, attending Mass together, or simply talking on the phone daily, they're very much in touch. "I'm a mix of American and also good Italian daughter," Francine says with a smile. "The only outrageous things I did were to go away to college and marry a man who isn't Italian. But my parents love him. So it's good. My brother Frank has a somewhat distant relationship with our parents. He only calls them maybe…oh, twice a week! And that can be a matter of contention between them. By his standard, that's plenty of contact. By their cultural standard, they feel nearly estranged from him."

In some families, the cultural split is darker. I once had a patient who was an immigrant from Afghanistan. I saw her in a worker's compensation psychiatric clinic because she was depressed about a work-related injury that was keeping her temporarily sidelined and causing financial stress for her family. She was working as a medical secretary and was her family's breadwinner. Her husband, a distant cousin eighteen years her senior whom she had been forced to marry when she was only sixteen, didn't work. He passed most of his time at the local mosque and spent much of their money on annual trips to Mecca—trips that he always made alone. He beat his wife, verbally abused her, and was trying to arrange a marriage between a cousin in Afghanistan and his bright, ambitious, American-born, sixteen-year-old daughter, who was dreaming of going to college and then medical school. My client wanted desperately for her daughter to have the educational and career opportunities she had never had. She wanted to escape her unhappy marriage.

However, when she went to her own parents, who lived about a mile away, asking for help, they threatened to kill her if she dared to defy her husband's wishes or to seek a divorce. Such moves would dishonor the family and, thus, justify an "honor killing." They told her that even if she went into hiding, even if she sought help at an abused women's shelter, they would find her and kill her.

Although one doesn't see a lot in the news in this country about honor killings, these types of threats can maintain cultural values and mores of the old country—even when the family has relocated to a Western country. And the possibility of violent consequences to acts that seem rational in this culture can influence choices and behaviors in several generations.

How to Avoid Culture-
Clash Estrangements

Ideas for Parents

Take a deep breath and try to stay calm when your adult child disagrees with you. While such disagreements might have been seen as a sign of disrespect in your country of origin, expressing differences in outlook and opinions can be a way of communicating and trying to find acceptable compromises in the United States. So try to keep yourself and the conversation calm. Listen and then respond. Don't command or demand.

Decide what matters to you and talk it over with your adult child. While your cultural differences may be in the foreground, it could be that, on certain matters very important to you, some sort of compromise is possible. For example, if matters of faith and of marriage traditions are high among your personal priorities, tell your adult child about how much these ideals matter to you and work together to find a compromise.

For example, among some Muslim American young adult women, wearing a headscarf is a sign of allegiance and respect. An arranged marriage is still important to parents and some find compromise in presenting their daughter with a choice of several men to consider before making the decision to marry—instead of giving her no voice in the matter.

Encourage your adult child to tell you what he or she wants to do with his life. Not everyone is cut out for a career

in the sciences, in medicine, or in law. Of course, you want your
children to do well and to have financial security. Most parents
feel this way. But there are many roads to success and to financial independence. And not everyone aspires to affluence. Some
would choose to make less money if they could build a career
doing something they love. As a parent, the prospect of your child
pursuing a less-than-lucrative career may make you wince. But
your adult child's personal happiness is important to you, too. In
listening, you can learn much, and perhaps find a way to guide
your child toward a career path that is rewarding in all ways.

**Think about what concessions you might make to
American ways.** Do you have a young adult daughter living with
you? Is your first inclination to protect her and forbid dating or
set a strict and early curfew? You might try talking the options
over with your daughter and coming up with a compromise or
two. Perhaps instead of forbidding dating, you could encourage
her to socialize with groups of friends. Instead of giving her a
curfew that makes things like going to the movies and then out
for dinner with friends nearly impossible, work together to find
middle ground with a curfew that makes sense but still keeps her
safe. Recognize the fact that strict old-world rules may feel quite
appropriate for you, given your own life experiences. However,
for young people who have immigrated to the U.S. or who were
born here, unrelenting old-world rules can isolate them from
friends and activities that have come to matter to them. Decide
how you can mix the best qualities of your old culture with those
of the new culture.

If you and an adolescent or young adult child have experienced an immigration-linked separation from each other, accept the fact that reconciliation takes time. Your young adult needs to know that he or she is a much-loved member of the family. Give him or her time to adjust, to move from relative stranger to totally included family member, before making demands.

"I felt that I was brought here from Guatemala three years ago—ten years after my parents went to work in the U.S.—not because I was loved and wanted, but to take care of their younger kids who were all born here during our separation," says Emilia, twenty. "I felt especially angry at my mother for leaving me behind. I'd say, 'What kind of mother leaves her child and then has other children while the first child waits and waits?' She would always cry when I'd say that. I know it wasn't her decision alone to leave me behind, and I understand now that it was very hard for her. But it was hard for me, too. I missed a lot of good years with my parents. So it was really hard to be brought here suddenly when I was finished with school and [to be] told that I needed to help with the younger kids and find a job to help the family. What about me and what I want?"

While perceptions of the same situation can vary widely between parent and adult child, being sensitive to the other's point of view is critical to reconciliation and rebuilding a family divided.

Ideas for Adult Children

Accept the fact that you and your parents may never agree on certain things. That isn't just a result of clashing cultures but also of differing generations. Your friends whose families have been Americans for generations still have disagreements with their parents. It just happens. Some of the expectations your parents have may differ from those of your friends' parents. Your parents may have more exacting educational expectations or feel that their role in shaping and directing your life extends into young adulthood and beyond. Pick your battles. Let some things go. Challenge others. And sometimes look for ways to agree to disagree.

Before you accuse your parents of not being able to leave old ways behind, realize that they may never have intended to separate themselves from their culture and traditions. Immigrants have many reasons for leaving their native countries. Sometimes it is to embrace a new country and new way of life. But just as often, it is to escape hardship and danger or to offer their children a better life than would have been possible in the home country.

"It took me a long time to stop being ashamed and angry at my parents, who are highly intelligent people, but who have clung, nevertheless, to many of the traditions of Romania," says Nick, a twenty-seven-year-old engineer. "I was just a baby when we came to this country, so I have no memories of life in Romania. But our home was like Little Romania. Sometimes it just drove me crazy. Then one day, when I was in college, it clicked. They came here for me, to give me better opportunities. And, in doing so, they made their own lives worse. My dad was a successful attorney in Romania. He drives a cab here. My mother was an engineer. She's an office clerk here. They've made huge sacrifices for me. How could I possibly challenge them when they want to find comfort in their old traditions? How dare I?"

Let your parents know what you value, admire, and accept about your family's cultural traditions. Instead of rejecting everything about old ways and traditions outright, think about what is meaningful and valuable to you. It may be the faith of your family or the way people care for each other or the strong encouragement to make the best of your intelligence and abilities. It may be shared love of your traditional music or holiday rituals. It may be family stories and the art of storytelling. Think about what makes you feel glad about being part of your family. Let those positive elements sustain you through conflicts about other aspects of your life together.

When you discuss cultural clashes with your parents, talk about the feelings you have about those specific interactions rather than criticizing their culture and beliefs. Your parents may well have grown up under vastly different circumstances, and their beliefs are firmly rooted in this past you may not have shared. Their beliefs are part of the people they've grown to be and may not be subject to change. That's why it's important to keep the focus on your feelings as someone growing up in a different time and place.

Express your discomfort or dissatisfaction with certain

expectations or family rules. At least initially, seek ways you might compromise. Let them know what you would like to see happen. Reassure your parents that, despite their concessions, you will be safe or on track in a career that works for you and eventually allows for some measure of financial security.

If this discussion might bring the threat of violence, weigh the risks and ensure your safety. If your family is from a culture where violence, especially toward women, is a danger, think carefully about challenging your parents' plans and beliefs and, before you disclose your disagreement with them, have a plan in place to ensure your safety. This may mean having a non–family member present for the discussion or putting it in writing from the safety of a shelter or safe home. It may mean that, as much as you may want to avoid family estrangement, in certain circumstances, estrangement may be lifesaving.

Take responsibility for the ways in which your family's culture of origin doesn't work for you, instead of attacking the culture itself. It takes at least two points of view to have a culture clash. You have valid reasons for feeling the way you do—and so do your parents. Instead of bashing your parents' cultural beliefs, take responsibility for the ways those beliefs aren't working for you.

"What I said to my parents was that I realized what I wanted to do was fairly outrageous from their traditional point of view," says Shahnaz, twenty-three, whose family emigrated from the Middle East twelve years ago. "I wanted an education, not an early marriage. I want a career, not seclusion at home. I want to find love on my own, not via an arranged marriage. That's a lot for them to absorb and, fortunately, they are not as strict as some immigrant Muslim parents. I told them that these wishes, coming from my being raised mostly in the U.S. and seeing all the opportunities for women, didn't mean I did not value our religion or all the values they had taught me. It hasn't been easy for them…or for me. But we're making progress. We're really trying to understand each other because, well, we love each other, that's all."

That's all…and everything.

CHAPTER FIVE

Parents, Adult Children, and Money Issues

There is nothing like money to spark family feuds and emotional divides. Whether it's a matter of giving too much or not giving enough, many parents and adult children find that, while they may disagree on a number of issues, money disputes can be particularly divisive.

Is this a problem for your family? It may well be if:

+ Your adult children expect you to come to their financial rescue repeatedly—bailing them out of credit card debt or supplying a down payment for a house or a new car (and perhaps cosigning loans).
+ You've needed to say "No" to your adult child's request for financial help and find that their anger and disappointment are creating a gulf between you.

✦ You're working two jobs to pay for your children's educations and other expenses of daily life, and now your elderly parents—who were rarely supportive of you in your struggling young-adult years—need help, and you're resenting this neediness at a time when you're trying to provide for your primary family.

✦ You've been generous with an adult child and have been met with not only a lack of gratitude, but with resentment that you're not giving them more and more.

✦ Your adult children are replaying some sibling rivalries when it comes to your money: if you help one with a special need in any emergency, another demands equal money for something else you may not consider an emergency.

✦ As a single parent of limited means, you've given your adult children everything they asked for, even jeopardizing your own financial security. Now that you're broke and have no more to give, they're not returning your calls, emails, or texts.

✦ After years of being alone—due to a divorce or widowhood—you've found love again and find that your adult children are incensed. Instead of being happy for you, they're angry and upset for purely financial reasons: they think of your money as theirs to inherit and feel it may vanish if you remarry.

✦ Your parents offer you money—hard to resist with all the obligations you have—and, as a result, they expect to have more power than you would like them to have over your decisions.

✦ You're upset with your parents because they always helped you here and there before they retired, but now the Bank of

Mom and Dad is closed as they travel and enjoy themselves while you continue to struggle.

WHEN PARENTS WIELD FINANCIAL POWER

Most parents want the best for their children—both growing and grown.

That can mean stretching the family budget or doing without, so that an adolescent or young adult child can enjoy a special opportunity or advantage.

It can mean rescuing a troubled adult child again and again— when he or she loses yet another job or is mired in credit card debt again or needs expensive medical or rehab care.

It can mean paying for frills that an adult child might not have otherwise.

Sometimes a parent's generosity greatly enhances an adult child's life and makes a major difference in his or her educational or career trajectory.

Sometimes a parent's inclination to give and give enables irresponsible behavior or fans an inflated sense of entitlement.

And, quite often, a parent's financial generosity can mask a desire to control a child well into adulthood, or an adult child's continuing financial dependence can perpetuate tensions and conflicts.

Financial contributions to adult children can mean an expression of power between the generations—perhaps seen as a kind of bribery. And adult children who can't seem to get it together financially, who have a heavy burden of debts, are twice as likely to be in conflict with parents.*

Helen is typical of both instances in her recent conflicts with her forty-eight-year-old son: even though she lives on a tight budget herself, she gives her son money he doesn't ask for so that she feels she has a say in his lifestyle choices, and then she criticizes the choices he does make—threatening to withhold the money he didn't request (but has become accustomed to receiving).

So she is paying for his cell phone bills, his car payment, and his daughter's music lessons, and she feels free to weigh in on purchasing choices that he and his wife make: "Oh, that's silly to think of going off to Hawaii, just the two of you, when we can all go to that condo by the lake again this summer," she told them recently. "And how is it, by the way, that your wife has bought herself those designer boots?"

So all family vacations thus far have been at places of Helen's choosing, with Helen present and calling the shots in all ways. And escalating conflicts with her son have all centered on his continued dependence on her.

"My son is mad at me right now," she confessed recently. "He's upset because when he refused to make his wife return her expensive boots like I told him to, I threatened to stop paying his cell phone bill."

---

*   Marc Szydlik, "Intergenerational Solidarity and Conflicts," *Journal of Comparative Family Studies* 39, no. 1 (2008): 97–118.

Studies have found that variations of Helen's conflict with her son are quite common. Parents who still contribute money to their adult children tend to report heightened tensions regarding adult children and their lifestyles—particularly how they tend to spend their time and their money.[†]

There are instances where these tensions can take a dark turn: several studies have found that mutual dependency between an adult child and a parent—most often with the parent offering primary financial support and housing the adult child—is a key dynamic in elder abuse. Researchers Kurt Luescher and Karl Pillemer, who reported similar findings in two separate studies of parents and adult children, found that physical abuse toward elderly parents sometimes stemmed directly from the sense of dependence and powerlessness experienced by the abusing adult children.[‡]

Even when financial conflicts fall short of abuse, the feelings of dependence and powerlessness, frustration and anger can lead to emotional distance and the beginnings of estrangement.

An anonymous comment left on my blog recently came from the mother of a twenty-one-year-old woman who had yet to find a direction in life or the means to achieve independent adulthood. Although the two were living under the same roof, "we haven't

---

[†]   Edward J. Clarke et al., "Types of Conflict and Tensions between Older Parents and Adult Children," *The Gerontologist* 39 (1999): 261–270.

[‡]   Kurt Luescher and Karl Pillemer, "Intergenerational Ambivalence: A New Approach to Study of Parent-Child Relationships in Later Life," *Journal of Marriage and the Family* 60, no. 2 (May 1998): 413–425.

spoken in weeks. We don't have a relationship. It's pathetic but
mostly heartbreaking. I know we love each other deep down. I
just wish we liked each other."

WHEN ADULT CHILDREN
EXPECT TOO MUCH

To get a real sense of what many adult children expect of their
parents and what all too many parents struggle to give them,
sometimes jeopardizing their own financial security in the
process, you only have to spend a day hanging around an active
adult community and listen to the stories.

There are stories one hears in a Sun City recreational pool
about foreclosures and bankruptcies suffered by retired parents
who took risks like cosigning student loans or taking on loans
themselves for their kids' college educations, or who emptied
their savings to meet requests or demands from their kids for
credit-card-debt bailouts, down payments on homes, new cars,
or special extras for the grandkids.

"Yep," said one man, floating lazily on a nest of pool noodles.
"If you let them, the damn kids will just drain you dry. Some
people would rather risk everything than say 'No' to their kids."

A couple in the pool, standing on the edge of the general
conversation, smiled uneasily as they told me the story of their
own financial risk-taking. Their daughter, a college student, had
decided after her freshman year that she couldn't abide dorm living
and asked them to buy her a condo. Soon after they closed on

her condo, their son—a drifter with a substance abuse problem, no job, and little motivation to turn his life around—demanded equal treatment: he wanted a house of his own. After some discussion, the couple took out a mortgage on their previously free-and-clear retirement home to buy their son a house, hoping that "putting down roots in a community [would] give him a new start in life." But they admitted that their generosity had put them in a bit of a precarious position with unplanned debt in retirement and a nearly empty savings account.

While it can be a pleasure to help the kids in a crisis or to obtain something they would not otherwise have, there is a limit. Each of us has a different limit. Some parents are willing to make major sacrifices in their own lifestyle to help their adult children. But some parents—who, for the sake of their own financial independence, need to be saying "No" to many of their kids' requests—seem unable to set limits as they finance their adult children's dreams to their own detriment.

"It's hard to say 'No' to my daughter," says Sherri, a newly retired widow. "She is always threatening never to speak to me again if I don't give her what she wants. And now there is a grand-baby, and she threatens that I'll never see my little granddaughter again if I don't cosign her car loan and give her money every month to rent a better apartment. It's a strain on my budget for sure. But the consequences of not helping would be unbearable."

Helping an adult child above and beyond the call of parental duty is no guarantee that estrangement won't happen.

Pete and Marilyn have a highly successful food-processing

company in Central California and are beginning to see the fruits of years of hard work and disciplined budgeting. "People don't realize what it takes to have a successful manufacturing business," Pete says. "We started from point zero. At one time, we had nearly $1 million in debts after buying necessary, but unbelievably expensive equipment. Now there's no debt, and we're hoping to have enough savings to be ready to retire in about fifteen years."

The one cloud on the horizon is their son. They paid in full for his college education in engineering. But he decided after working for a few years that he didn't like the field at all. By that time he was married to a local woman who urged him to move back to his hometown so she could live close to her mother and he could join the family business. Pete happily brought him into the business and built a lovely home for the son and his wife. Pete was pleased when his son seemed to embrace the family business with a passion he had never had in his brief engineering career.

Three years later, the son and his wife confronted Pete and Marilyn with a shocking demand: to hand over the entire business to the son or face estrangement from him and his family, which now included three beloved grandchildren.

Pete and Marilyn were stunned. "We gave him all we could to get a good start, something we never had when we were young," says Marilyn, wiping tears away with a crumpled tissue. "And of course when we retire, we would be happy to see him take over our business. But we're not ready to retire. We can't afford it yet. We need at least ten years, preferably fifteen, before we're at that point. We've offered him more responsibility and a greater share of the profits. But no. Now it has to be everything we own—or we don't have a relationship with any of them. So, at the moment, we're totally estranged, and it breaks our hearts."

The fact is that sometimes kids expect too much and parents give too much. Still, as we have seen, that may not be enough to prevent conflict and estrangement.

WHEN PARENTS AND ADULT CHILDREN CLASH OVER MONEY DECISIONS

Money decisions—from wills and trusts to special help for one adult child or for money given as a loan, not a gift—can cause heated conflicts between parents and their adult children.

"I guess our mistake was even talking about our will with our three grown kids," says Marla, seventy-three, who, with her seventy-seven-year-old husband Charles, recently updated their will after his heart surgery and her cancer diagnosis. "We have three kids and one granddaughter, who is eleven. We have been putting money in her college fund since she was born and have paid for dance lessons and camp every summer. Our will divides our estate equally between our three adult children. We thought that was only fair. But our eldest daughter—the mother of our grandchild—is furious and refuses to speak with us, saying that the estate should have been divided four ways—with her daughter receiving a share equal to that of our three kids. Our other daughter and our son have actually been much more helpful and connected with us over the years and have asked for nothing. How could we even think of giving half of our estate to our daughter and her child—after we've given them so much already? I don't understand her way of thinking—and she doesn't understand ours. So there you are. We're not on speaking terms."

Sometimes the financial dependence of one adult child on a parent can spark conflict with other offspring.

"We have a tough situation with my seventy-year-old mother, who has been a widow for years and who has indulged my younger brother well into adulthood," says forty-six-year-old Teresa. "He is forty-one and has never worked. He still lives with Mom. She is having some trouble paying her bills, and my older brother, and I have agreed to help her. But I was very clear with her about one thing: if I find she's giving the money I send her every month to Gary instead of paying her bills, I'll cut off that financial spigot immediately. She thinks I'm heartless. But she has played a part in enabling Gary's laziness and lack of motivation. What will he do when she's gone? We're sure not supporting him. So he needs to get his ass off the couch and find a job now."

For Mandy and her parents, the sticking point is the $2,500 she requested from them after breaking up with her live-in boyfriend and having to find an apartment of her own close to her workplace in a city more than a thousand miles from her hometown.

"They've helped me out lots of times before and have never expected me to pay the money back," she says. "But now, when I'm feeling so down and finding it hard to make ends meet on one income, they want this money to be a loan, for me to be paying it back on a regular schedule month after month. It's not like they're struggling. I think they're being so unfair!"

Her mother Janet has a different perspective. "Mandy has had one financial crisis after another, and we've probably been too quick to bail her out time and time again," she says. "She needs to learn to meet her obligations, including the obligation to pay us back for the $2,500 we lent her recently. We've made some pretty big sacrifices to help her, including foregoing a special vacation that $2,500 was earmarked for. So, yeah. We expect to be paid back. We're asking $50 payments the first of every month. It's an interest-free loan, and we're keeping the payments small. But they need to be regular and on time. It's important for her to do that... and it may make her think twice about making more demands on the Bank of Mom and Dad!"

WHEN FINANCIAL CIRCUMSTANCES CHANGE AND CAUSE CONFLICT

Financial changes and challenges can happen to both parents and adult children and spark conflicts between the generations.

These can include a job loss or major illness or injury, resulting in increased need for financial help or decreased ability to help.

"My dad lost his job in a corporate merger and was never able to find another one," Julienne, twenty-seven, remembers. "This happened just before my junior year of college at NYU.

"Staying there became totally unaffordable, even with some emergency financial aid from the school. I had to go back to L.A. and enroll at Cal State L.A. I was just devastated. I guess I should have been grateful I could stay in school at all. But that was such a huge disappointment. I know I shouldn't blame my dad. He feels worst of all about this. But I have to say, I've lost a lot of respect for him, and I'm scared that it won't be long before my parents will need my financial help, and I resent that. I mean, you think he could get something, some kind of job, and my mom could go back to work. I don't see them doing anything to help themselves, and that makes me angry."

Conflicts can happen when a change in financial circumstances requires major life changes that impact, to varying degrees, everyone in the family.

"Our kids were definitely not happy when we made the decision to sell the family home where we had lived for thirty years," says Marlene, sixty-seven, who retired from her teaching job two years ago and, along with her husband, Joe, moved to a less expensive home out of state. "We had lost a lot of our retirement savings in the crisis of 2008 and needed the equity from our California home to buy another and have cash left over. So we sold the house that all of us loved and that held so many memories for us and bought a new one in Arizona. Our son refuses to visit us because he has this irrational hatred of Arizona. Our daughter can't understand why, if we got all this money from selling our longtime home, we can't share some of that with her. What we're trying to do is to have a self-sufficient retirement and not be a burden to our kids. Part of that plan for self-sufficiency is safeguarding our savings. The kids think we're being selfish. We call it being prudent. There are a lot of hard feelings about this. Our son rarely calls, and our daughter isn't speaking to us at all."

There are times, too, when changing family circumstances mean that certain patterns of intergenerational behavior need to change as well.

Joan and Clem, both seventy, retired recently and put their middle-aged daughter Patti on notice that she would have to handle her own financial challenges from now on. "We have indulged her too much over the years," Joan admits. "When she couldn't make ends meet, we'd always step in with financial help. But she's still living beyond her means and not taking care of business—and that can't be our problem anymore. We simply can't afford to keep bailing her out of financial trouble. And suddenly, she doesn't want to know us. I can't begin to tell you how much that hurts."

How to Avoid Financial Estrangement Triggers

Ideas for Parents

Make your own financial security your first priority. Remember the emergency instruction you get before taking off on a flight: secure your own oxygen mask first and then assist your child? It's as valid when you're trying to decide whether or how to help an adult child in need. Trying to decide whether to take out loans for your child's college education so he or she can be debt-free? Trying to decide whether to help with a down payment for a home or expensive car? Mulling over an adult child's request to cosign a loan?

Before you say "Yes," consider how this will affect your own financial situation. If you're thinking of raiding your retirement fund or taking another mortgage on your house to help an adult child, think again. Young adults can get loans for college. You can't get a loan for retirement. And taking on long-term debt in late middle age or, worse, the retirement years, can be especially precarious. It's very hard to pay off debt on a fixed income. Some parents say they plan to work longer or take a second job to handle the debts acquired by helping their kids.

"But how can they ensure they can hold onto their job or find another to fund the gap?" asks financial columnist and expert Jill Schlesinger. She recommends covering the big three considerations for your own financial security: paying down your own consumer debt, establishing an emergency fund, and continuing to fund your own retirement before thinking about giving your kids—college students or young adults—financial help. She contends that when parents cut corners with the big three, however loving their intentions for their children, they may well be creating a future burden if they end up struggling in retirement and need help from their kids. She quotes the playwright Tony Kushner in giving this advice: "Sometimes self-interested is the most generous thing you can be."*

---

*   Jill Schlesinger, "Cashing in Some Retirement to Pay for College Is a Bad Trade," Jill on Money, Tribune Media Services, August 18, 2016.

Learn to make a clear distinction between a true emergency and an adult child's whim or habit of depending on you financially. It's one thing if your adult child, his spouse, or his child is experiencing a major illness, or if an adult child with a responsible and steady history of employment and prudent financial management suddenly loses a job. It's quite another thing if you have an adult child who is chronically unemployed, losing one job after another, and making a habit of looking to you for a bailout. Or if you have an adult child who asks too much and whose situation is decidedly not an emergency.

For example, mortgaging your home to buy a house for an unmotivated drifter of a son or to buy a condo for a college student daughter because she doesn't like dorm living, or using retirement savings to bail kids out of credit card debt, sounds less like kindness and more like sheer lunacy. A college student can learn a great deal about compromising and getting along with others by living in a dorm. A financially challenged young adult can learn much more about managing credit card debt by working with a credit counseling service agency than by being rescued once again by his or her parents.

Loan money only if you can afford to lose it. While some adult children may be very responsible about paying back loans, others may have a tendency to regard any money from you as a gift, even if you say that it's a loan. If an adult child is struggling to pay existing debt, he or she may be unable to pay you back in a timely fashion. And if you're loaning money during a true emergency for your child, it may take a long time for him to get back on his feet and pay you back. So, even if you are clear that this is a loan and that you do need to be paid back, don't hold your breath. And don't part with money earmarked to meet your own immediate needs.

Don't give your adult child money with the hope of getting closer emotionally or of being cared for in your later years. Giving with an agenda all too often backfires. As we have seen in studies cited earlier, when an adult child is financially dependent on parents, this can lead to tension in the relationship as the adult child feels powerless and the parents may feel justified in making comments and judgments about lifestyle choices. And making dependence on adult children part of your retirement plan can also lead to tensions, with the adult child resenting the burden of helping elderly parents just when his or her own child-rearing expenses are escalating.

Offer help in nonmonetary ways. Perhaps you can care for grandchildren while your adult child job-hunts or works a temporary part-time job that pays too little to cover child care. Perhaps you can offer to help an adult child work out a plan for getting out of debt on his or her own. Or you might offer an unemployed or financially strapped adult child a place to live for a certain, very specific, amount of time. There are many ways you can help without emptying your own bank account in the process. Give of your time or your expertise. Give loving support. But don't give away your own financial security.

Start saying "No" with love. Saying "No" when you need to and when it makes sense can be the most loving move you can make. Throwing cash at an unmotivated or irresponsible adult child does no one any favors. And using irreplaceable savings to finance whims and frills doesn't make sense either. Your granddaughter wanting a trip to Europe as a graduation present is not an emergency. Europe can wait until she is working and can afford to pay for the trip herself—and she might appreciate it more by then.

Remind your disappointed kids and grandkids that hanging onto your money and saying "No" is an advantage for all if it enables you to keep your financial independence. And refusing money requests doesn't have to be harsh if you let your adult children know that even when you're not able to give them cash, they have your love and emotional support forever.

Ideas for Adult Children

Keep this fact in mind: your parents' money is theirs—not yours. This may not be obvious, especially if you've been a close family and your parents have shared their resources to give you many advantages over the years. But the fact is that your parents have worked hard for their money, and especially when you're a young adult on your own at last, they may be redirecting more of their resources toward funding their retirement or enjoying experiences they have long deferred. Some adult children begrudge their parents these perks—either wanting more help now or fearing that their parents are busy spending their inheritance.

"They're being selfish," says Paula, thirty-four, of her fifty-something parents. "You'd think they'd take the family along instead of going to Hawaii all by themselves. And they just bought a new car after telling me I'd have to save for a down payment for a new car. And they should be putting more in the grandkids' college funds. The way they're spending, there will be nothing left to inherit!"

If you find yourself echoing Paula at times, wrap your mind around the fact that no one is owed an inheritance. Or a new car. Or an expensive family vacation. It could be that Paula's parents need a vacation for two to get reacquainted after years of putting family first. And this new car may be a treat after years of going without new cars in order to fund their own children's educations. Putting money aside for grandkids' college funds is a wonderful gift. It should be appreciated, but not expected.

If your parents are like most, you're still high on their financial priority list. But at this stage in their lives, they also need to focus on themselves: to readjust to an empty nest, to rediscover each other, to relax and enjoy themselves, to save aggressively for retirement.

Keep in mind that when your parents take care of themselves, particularly when it comes to planning for the future with savings and insurance plans, you benefit, too, by not needing to come to their financial rescue in their later years.

See a parental "No" as a positive. What? It's true: sometimes a parent's refusal to bail you out of a financial bind once again can be the beginning of your journey toward true independence and financial responsibility. If a parent is unable or unwilling to help you at this time, put a positive spin on it: if you're financially independent, even if you're struggling, you're free to make your own decisions. If your parents were financing your lifestyle, they might well feel that they have a vote in the choices you make. There might be tension, spoken or unspoken, when you're still dependent on your parents well into adulthood.

Don't let your parents' inability or refusal to help keep you from achieving a goal. If parents can't or won't pay for your college or for special training, or help you with a down payment toward a house, don't let your dreams be derailed by what looks like a setback. Decide to achieve your goals on your own. To be sure, it will be harder than if your parents had been willing or able to help. You may need to make adjustments to your plans and your lifestyle. It may take you longer to get that degree or buy that house, but you can do it. And achieving a major goal on your own—as hard as it may be at the time—can be immensely satisfying.

My brother Mike and I were talking about this recently. Our father, who was alcoholic and mentally ill, lost his job on my thirteenth birthday, and he never got another one. Our family sank into a kind of genteel poverty—with a paid-for house in a nice area but not much else.

We had no expectations that our parents could contribute to our college educations. But there was a further obstacle: our father was too ashamed to fill out the FAFSA, the parents' financial disclosure document required for financial aid. I got through college with help from other relatives during my first year. After that, I worked and also, once emancipated, applied for financial aid on my own.

During his undergraduate years, Mike lived with our widowed maternal grandmother, helping her on her farm and attending a small state school near her home. He graduated during the height of the Vietnam War with a low draft lottery number and found himself in the middle of the action. He promised himself that if he survived his combat duty, he wanted to do something beneficial for others, and he decided to become a doctor.

He applied to medical school after getting out of the service. He was twenty-nine years old when he enrolled at Stanford. And there was an unpleasant surprise: even though he was well into adulthood, our parents would need to fill out a FAFSA in order for him to get financial aid. Once again, our father adamantly refused to do so. Rather than let his dream slip away, Mike decided to make it happen on his own. He had saved some money during his military service. During medical school, he worked nearly full-time at two different part-time jobs, with most of his earnings going toward tuition. He drove our late grandfather's battered twenty-two-year-old Oldsmobile and rented a tiny room in the home of an elderly woman (who became a dear friend). It was far from easy, but he got his MD on time. And, looking back, he feels fortunate. He's convinced that if our parents had filled out that FAFSA, he would have applied for financial aid and graduated burdened by hefty student loans.

It's true that the cost of everything—from college to cars to houses—has exploded over the past few decades. It's harder than ever to pay for those major expenditures on your own. But it can be done.

Your plan of action might look something like this: attending a community college, living at home or in a rented room or with more roommates than you would prefer. It may mean riding public transportation longer than you had planned or driving an aging clunker or, eventually, buying a smaller, more modest starter home. But you can make it happen.

And that's a much better situation than spending a lifetime grumbling that you weren't able to meet an important goal because your parents wouldn't help you.

If a parent needs support from you, give it in other ways if you can't afford to give money. Help your aging parent to find much-needed resources. Offer occasional help with food supplies or medicine. Offer rides, or your time, or your warm embrace. Offer reassurance that, though money is tight for you right now, you will be there for your parent in other ways. And if you can contribute money on a regular basis, decide how much you can give without jeopardizing your resources for your own family's needs. If you give more than you can comfortably manage, there will be tension and resentment. Set a limit—and then see what else may be possible from siblings or from community resources.

Put the people in your life ahead of any financial concerns or disappointments. Some young adults are tempted to erupt in fury when parents are unwilling or unable to give them the financial help they would like. Many estrangements have started in this way. Before you say things that can't be unsaid or cut emotional ties with your parents, think about what will matter most in a year or two, or ten, or twenty. As we grow in our adult lives, we come to realize—sometimes too late—that the stuff we thought we needed, or the financial rescue that seemed so crucial once upon a time, pales beside the comfort and the joy of strong and loving relationships with those who may sometimes say "No" or otherwise disappoint us, but who love us deeply and forever.

CHAPTER SIX
Marriage—Yours and Theirs

As much as marriage can mean a loving joining together, it can also drive families apart, as troubles in a parents' marriage can divide or triangulate adult children, and a parental remarriage can be a seismic event even after the kids are long out of the house. When adult children fall in love and marry, there can be emotional minefields aplenty.

Do any of these scenarios sound familiar?

+ Immediately after your son and daughter-in-law were married, he became part of her family, and you were left out in the cold.
+ You voiced your disapproval of the man your daughter inexplicably decided to marry, and now neither of them is speaking to you.

+ You and your spouse of many years have been struggling quietly for a long time, but a recent argument in front of one of your adult children has prompted all your children to take sides and is forcing you apart even further.

+ You've done everything imaginable to have a good relationship with your daughter-in-law, but she keeps overreacting to everything you say and do and building a painful barrier between you and your son.

+ Your son-in-law is a control freak, and you feel that he is putting pressure on your daughter to cut ties with you.

+ Although you and your ex-wife were divorced seven years ago—after your youngest child left home—the kids have reacted very emotionally to the split. They weren't thrilled when your ex-wife remarried two years ago. But now they're going ballistic over your plans to remarry, and even they can't tell you exactly why.

+ Your mother can't understand why you're not willing or able to talk to her on the phone for at least an hour every night now that you're married. She's blaming your husband for coming between you, and that's not the case at all!

+ Your parents seem to hate everyone you date, and you're beginning to wonder if they have your best interests at heart—or not.

+ Your dad is remarrying, and your feelings are decidedly mixed. You're happy for him but sad for you, wondering how and if you'll fit into his new blended family.

When Your Marriage or Remarriage Causes Conflict with Adult Children

Through their many years of a difficult marriage—complicated by early and continuing resentments—Jack and Priscilla have suffered quietly, united in their desire to create a loving, secure home life for their three children, all now young adults.

Unbeknownst to their adult children, they have been getting marriage counseling for the past year. The counseling sessions are starting to feel like an exercise in futility, and with trepidation and great sadness, they have begun to consider divorce after more than three decades of marriage.

Recently, an argument that started in a marriage counseling session erupted once more at home in the presence of their visiting eldest daughter. She immediately jumped in to defend her mother's point of view. The youngest daughter, still living at home, vociferously took her father's side. Jack decided to leave the house until tempers cooled. He hasn't spent another night there since.

"I wouldn't say that the kids determined the outcome of our marital crisis," Jack says. "But their involvement at that awful moment hastened our path to divorce. And the rancor of that family argument has been divisive to this day, making the whole process more acrimonious than it might have been otherwise and causing a rift that continues between my eldest daughter and me."

Perhaps nothing can spark a family feud like a parental

remarriage—whether this happens years after a parental divorce or is the result of a more recent "gray divorce" between long-married parents of adult children.

According to Dr. Wednesday Martin, the single greatest predictor that a marriage will fail is the presence of children from a previous marriage or relationship. The divorce rate is 50 percent higher in remarriages with children than those without—and it doesn't matter how old the children are.*

In a survey of professional studies of the impact of adult children on remarriages, Dr. Martin found that adult stepchildren resent stepmothers the most. Whether the stepmother was a factor in their parents' breakup or came into the picture some time later, the stepmother was most likely to be the lightning rod for the husband's kids' unhappiness and anger. Stepmothers are resented more fiercely and far longer than stepfathers. Adult children can harbor unresolved anger and grief over their parents' divorce, hostility toward a new person shaking up the family nest further, and anxiety about the impact the new marriage may have on their relationship with their parent. They may also have concerns about their continuing ability to spend time alone with the remarried parent. Financial concerns may surface too: about how this new marriage will affect their financial life—from getting parental financial help now or via a future inheritance.

Some studies show that the mix of divorced parents, adult

---

*   Wednesday Martin, "Guess Who Has the Power in a Remarriage with Children?" Stepmonster (blog), *Psychology Today*, October 7, 2009. https://www.psychologytoday. com/blog/stepmonster/200910/guess-who-has-the-power-in-remarriage-children.

children and a new spouse can be volatile. Research by Dr. Richard Warshak has found that the underlying dynamics of this conflict can include jealousy, narcissistic injury, desire for revenge, competitive feelings, and parent-child boundary violations.[†]

"How am I supposed to feel?" asks Annalise, the twenty-five-year-old daughter of a father who remarried last year, six years after her parents' divorce. "They had been dating for two years before that and all I would hear when I was alone with him—which wasn't often because *she* was usually hanging around whenever I visited—was how great she was, how, unlike my mother, she was a really hot number in bed. Oh, my God! TMI! I don't want to hear that kind of stuff. And now that they're married, we're supposed to be lovey-dovey family with her and her two brat kids from her previous marriage. And now they're talking about having another child of their own! And I'm not sure where I fit in all this, or if I fit in at all. I feel like this has destroyed whatever closeness I had with my dad...and maybe that isn't even a problem for him. I'm beginning to think he doesn't even care about my feelings."

A similarly unhappy adult child was the topic of a recent letter to "Dear Abby." A fifty-four-year-old mother who had been divorced for ten years and remarried for two years reported that her twenty-five-year-old daughter, who was married and had two kids, was furious over her remarriage. Her daughter angrily asserted that she, not the new spouse, should come first in her

---

[†]   Richard A. Warshak, "Remarriage as a Trigger of Parental Alienation Syndrome," *American Journal of Family Therapy* 28, no. 3 (2000): 229–241.

mother's life. She stopped calling her "Mom," substituting her mother's first name, and forbade any contact between her and the grandchildren. The mother, heartbroken, said that she had no intention of leaving her husband to please her daughter, but that it was very painful to be cut out of her daughter's life.

Some of the anger behind such conflict is due to a shift in the ways that adult children see their parents. Falling in love again and remarrying sends a message to children of any ages, even independent adult children with families of their own, that it is more important for the parent to have a life of his or her choosing than to remain in their prior and primary role of mom or dad.*

WHEN YOUR ADULT CHILD'S MARRIAGE IS CAUSING CONFLICT

The road to estrangement is well traveled by parents and adult children when love and marriage are involved. Some of the more common conflicts are parental disapproval of the new spouse, a parent's unwillingness to play a secondary role in their adult child's life, family competitiveness, personality or cultural clashes with a new son- or daughter-in-law, and differing ideas of what it means to be family.

As we saw in an earlier chapter, researcher Dr. Megan Gillian

---

*   Linda Bernstein, "What to Do When Your Adult Kids Hate That You're in Love Again: 6 Tips for Negotiating the Shark-Infested Waters of Remarriage After 50," NextAvenue.com, February 11, 2013, http://www.nextavenue.org/what-do-when-your-adult-kids-hate-youre-love-again/.

of Iowa State University found that when a mother disapproves of an adult child's new spouse or of the marriage itself such as when a marriage violates a treasured value by going outside the family's religion, there is a much greater chance of estrangement than if the adult child had run-ins with local law enforcement or was even in prison.[†]

"My parents were totally enraged when I chose to marry outside the Catholic Church not once but twice," says Alexis, thirty-seven. "There was no other consideration—like whether I was marrying a good person or whether we might, just might, be happy together. Both marriages failed. I won't say it's because my parents were so unaccepting of these relationships. But it sure didn't help get us off to a good start either time."

There are times when vehement parental disapproval can actually push a young adult child *toward* an ill-advised marriage.

Jillian, now thirty-nine, thoroughly alarmed her parents when she married a drug addict, divorced him, and then married another very similar man. She says now that she wishes that her parents had gently expressed their concerns rather than screaming their opposition to her two marriages.

"If my daughter announced that she was going to do something as dumb as I did, I would take the soft approach so that she wouldn't get defensive and run off to spite me," she says. "I wish my mother had said 'Honey, I know you have a kind heart

---

[†]   Megan Gilligan, J. Jill Suitor, and Karl Pillemer, "Estrangement between Mothers and Adult Children: The Role of Norms and Values," *Journal of Marriage and Family* 77, no. 4 (2015): 908–920.

and like to help people who are in distress. That's something I really value about you. I just want to suggest that perhaps you take your inclinations to help those who are down and out and become a social worker or nurse rather than trying to help someone by marrying him. Unfortunately, often we are least able to help and rehabilitate those who are closest to us. You might end up being a better friend to this man by simply being a friend, not a spouse."

Jillian, who did eventually become a nurse, says that she has totally sworn off trying to fix lovers and potential spouses. "I'm getting my helping fix professionally," she says. "And I don't try to change my current boyfriend, who is also a professional and who doesn't drink or smoke or do anything else that's heinous. It's such a relief to be with a true adult person. I'm just sorry that it took me two awful marriages while breaking my parents' hearts to learn what a real loving relationship might be."

Even when parents approve of a new in-law, there can be conflicts inherent in the major shifts in alliances within the family. The new spouse becomes primary in the adult child's life, and the young couple may struggle to balance their own time and their own needs as a couple with their ties to parents and other extended family members.

This balance can be difficult to achieve when one or both of the young partners has not yet achieved separation from the parents, or when there is contentious competition between the two families for the young couple's loyalty.

In such loyalty battles, it is often the parents of the son who lose. Researcher Dorothy Jerrome has observed that family ties tend to be stronger among women, and that women are responsible for creating the culture of the home. The wife's parents may feel more comfortable in their daughter's home than the parents-in-law do. This tilt toward the wife's family of origin produces the most tension between the young wife and her mother-in-law, especially when the older woman seeks to continue active parenting.* Such agendas can set up struggles for primacy in an adult child's life that alienate not just your new son- or daughter-in-law, but also your adult child.

So many times parents—often unwittingly—speak before they edit themselves, revealing troubling feelings of ownership, of desires for unchanged primacy, of betrayal over the necessary changes in their relationships with adult children when the children marry.

Resisting the reality that life must change when adult children marry, being competitive with the spouse's family of origin and continuing to express disapproval of the match can quickly lead to greater emotional distance and, too often, estrangement between parents and their married children.

Two comments I received not long ago on my blog reflect this unhappy reality:

> *"My mother made the mistake of rejecting my brother's wife. Mothers can be possessive over their sons and think no*

---

*   Dorothy Jerrome, "Family Estrangement: Parents and Children who 'Lose Touch,'" *Journal of Family Therapy* 16 (1994): 241–258.

woman is good enough for them. As a result, my brother has now cut my mom off from his life. He is an adult now and had to choose between his wife and his mother. So he chose his wife."

"If you don't like their spouse and you communicate that through judgments, actions, and criticisms, you are surely destined to never see your child again. Their allegiance is to their spouse, just as yours was when you got married."

Of course, estrangements don't always come from parental misdeeds. Sometimes an adult child's new spouse plays a major role in creating a rift between parents and an adult child.

The new spouse may have a history of a more distant relationship with their parents and may see more frequent contact with parents as intrusive. Or the new spouse may sense or anticipate criticism where none is meant. Or he or she may be controlling and try to isolate his or her spouse from extended family.

"Our daughter's husband is highly controlling, though she swears that he doesn't abuse her," says Janet, sixty-eight, the mother of three adult children. "He's an evangelical Christian and sees us as nonbelievers and a bad influence on his family—our daughter and the two grandchildren with whom we have a very distant relationship despite living only forty-five minutes apart. All three of our children married people for whom religion is a major part of family life. We honor their beliefs, even if we don't share them, and we would never try to influence the grandchildren in a way that would detract from their faith. The other two kids and their families are closer to us. I wouldn't say *close*. But at least they're not estranged. With our daughter, birthdays and holidays pass without a word. She did come see us for a couple of hours two Christmases ago. She came alone and only stayed an hour. And she cried and apologized. I had such hope. But the estrangement pretty much continues unless her husband is out of town on business. It's so sad. For us and, I suspect, for her. We always give her the message that our door is always open—to any of them."

TIPS FOR AVOIDING ESTRANGEMENT

Ideas for Parents

Create an open-door policy. Even if you and your adult child seem impossibly at odds over his or her marriage—or yours— let your adult child know that your door is open, both literally and figuratively. No matter how angry or hurt or disgusted you're feeling, don't cut off all possibilities of reconciliation. Though there may be an angry silence between you at the moment, let your child know that you're open to talking, to listening to his or her point of view, and to finding a way to be together again.

Be the first to apologize—even when you're sure you're right. This can be a tough one to swallow. But sometimes that what's it takes to reconcile. And when people who love each other are alienated by their differences there are usually two sides to the story. So take the initiative and apologize for your part in your falling-out. Remember, as we discussed in chapter 1, parents usually have more of an emotional stake in remaining close with their grown children than the adult children have in maintaining ties with parents. It's easier—though generally not painless—for the kids to simply walk away from having any relationship with you than it is for you to sever ties. So even if you think apologizing is out of the question, think again. If you want to have an ongoing, loving relationship with your adult son or daughter, you can't be relentlessly right.

If your adult children are exacerbating your marital woes, call a halt. They may be taking sides, making suggestions, or getting triangulated into your marital disputes. Sit down with your adult child or children, preferably with your spouse, and explain that, although they might feel quite affected by the tensions between you and your spouse, the responsibility for resolving these issues is between husband and wife—and that even other family members can't really know or understand the complexity of the marital dynamic. Reassure them that you're both working hard on your issues but that, in order to reduce the tensions and find a reasonable solution, you two must be left alone to work this situation out. Well-intentioned interventions by adult children can only exacerbate the pain. Ask for their support, for their prayers, and good thoughts for both of you—but they need to leave it at that. Just as you would be expected to stay out of their marital disputes, they need to stand back and let you deal with yours on your own.

Before announcing a major change, be sensitive to your

adult child's emotional ties to the way things used to be in your family. Even when they're grown, many adult children still have a strong emotional attachment to their original family—even if that family hasn't been an intact unit for years. Many parents wait until the kids are grown and out of the house before making the decision to separate or divorce. But even though they are not under the same roof now, adult children can feel tremendous grief when their parents part. And they share many of the emotions of younger children when a single parent finds a new love or remarries—feelings like jealousy, a sense of betrayal, divided loyalties, grief over the loss of the family they once loved, and anxiety about where they will fit into this reconfigured family. While it's not necessary or even desirable to keep your adult children posted on your love life, it is essential to let them know when things are getting serious and to give them time to resolve their feelings about the situation. Don't expect them to share your joy immediately—or perhaps ever. But steer clear of ultimatums or forced togetherness when they're still trying to wrap their minds around your being with a new partner.

Make one-on-one time with adult children a priority. No matter how serious your new romance or how close you feel with your new spouse, make one-on-one time with your adult child a high priority in your life. Many of the negative feelings adult children may express when they hear the news that is making you so happy consists of wondering whether the new spouse will be a barrier to continued closeness with you. Though they need to get to know your new partner, they also still need time alone with

you. And in the tumultuous early months and years of a remarriage, perhaps this alone time—reassuring the adult child that
he or she is still loved and important in your life—is even more
important than new-family time with everyone together.

**Take a low-key approach to your adult child's new love,
even if your initial reaction is revulsion.** If you dislike your adult
child's romantic partner or feel that he or she is not quite the right
fit for your child, find something positive about your child's new
love and mention that, along with any reservations you may have,
rather than voicing relentless displeasure. And voice those reservations gently, more with questions than as statements.

For example, you might say, "Denny seems to be a really fun
guy and I enjoy his humor and his energy, but I wonder how your
differences will play out long-term. Have you discussed what it
would mean to have you working long hours and trying to get
ahead in your job while he is more laid-back? Would you both be
happy with that? Have you discussed what problems, if any, your
religious differences might bring up?"

Even with a nightmare scenario like your son falling in love
with a woman you consider a hopeless drunk, or your daughter falling in love with a guy who has done time both in jail and
in rehab for his drug activities, screaming "Have you lost your
mind?" could drive your love-besotted adult child straight into
the addict's arms, purely as a reaction against your negativity.

Give your adult child's new love the benefit of the doubt.
People get together for a lot of reasons, and what initially looks
like an imperfect match might work wonderfully over time.

For example, an ambitious go-getter might do well married to someone less driven if each complements the other in the relationship dynamic. Religious differences might matter more to you than to your adult child. An alarming first impression may mellow with time into an affectionate bond between you and your son- or daughter-in-law. Give the person a chance, and give yourself a chance to establish a warm connection with the couple, preferably before they make their relationship permanent.

Don't boycott a wedding, even if you disapprove of the match. Being present at this life transition, even if your heart is breaking, sends a message of love and emotional support to your adult child. So show your love by showing up, by smiling, by avoiding criticism or emotional scenes. If your adult child is truly making a terrible mistake, he or she will remember your support and will know that you will be there for him or her through all the changes and challenges of life. And if the match turns out to be a good and lasting one, your willingness to share that special day with them is a good way to get past old pain and build a new relationship.

Susan, a former client of mine, was, at least initially, opposed to her son Joe marrying Lisa. She told her son, "I have reservations about Lisa, as you know, but I want to reassure you that if you marry her, I will respect your choice and I will never say another word against her. I will make every effort to make her feel welcome and part of this family." And she held to that promise. Life wasn't immediately easy, for Lisa had been hurt by Susan's initial coolness toward her, but over time they built a good relationship.

Think back, remember, and understand the pressures that a newly married young couple face. When adult children marry, it does change your relationship with them, for better or for worse. While some adult children grow closer to their parents when they marry and have children of their own, others feel new conflicts as they struggle to maintain relationships with both sets of parents while building a marriage and an independent life.

The young couple may face logistical problems balancing busy work and commuting schedules with time with friends and family, and time alone together. They have the challenge of maintaining relationships with their own and each other's families of origin, and this task can be made more difficult if one or both sets of parents are competitive or demanding. Don't set up conflicts between families And don't ever try to force an adult child to choose between his or her spouse and you.

Keep clear boundaries with your adult children, especially when it comes to their marital problems or their sex lives—or yours! Be very careful when it comes to your adult child's marriage. If he or she tells you about marital problems or complains about a spouse's habits or personality quirks, don't immediately join in with critical observations. It is much more helpful to say something like "I'm concerned for you and love you so much. I'm sorry you're going through a difficult time. I hope that, however you work this out, it will be for the best."

Taking sides could come back to haunt you when or if the crisis passes and the young couple reconciles. Encourage careful thought before acting. Suggest marriage counseling to improve communication skills. Share your thoughts about all marriages having ups and downs, times of closeness and times of distance, and caution your adult child not to panic at the first signs of trouble, but to see difficulties as a sign that some change needs to happen.

In the same way, don't involve your adult children in your own marital tensions, complaining about their other parent and expecting them to take sides. If you're a single parent, it can be tempting to make an adult child a buddy and confidant. But as close as you may feel, there are some things adult children don't want or need to hear.

"When my parents divorced and my dad was dating again after thirty-eight years of a faithful but increasingly antagonistic marriage, he was eager to share all the details with me," says Eric, twenty-nine. "It was like we were just two guys talking about women. Except we're not just two guys. He's my dad. And I really don't want to hear about his sexual adventures. It isn't a matter of resenting his dates or being loyal to my mom. Even if he and Mom were still together and suddenly happy and passionate with each other again, I'd be happy for them, but still I wouldn't want to know the details. It's more information than I ever want to know."

Respect the privacy and primacy of your adult child's marriage and parenting. Don't drop in. Don't force an adult child to take sides with you against his or her spouse. In the absence of abuse or obvious neglect, don't question their rules and routines for their children.

If you're feeling bad vibes or feeling judged by a new in-law, don't act in kind, with criticisms or judgments in return. Instead, look at the situation and see how you might be contributing to the conflict. Are you expressing your opinions a bit too assertively? Are you undermining the importance of the new spouse's voice in making decisions for the couple? If there is nothing you have done to prompt such tensions, you might choose to see these behaviors as insecurity on the part of the young spouse and find ways to build ties despite your differences.

Treat differences in values gently. Religious and cultural differences are practically inevitable these days as our society becomes more diverse, and marriages are likely to reflect that. Whether your adult children and their spouses share your faith or your sexual orientation, whether a new spouse is of a different race or ethnicity, are all less important than whether they are happy, living with love, and able to care for themselves.

It's time to let go of the old expectations that you and your adult child will always agree and that your relationship with him or her will never change. This letting go isn't always easy.

There are instances where parents behave wonderfully and still get rejected by a son- or daughter-in-law and/or their own adult children. There are times when young couples are totally unreasonable and when time does, indeed, take a decidedly unfair turn.

Letting go of your adult children—and of any expectations that you will continue to have a central role in their lives—can free you to be happy in other ways, and free them to live their own lives. This sense of freedom may bring you closer together over time. Being close will be an active choice, not a dreaded obligation.

Ideas for Adult Children

Give your parents time to adjust to your new love, especially if there are significant differences that are of concern for them. They may need time to embrace a new person in your life whose religious belief, lifestyle, race, ethnicity, or gender is at odds with their beliefs. Give them some time and space to think about how this relationship works for you and to come to share your happiness. Don't immediately label them as sexist, racist, or homophobic. They may or may not be those things. But, in the interests of family harmony, give them the benefit of the doubt and let them know how much this relationship means to you.

"My parents really didn't know what to make of Bree when they first met her," Jake, thirty-three and married for two years, remembers. "My parents are pretty set in traditional sex roles, with the ambitious, breadwinning man and the stay-at-home wife and mother. That's how they live and what has worked for them for forty-two years. So they were shocked when I got serious about Bree, who is a physician and very dedicated to her career. She has more ambition than I do and more education than I do, and to them, it just didn't seem right. But after spending some time with her and seeing that we really loved each other and agreed in so many ways and truly complemented each other's lives, they fell in love with Bree, too. But it did take a little time. There were times when I wanted to scream at them in frustration. But I didn't, and I'm glad now. There were no angry barriers to their getting to know her and they're coming to appreciate all her good qualities."

If your parents are having marital problems, stay out of the fray as much as possible. Make an effort to express love and support for both parents (even if you feel that the trouble is more one person's fault than the other's). The fact is, even close family members can't know what a marriage is really like for the two partners. So even if one partner has been unfaithful or more agitated and argumentative than the other, there may be reasons or a backstory there that you will never know. Stay on the sidelines, express your love, and don't complicate matters by taking sides or expressing opinions.

If your parents and friends continue to have reservations about your love, consider what they're saying and hear it as love, not criticism. Try not to immediately reject what they say. It could well be that they have the wrong impression of the person you love. But when you're hearing some of the same comments from people who love you and whose opinions you usually respect, stop and think about what they're saying before challenging them or abruptly cutting ties with those who have reservations about your new relationship.

"My parents, my sister, and my best friend all felt that Jared was too controlling and too critical of me," says Emily, twenty-eight, of her now ex-love. "I saw and felt it as love and devotion and a wicked sense of humor. But when I considered their observations and then thought about how his possessiveness and barbed comments made me feel, it was a real awakening. I really resisted their perspective for a long time. There was a lot I liked about Jared. But I had to admit, quietly at first, that this relationship wouldn't be good for me long-term. I eventually broke up with him. Everyone around me was relieved, but no one said 'I told you so!' I'm so glad they spoke up early on and that I didn't marry Jared."

If a new love or new spouse is trying to isolate you from family and longtime friends, discuss it with him or her to find out why. It could be a feeling of discomfort and insecurity around your family and friends. It could be dislike or disagreements about their values or beliefs. He or she may feel that you don't have enough time together as a couple, or may have a differing sense of what it means to be close to family. In these instances, some compromise may be possible in terms of your keeping up ties with people with whom he or she would prefer not to spend a great deal of time.

Michael, a longtime friend of mine who was raised in a quiet, conservative family with ancestral ties to Austria, married into an exuberant, gregarious Iranian immigrant family. I once asked him the secret of his marital success despite significant differences in beliefs and life experiences.

"We allow each other to be authentically ourselves," he replied. "Persians love to party, and you really haven't lived until you've been to a Persian party! Frankly, though, a little goes a long way with me. I'm a quiet guy, as you know. If my going with her to a particular gathering is important to my wife, I go happily, without hesitation. Otherwise, I just as happily stay home and encourage her to party on. That might not work for everyone, but it does for us!"

There may be times, however, when a spouse's moves to isolate you from those you love have a darker side. Often, an early sign of emotional abuse is the attempted isolation of the victim from others. If your new love has strong negative feelings about your being in touch with loved ones, it could be a red flag that he or she is abusive and a sign that you need to be vigilant and, perhaps, reevaluate the relationship.

Think twice before excluding your parents from your wedding or from your children's lives, even if they have been critical and problematic. Deliberately excluding your parents from your wedding makes a statement that keeps on hurting, even years later, and can damage your relationship with your parents significantly. This is a major life event that parents may have dreamed of sharing for many years. While your choice of spouse may not have coincided with their dream, they may still very much want the option of being there for you on such an important day in your life. It might make sense to talk with them beforehand and agree on some rules of behavior—no outbursts, no criticism, no wailing in distress—during the wedding and reception. But do think twice about excluding them altogether.

Incidentally, the same holds true for excluding your parents or your in-laws from your children's lives. If they have been undermining you with the children—for example, saying "Yes" after you've firmly said "No"—it's time to speak up and let them know they're out of line. If they are passing on comments or values you don't share and don't appreciate your children hearing, let them know how you feel. And, if your children are old enough for such a discussion, tell them that you love your parents even though you disagree with them on certain matters, and let your children know how and why you disagree.

If the grandparents were harsh or distant or otherwise imperfect parents, don't exclude them on that basis. Quite often, your parents may be quite different with their grandchildren than they were with you.

"I couldn't believe how wonderful my father was with my daughter!" says Steve, thirty-seven, whose family has now expanded to include three children. "He was kind of cold and distant with me, distracted at best. But he was wonderfully warm and silly with her, cuddling her, singing funny little songs! I was just amazed. While the wistful child within me was running around begging him to give *me* that kind of attention, my adult self was just delighted, so happy to see what a wonderful grandpa he turned out to be!"

It makes sense to try to work out differences and agree on rules of the house rather than to exclude a grandparent from your child's life. When that happens, everyone loses so much.

If you're uncomfortable with your parent's lack of boundaries, say so and create your own. Speak up if your parent is telling you too much about his or her private life—or asking about yours.

"My mother never did have good boundaries, ever," says

Ashley, the only child of parents who have always been at odds in their intimate life. "When I was, like, ten years old, she'd be complaining to me about my dad wanting sex too much. And I'd be thinking 'I don't want to know this!' but I was a kid and didn't know how to say it. I was just so, so embarrassed. But lately she was telling me what a drag it is now that Dad's diabetes has made him generally impotent and the only thing he likes is manual stimulation. She was saying, 'He wants me to jerk him off, but it takes ages for anything to happen. It's such a chore.' And I said, 'You know, Mom, I love you and Dad. But some realities of your life are not for my ears. I don't need to hear this. If you want some help or advice, why don't you talk with his doctor and see if there's anything that could help. But please don't talk to me about your sex life. I'm your daughter and I love you, but I don't want to know.' She pouted a little a first, but she has taken that to heart. So I'm not getting too much information, and she's not asking too much about me and my life. And we're still close. That's a relief for both of us, I'm sure."

Before rejecting a parent's new spouse, take a deep breath and think about what you would like to have happen. Maybe your fondest wish is that this new person would just go away forever. Unless this person is abusive to your elderly, vulnerable parent (in which case you might want to intervene legally), it may well be that this new love is here to stay in your parent's life. You may find yourself longing for the family configuration that once was. You may be heartbroken about your parents' split, whether it was years ago or much more recent. You may consider this new person a pathetically poor substitute for your other parent.

The fact is, this new person will never take the place of a parent. But he or she could, in time, be a friend.

Consider this: if you have at least a cordial relationship with your new stepparent, this can help you to maintain a close relationship with your biological parent, who will appreciate your making an effort to accept the new love in his or her life.

If you feel that the new relationship is making it difficult to have a close, one-on-one relationship with your parent, discuss this privately with him or her. Let your parent know that you accept the new love, but that you miss having times alone together—while expressing willingness to socialize with the two of them at times.

"What I said to my dad was 'I need to still feel important in your life!'" says Liz, thirty. "I added that, to me, this meant having some alone time with him as well as time shared with both of them. He understood, especially since I wasn't being critical of her or expressing it in a way that made him feel that he had to choose between us. So now we have our own private lunches or meet for a run together some weekend mornings."

Respect the fact that your parent is not just Mom or Dad, but a complex person with a variety of feelings and needs. If your parent is like most, he or she needs and wants to have a loving relationship with you, to love and enjoy the grandkids, and to find a special partner to love. There is so much more to your parent than living the role of Mom or Dad.

Adult children who try to confine their parents to parental roles without seeing them beyond that can set up conflicts that lead to estrangement when certain aspects of the parent's life change.

"My thirty-five-year-old daughter was totally scandalized when I started dating ten years after her father's death," says Betty, sixty-three. "She thought I should just be a devoted mom-advisor and loving grandma. She couldn't see the sense to my dating or, heaven forbid, having a sexual relationship. She thought it was being disloyal to her dad and also completely pointless at my age. *At my age?* There's a lot of life left in this old gal. Now, I loved my husband very much and was so devastated by his fatal heart attack that I grieved for years. I'll always miss him. But it's time to get back into life. And there's a lot more to living my life than being Mom and Grandma—though I treasure those roles. I want to live my life to the fullest. Have a fling! Have fun! And, someday I hope to fall in love again. I hope my daughter comes to understand this. If she doesn't, well, that's her choice."

• • •

When it comes to accepting and understanding new love in your life—or in your adult child's life—it's important to embrace the fact that life itself is forever changing. And the best relationships grow with the changes.

Those who resist change and try to keep relationships exactly as they were once upon a time may feel betrayal when new love comes into another's life. They may say things like "After all I've done for you and all the sacrifices I've made for you, you go and do this to me?" or "Why do you need to find a new partner? I'm your daughter. Aren't the grandkids and I enough for you?"

Wise and loving parents and children celebrate the changes in their lives together and with love. This was quite evident in a comment by the parent of several adult children who wrote to comment on a blog post of mine recently:

I would never, ever pull the 'how much I have sacrificed!' card on my kids. The truth is, I didn't sacrifice anything in raising them. All the love, caring, laughter, and tears were all willingly given. My kids do not owe us anything more than to be the terrific adults that they have become. And they have all chosen to marry wonderful people.

When you look ahead and embrace change, expecting no payback for the past—only celebration of what is at the moment—life for you, your children, and the people you've chosen to love will be easier, sweeter, and filled with shared joy.

CHAPTER SEVEN

Divorce—Early or Late

The roots of estrangement may lie in the legacy of a long-ago parental divorce when the relationship between the noncustodial parent and child was broken by distance, by a hostile ex-spouse, or by one's own mistakes in parenting through this painful family transition. Or the challenges may be due to a "gray divorce," a divorce between longtime spouses over the age of fifty.

Do any of the following sound familiar?

+ You were divorced from your children's father when the children were very young. You did everything you could to give them a good life. But now that they're grown, the kids are flocking to your ex-husband and ignoring you.

+ You're close to retirement age and can't imagine being retired and with your spouse 24/7. You've been unhappy for a long time, but haven't left for many reasons: guilt, fear of upsetting the kids at important transitions in their lives, fear of the unknown, dread of the battle, anxiety about finances. You're wondering if this might be your last chance to be happy…or if it's already too late to make such a major change in your life and upset the whole family.

+ Your parents divorced when you were a young child and shared custody, which meant you never had a consistent home, moving back and forth between them. Now that you're grown and in your own place, you're feeling resentment toward both of them because it seemed that their needs always came first.

+ Your mother's hatred for your father hasn't abated in all the years since their divorce. Whenever you make an effort to maintain some sort of relationship with him, she sees this as a personal betrayal.

+ Your parents just filed for divorce after more than forty years of marriage, and you're finding it hard to take, especially since the grandkids are just babies and will never know an intact extended family. You're furious with both parents for not just hanging in there.

+ Now that your parents have divorced after many years of marriage, your mom has latched onto you to do all the things your dad used to do—fix things around the house, drive her places, take care of her after her latest foot surgery—and you feel like running away, leaving no forwarding address.

+ Your dad is dating again after ending his marriage to your mom after forty-one years, and the whole idea of this is just grossing you out. You really don't want to see this newly cool dude and hear about how happy he is when everyone else is miserable.

Whatever issues you may be facing in the wake of your own or your parents' divorce, you're far from alone.

Although there was a slight decline in overall divorce rates between 1990 and 2010, the divorce rate among adults over fifty doubled during that same time period.*

Whether divorce happens early or late in the life of a family, it can profoundly affect both young children and adult children's relationships with parents.

WHEN DIVORCE IS A PAINFUL LEGACY FROM THE PAST

When parents divorce while children are still young, there can be custody issues, financial considerations, and logistical challenges not shared by families facing divorce after the kids are grown.

"The most painful part of my being a child of divorce was feeling that, whatever I did, I was upsetting someone," says Dave, now thirty-four. "My parents spent years at each other's throats and running to court over money or me. I lived with my mother, who made constant nasty comments about my dad. I

---

*   Susan L. Brown and I-Fen Lin, "The Gray Divorce Revolution: Rising Divorce among Middle-Aged and Older Adults 1990–2010," *Journal of Gerontology, Psychology, Science, and Social Service* 67, no. 6 (2012): 731–741.

was supposed to see him every other weekend. But she made it so difficult that, after a while, he stopped trying so hard to see me. When I got older and could drive, I'd go to see him and, as an adult, I've tried to re-establish the closeness we had when I was a small child before the divorce. But there are so many things you can't get back—like time. I still feel angry at my mother for making a painful situation worse by trying to alienate me from my dad. She was very selfish in her anger. Still is. And that has definitely come between us."

Parental Alienation Syndrome, when one parent deliberately alienates a child from or denies the child access to his or her other parent, creates an environment filled with anger, hatred, and vicious remarks about the other parent. As a result of growing up in this toxic situation, children have an array of problems: guilt over their feelings toward the targeted parent; lower levels of achievement (measured in terms of having a college degree, gainful employment, and economic stability); impaired relationships; and lower self-esteem.[†]

Other studies have found that those exposed to parental alienation as children are more likely to experience depression, drug or alcohol abuse, lack of trust, alienation from their own children, and divorce later on in life.[‡]

[†]   N. Ben-Ami and Amy J. L. Baker, "The Long-Term Correlates of Childhood Exposure to Parental Alienation on Adult Self-Sufficiency and Well-Being," *American Journal of Family Therapy* 40, no. 2 (2012): 169–183.

[‡]   Amy J. L. Baker, "The Long-Term Effects of Parental Alienation on Adult Children: A Qualitative Research Study," *American Journal of Family Therapy* 33, no. 4 (2005): 289–302.

Some mental health professionals consider alienating a child from the other parent to be a form of emotional abuse—whether the child is completely cut off from the other parent; whether his or her relationship with the other is sporadic, dependent on the whim of the custodial parent; or whether the child is subjected to emotional manipulation such as withdrawal of love, the creation of loyalty binds, and cultivation of dependency. However it occurs, parental alienation disrupts the attachment between the child and the targeted parent.*

Even when children of divorce have not been subject to Parental Alienation Syndrome, the impact of their parents' divorce can influence their lives for years to come. As adults, children of divorce often report symptoms of anxiety and depression as well as reduced belief in their own ability to succeed.†

"I think my parents' divorce made me aware of the fragility of relationships and also the fact that you can think you have it made, financially and otherwise, and then everything falls apart," says Terry, a single, twenty-six-year-old flight attendant. "I don't expect relationships to last. I pick fights with boyfriends and am not surprised when we break up. And I'm very careful with finances. I live below my means. I remember so well what it was like for my mom, when my dad, an attorney, wanted a divorce. She went from having everything she had always wanted to

---

*   Amy J. L. Baker, "What the Research Says about Adult Children of PAS," *The Attached Family*. November 8, 2008, http://theattachedfamily.com/membersonly/?p=310.

†   J. S. Wallerstein and J. M. Lewis, "The Unexpected Legacy of Divorce: Report of a 25-Year Study," *Psychoanalytic Psychology* 21, no. 3 (2004): 353–370.

having nothing but me and a bunch of bills. I don't ever want to be in that kind of bind."

Avery-Ann remembers that she was five when her parents split and that it was the beginning of feeling "at the center of everything and, at the same time, totally invisible."

"I know that sounds contradictory," says the thirty-two-year-old married mother of two with a faint smile. "But that thought resonates with me. My parents fought over custody and money and came to an agreement where I would spend half my time with one parent and half my time with another. It worked for them. It didn't really work all that well for me. I never felt that I had my own safe place. I never had a lot of friends in either place. I felt like I was living out of a paper bag, carting my belongings around. My parents were satisfied that they were being involved parents. But whether I was with one or the other, I never felt like I was at home. I was just in Mom's place or Dad's place. There really wasn't a place—a home—for me and my feelings."

"I felt disposable," says thirty-one-year-old Denise, whose mother was married four times before Denise had finished high school and whose father, her mother's first husband, totally abandoned the family. "I had one stepfather when I was a child who was kind to me. I called him Daddy. I thought he would be in my life forever. But when he and Mom divorced, he moved on and left me behind, having a family of his own with his second wife. I've had a battle with depression all my life. I cling to relationships until there is no life left in them. I wonder if I'll ever have real love in my life. At the moment, I feel pretty much alone."

For some children of divorce, trying to put the pieces of their original family back together to fashion an extended family in adulthood can be a challenge.

"I grew up pretty much away from my dad," says Jake, twenty-eight. "It wasn't like my mom kept me from seeing him. He just sort of went on with his life. He had another family with a new wife, and they were closest to the grandparents on that side of the family. So I kind of drifted away. I have a lot of anger and resentment about that, but also a lot of sadness. I'd like to be close again. But distance has become this entrenched habit with us. I try to get closer at times. And, then again, at other times, I wonder why I even bother."

THE SHOCK OF GRAY DIVORCE

Even when a couple has struggled for years with a difficult relationship, a late-life divorce can be a shock to their adult children.

"You think, well, they've managed to get this far together," says Sandi, the forty-five-year-old daughter of divorcing parents. "You think that if they've managed to live with a certain level of discomfort with each other for all that time, they would just go on doing that. And I think that, whether you're a young child or an adult child, you always, deep down, prefer that your parents would stay together."

Kevin, who left a forty-eight-year marriage two years ago, has a different perspective. "A lot of people assume that a gray divorce is a matter of middle-age or older-age craziness or an old fool lusting over some young woman," he says. "That may be true in some instances. But my perspective is this: you don't leave a relationship of four or five decades on a whim in your senior years. I wanted to leave for many years, but didn't for so many good reasons. The main reason I stayed was that I loved my family so much. But I got to the point where I just knew that if I stayed in the marriage and continued so feel such stress and unhappiness, I would die sooner rather than later. I know it sounds dramatic, but it felt true for me: I needed to leave in order to live. It took that life-or-death certainty for me to leave."

Gray divorce can significantly change parent–adult child relationships. This is especially true in the case of fathers in late-life divorces who have daughters. Daughters are more likely to be angry with their fathers and blame them for the divorce.*

Other researchers have found that while father–adult child relationships are especially vulnerable in the wake of a late-life divorce, the mother–adult child relationship can become closer—or not. In some instances, newly divorced mothers may see more of an adult child as that young adult steps in to help her with tasks formerly performed by her husband. On the other hand, some mothers, among them those who lean too heavily, who ask too much, may cause adult children to back away and even become estranged.†

---

* W. S. Aquilino, "Later-Life Parental Divorce and Widowhood: Impact on Young Adults' Assessment of Parent-Child Relationships," *Journal of Marriage and the Family* 56 (1994): 908–922.

† Adam Shapiro, "Later-Life Divorce and Parent-Child Contact and Proximity," *Journal of Family Issues* 24, no. 2 (2003): 264–285.

Some newly divorced parents are more likely to place greater demands on their adult children, from daily tasks to caregiving. These new, often intense, obligations can weaken intergenerational ties.*

"Everything seemed to change so quickly," says thirty-five-year-old Jan, who is nursing her mother through hip-replacement surgery while juggling a busy work life and responsibilities as a wife and mother of two elementary-school-aged children. "Mom has always been having health issues, but Dad was always there at her side. Now he has left and is living several states away, and Mom is all mine. I can't say that I'm happy about him going on with a new life while I'm trying to keep all these plates spinning."

Jan's sentiments are echoed by many adult children who feel burdened or uncared for, torn by divided loyalties, or abandoned as their parents divorce and move on with their lives.†

Young adult children can be impacted by parental divorce in other ways. Some, still in college or not quite financially independent, may feel a loss of financial support and, for some, this can bring some dramatic changes to their own lives or educational goals.‡

After their parents divorce, adult children of all ages may

---

*   Susan L. Brown and I-Fen Lin, "The Gray Divorce Revolution: Rising Divorce among Middle-Aged and Older Adults 1990–2010," *Journal of Gerontology, Psychology, Science, Social Service* 67, no. 6 (2012): 731–741.

†   M. Campbell, "Divorce at Midlife: Intergenerational Issues," *Journal of Divorce and Remarriage* 23 (1995): 185–202.

‡   N. Long and M. Pett, "Parental Divorce: The Adult Child's Experience," *Family Perspectives* 26 (1992): 121–146.

experience difficulties and uncertainties around their own love relationships. They may have difficulty finding a mate and creating a lasting relationship or, if already married, they may question their own marriage in the wake of the breakup of their parents' long marriage.[§]

"I'd say that my own marriage is pretty happy, not perfect by any means, but okay," says thirty-year-old Brittney. "But when my parents, who always seemed to have a pretty near perfect relationship as far as I could see, split up, I began to wonder if Greg and I even have a chance. If divorce could happen to them after all those years…well, it makes me nervous about us."

Adult children may also find themselves grieving what was: the solidarity of the family they have known since early childhood.[℃]

"I'm just very sad," says Anna, twenty-nine, who is single and an emergency room nurse. "I miss our family get-togethers, just hanging out together, going on little vacations to visit other family members," she says. "Since the divorce, it just seems like family doesn't matter as much. And spending time with my parents is more complicated. I can't just go hang out with them on a Sunday. It has to be more…planned and balanced. Heaven forbid I should spend one minute more with Dad than with Mom. And some of the more extended family gatherings don't seem to be

§   C. L. Wright and J. W. Maxwell, "Social Support during Adjustment to Later-Life Divorce: How Adult Children Help Parents," *Journal of Divorce and Remarriage* 15, no. 3–4 (1991): 21–48.

℃   Holly Uphold-Carrier and Rebecca Utz, "Parental Divorce among Young and Adult Children: A Long-Term Qualitative Analysis of Mental Health and Family Solidarity," *Journal of Divorce and Remarriage* 53, no. 4 (2012): 247–266.

happening…or we're not invited. I miss the warmth and closeness of the family I grew up with. Things are not the same now that my parents are living apart."

Parents, too, can grieve family solidarity. Martin, who left his marriage of thirty-seven years last year, found himself overwhelmed with sadness and wistfulness last summer when his adult children, grandchildren, and ex-wife spent time together vacationing at the family's beach condo in San Diego, which his ex-wife got in the divorce settlement. "It isn't that I begrudge her that place," he says. "The condo meant much more to her than it did to me. I'm not jealous that the kids and grands are with her. I'm just sad because I'm the only one missing from the traditional family vacation this year. I miss the closeness and the fun of those days at the beach. Even though I have loving relationships with my children and grandchildren, I'm just wistful that I'm not there with them in that lovely, relaxed setting. I miss the good times of our life together."

How to Avoid Divorce-Related Estrangement Triggers

Ideas for Parents

Avoid making your adult children confidants for your marital or divorce woes. Just because your children are adults doesn't mean that they want to hear all the gruesome details of your disintegrating marriage. Even though they may offer you loving support during and after this painful time of transition, they have their own feelings of sadness, anger, and loss. As you divorce, they're losing the security of the only family they've ever known.

"On one level, I could really understand why my parents decided to divorce," says Alyssa, thirty-one. "They have little in common except us kids. They've been growing apart for a long time. My mom's spending sprees and my dad's affair two years ago just pushed them further to the edge. I understand all that. But I'm very sad about losing what I always considered home: the house I grew up in with both parents there. Now they're moving into their own separate places and neither feels like home. I love them and want to be supportive. But hearing the details from one or the other? Not so much. I know as much as I need to know."

Instead of engaging an adult child as your confidant, talk to an older family member, a close friend, or a psychotherapist.

Give the kids news on your pending divorce in person, preferably when they're all together. Unless distance dictates otherwise, telling your adult children about this life-changing event in person, preferably with your spouse and all your children present, is preferable. Especially when the divorce is unexpected, an out-of-the-blue phone call or email can feel like a bomb, leaving the adult child feeling shell-shocked and profoundly alone.

When you can share the news and deal with your feelings as a family, it can reassure adult children that they still do have a family, that their feelings matter, and that this is a painful event you will all get through together.

Don't seek to align your adult children with you against your ex-spouse. Expecting your adult children to choose sides adds greatly to the stress of a divorce—for them and for you. Don't add a layer of guilt or inquisition when they get together with their other parent.

It's important not to compound mistakes of the past with continuing bitterness and expectations of loyalty and exclusion. If, in your anger and bitterness over your divorce or your spouse's behavior years ago, you attempt to limit your children's contact with their other parent, this can have unhappy consequences in the present. No matter how he behaved or how much child support your ex-husband didn't pay, your adult child may be seeking to re-establish a relationship with his or her father. No matter what your ex-wife's transgressions in the past, your adult child may choose to form a new bond with a long-lost mother, and will resent any efforts on your part to interfere further.

If your adult child seems to prefer the company of the alienated parent these days, it could be due to a number of feelings: resentment over the alienation; guilt over the angry, hateful sentiments they may have adopted in the process; assertion of the independence of young adulthood; and the discovery that this parent, rather than being the personification of evil or the poster person for bad parenting, is, instead, a complex person with some strengths and some weaknesses.

Even if you never consciously thought to alienate your child from his or her other parent all those years ago, if you confided your anger to them and criticized the other parent relentlessly (even if much of that criticism was warranted), this could have caused a certain amount of parental alienation. Don't discourage their efforts to reconnect. Don't tell them that this is a betrayal and that they have to choose between you and their other parent. In doing so, you could be building an emotional barrier between you and your adult child.

Allowing your adult children the freedom to have their own time with, and feelings about, you and your ex-spouse can enhance the quality of your relationship. Focus on enjoying your time with your adult children without trashing their other parent or seeking information about your ex-spouse. Once you're divorced, information about your ex's love life or lifestyle choices really isn't your business. Nor should he or she be making inquiries about yours. Feeling an urge to know everything is a sign that you're still feeling connected, even if only through anger, and that you may need help resolving your feelings in order to let go and move on with your life. If you do need help with this, professional counseling and talking with your pastor or with friends are all better alternatives than involving your adult children as confidants or spies.

It's important, too, to avoid making your marital split a continuing area of contention that takes center stage at your children's own major life transitions. Weddings, especially, can be a minefield as divorced parents make ultimatums about the ex-spouse and/or his or her new spouse attending the festivities. The wedding of an adult child is about him or her—not you. Even if you're footing some or all of the bill, this is your adult child's day to share with all family members. Just for that day, honor those wishes.

Sally and Ron weathered a contentious divorce with lingering rancor for years afterwards. They had been divorced for twenty years when their daughter Jessica got engaged. Although the ex-couple had not seen each other for years and communicated only through their attorneys, both agreed to walk Jessica down the aisle together and to put aside the acrimony in honor of her special day. The wedding pictures show a family briefly united to celebrate Jessica's happiness, and the photo of her parents smiling as they walk her down the aisle is one she particularly treasures.

"I felt so totally loved that day," Jessica says, smiling through tears. "It was truly the best day of my life so far. I have the most wonderful husband and loving marriage—and I felt my parents' love for me so strongly when they put aside their own discomfort to be there for me. It meant so much to me! I've seen friends' weddings get ruined by parents who [each] refuse to come if the other does, or who get into a fight during the reception. My parents were both wonderful at the wedding and reception. It makes me love them more than ever!"

Take care of yourself as much as possible. Don't lean on the children, expecting them to take care of you the way your spouse used to. Don't expect a daughter, whether single or married, working outside the home or not, to take care of your household duties or to cook for you on a regular basis. If you haven't cooked for yourself or done laundry or cleaned the house for years—or ever—it's not too late to learn. If you have the resources, hire a cleaning person. Don't expect your adult children to fill the void your ex-spouse left. Don't expect a son to run over to fix whatever isn't working or to drive you to appointments. Drive yourself. Take public transportation. Ask a friend. Hire a handyman to do the household tasks and repairs you can't handle. Don't just expect that your son or daughter will take care of everything. Such expectations, especially when the adult child is busy with work or a family of his or her own, can create considerable tension between you and your son or daughter.

"It just got to be too much," says Ric of his newly distant relationship with his divorced mother. "In the divorce, she got the house. She got the dog. But she didn't really want to take care of either [one]. She expected me to drive forty miles each way a couple of times a week to take her grocery shopping, to do yard work, and [to] pick up dog droppings from the yard. She can drive. She just prefers not to. She could hire someone to do the yard work. She has a small yard. It would be less than $50 a month. I'd even pay it. And she needs to get out of the house and walk her dog and pick up after him. I have my own life. I work long hours. My wife and I need our time together. We have two teenagers. Need I say more? I don't need to be making eighty-mile round-trips three or four times a week to pick up dog crap. It made me feel used and manipulated. Mom is healthy and in her late fifties. She's perfectly capable of doing for herself."

If you're still feeling a lot of anger and bitterness toward your ex-spouse, find other ways to deal with it (instead of

venting to your children). Dispel some of that angry energy through exercise—run it off, learn kickboxing, hit tennis balls with new ferocity. Pummel a pillow. Vent to a friend or talk with a psychotherapist. Write a letter to your ex saying exactly what you think. Then tear it up. Keep a journal and write all of your feelings for your eyes only.

"Journaling was a tremendous help to me," says Shari, fifty-seven, and divorced for three years. "It still is. I can say anything on paper without having to deal with another person's feelings. I used to complain all the time to my daughter until she told me that she had heard enough and was feeling sad and frustrated. A friend suggested that I try journaling, and it feels great. Not only do I get to say whatever I'm feeling, but I can also go back and read earlier entries in my journal and realize how far I've come from where I was emotionally even a year ago."

Expect moments of sadness and wistfulness despite your firm resolve to move on. Especially as your anger begins to fade, you may begin to miss some of the good times you shared as a family. This doesn't necessarily mean that your divorce was a mistake, but that, like any relationship, your bond with your ex-spouse was a mixture of good times and bad, love and anger, sharing and resentment.

Particularly when your adult children and ex-spouse get together for a holiday, it can be difficult. You may feel wistful about all those holidays you shared together. You may feel sad about being the one left out and resent that the kids are choosing to spend time with the other parent on this particular holiday.

Instead of quietly resenting your kids and your ex-spouse or expressing your feelings to your adult children, accept these feelings as your own, as part of the experience of being divorced or separated. Deal with these feelings in ways that don't guilt your kids or otherwise put them on the defensive. You might choose to journal or talk with a friend. You might choose to plan a holiday celebration for other single friends—or to spend time with one special friend. You might decide to work as a volunteer at a holiday event for those less fortunate.

It's time to reflect on what was good about your life with your ex-spouse, and the blessings you still have in your life today, and to take steps to build a happier, more independent life in the future. When you're in charge of your own life, when you can begin to look back with love and forward with hope, your adult children may be increasingly inclined to spend more good times with you.

Ideas for Adult Children

Be aware that taking sides in your parents' divorce can damage your relationship with both parents. If one parent is totally trashing your other parent and encouraging you to cut ties with him or her, you could get caught up in the moment and then later resent your alienating parent for urging you to take sides. Or you could distance yourself from the parent you blame for the divorce, only to discover later that things were not quite the way you initially imagined.

Even though emotions can be raw in the early stages of a marital breakup, try to avoid passing judgment or distancing yourself from a parent because of what you think you know. Even though you've lived a lifetime with your parents, it isn't possible for you to know all the intricacies of their relationship.

In most divorces, there are two sides to the story. It's likely that both parents contributed, each in his or her own way, to the marriage falling apart. There may be old hurts that have eroded martial good will. One may have taken the other for granted or have withheld sex to signal his or her unhappiness. There is so much you may never know. So don't rush to judgment. Try hard to be loving and supportive of both parents during this painful time in all your lives.

Clarify with your parents how your life may need to change as a result of this divorce and develop a plan for yourself. If you're still in college or not quite financially independent, it's important to clarify with your parents what financial help, if any, they will be able to offer you in the wake of the divorce—and then plan accordingly. You might need to work more and go to school part time. You might need to transfer from an expensive private college to a state school. Or maybe nothing will have to change. But—if you're worried about the impact of your parents' divorce on your own educational future—it's good to find out sooner rather than later what will be possible.

"I lived with uncertainty for the whole first year my parents were divorcing," says Rob, twenty-one. "My tuition was paid for that year, but I just didn't know how things were going to go and hesitated to bring it up. I just worried quietly, hoping nothing would change. But everything did change, and when my parents started the conversation with me later on, I felt resentful, like I wasn't in control of my own life. I ended up transferring from my dream school, a private Eastern college, back to a state university back home in California. At first, I was upset. Then I discovered a new major that excited me, and it turned out great. I'm grateful to be able to finish college at all, let alone in a program that has given me a whole new goal for the future. I guess I just wish I had taken the initiative and discussed the possibilities with my parents before changes were absolutely necessary. Even though things have turned out well, I would have felt better at first if it had been more my own idea."

When you initiate such a discussion with your parents early on, you have more of a voice in the decisions that concern you and, perhaps, more control over your own destiny, particularly if you are willing to make changes and sacrifices given your family's new financial realities.

Set limits on a needy parent. You may be feeling torn when your parents divorce, and suddenly one or both are leaning on you more for support and practical help. You love them. You feel bad for them. You want to help. But you also have your own life and responsibilities and are quickly feeling overwhelmed and, perhaps, a bit resentful.

Letting your parent know what you can and will do—and what you can't—may decrease rather than increase hard feelings.

"When I told my Mom that I would talk with her on the phone for twenty minutes every other evening, she didn't like it one bit," says Jennifer, a busy forty-one-year-old corporate project manager and the mother of two teenagers. "But when she realized that she could count on hearing from me at a specific time, she came to accept it and depend on friends and her sister to talk with in the times in between."

Decide in advance what is possible for you, and then stick to you plan. Don't let guilt make you agree to do things that you don't have the time or inclination to do. Help your parent find ways to meet his or her needs by calling on different family members, community resources, or services.

Keep boundaries firm. There are two major challenges when you're an adult child with divorcing parents: keeping out of their fights and feuds with each other; and letting them know what you're willing—and what you're not willing—to hear.

It could be that one parent crosses the line by complaining endlessly about your other parent or by trying to get you to act as an intermediary. It could be that a parent, newly single and dating for the first time in years, is acting like a besotted teenager and telling you more than you ever wanted to hear about his or her romantic adventures. It could be that a parent wants to share more details of the failed marriage than you care to know.

It's time to call a halt and tell your parent kindly but firmly that this is all too much information and that you refuse to get into the middle of what needs to be a private matter between your parents.

You might draw a line in the sand by saying something like "I really love you and care how you're doing, but I find it very hard to hear about [fill in the blanks!]. I don't want to get in the middle of things and keep you guys from working out your feelings or the divorce settlement on your own. I love you both. I want to be there for you. But right now, it's just too painful for me to listen to all these details."

Understand that, even though you're no longer a child and have your own life, a parental divorce can hurt—a lot! A variety of feelings can come up when you hear the news that your parents are divorcing. You may feel intense sadness at the loss of your intact family of childhood. You may feel angry at one or both parents for not making their marriage work. You may feel guilt over somehow not being able to help them manage to stay together. You may have some resentment over ways this divorce will change your life, available resources, and educational or career options. You may harbor some anticipatory dread over living through this divorce with your parents over the next few months or years. You may wonder if love is worth all the pain and if this kind of unhappy ending is inevitable.

"I have to say, I was a mess when my parents were divorcing, even though I was thirty-five and married," says Gina, now four years past her parents' split. "I cried. I was angry and sad and had spats with both of them. I went through a period of depression. I felt like I wasn't handling it well at all. Come to find out, it's quite common. Kids of all ages don't like seeing their parents divorce. Only there's a lot more support around for young children of divorce. Adult children of divorce are, too often, left hanging or told to grow up and get on with life."

It's important to know that all these feelings are very common, normal, and natural in the wake of this major life transition. You're losing your family as it has been all your life. Your children may be losing, or may never know, grandparents who welcome them into a shared home. And you may, quite understandably, grieve this loss for all of you.

Although support groups for adult children of divorce are not nearly as common as those for younger children, check to see what might be available in your community. Talk with friends who share this experience. Talk with siblings or other family members. See a psychotherapist to work through your feelings of loss, of anger, and of grief. Cry when you need to.

The passage of time and adjustment to this new normal in the life of your family of origin will help. In time, you will be not only better able to deal with the fact that your parents are no longer together, but also able to look back on the happy times you shared as a family without quite so much sadness and longing. You may come to the point when you feel grateful for the warm memories and accept the fact that not every love story—even one that once seemed nearly perfect—has a happy ending.

Don't give up on love. When you've lived through a parental divorce as a child and have seen how love can turn to rancor and how often remarriages don't work out, you may be a pessimist when it comes to romance. At any age, when you see your parents' marriage in ruins, you might start feeling pretty cynical about love relationships in general. You may wonder if taking the risk of loving another is even worth it. You may wonder if you'll ever be able to trust another or find someone wonderful to love. You may worry about the fate of your own marriage and whether it can withstand the stresses that life brings in middle age and beyond.

It's important to realize that each relationship is unique, with its own strengths and its own points of vulnerability. There are some ways to safeguard your relationship if you are an adult child of divorce. Realizing your uniqueness as a couple is a start.

It's also important not to panic when you feel some stress or distance in the relationship. All marriages go through times of closeness and times of distance in an endless cycle. As a therapist, I've seen many couples panic at the first disagreement or that first cycle of distance and hasten to call it quits. And that's sad. Because on the other end of feelings of loneliness or anger, there can be reconciliation and rediscovery. If you simply assume that your relationship is fated to follow your parents' path, you'll miss so much.

Paying attention is another relationship strengthener. When you feel at odds with each other, reach out. Express your love, even in conflict, and your commitment to work this out. The same is true when you have a sense of distance, even if you can't pinpoint the reason. If you believe in your relationship and want it to work, you take notice. You may be going through one of those predictable cycles in marriage, but it's important to let your spouse know that you're there for him or her and that you're fully committed to this relationship.

Don't take your partner or his or her love for granted. Talk with each other. Listen to each other. And don't assume that a dire family history of broken marriages will doom yours. You have the power to be different. Make a promise to yourself and each other that your love and commitment will endure.

CHAPTER EIGHT
Divergent Memories

From family stories to photo album narratives and family in-jokes: all of these ways of remembering can add to the bonding of family members, including parents and adult children. But our memories can also divide us.

Do any of the following sound painfully familiar?

+ As a parent, you're puzzled. You have wonderful memories of fun and loving involvement with your child when she was young. But all she can remember is the negative aspects of those times.

+ You and your adult child had a good relationship until she went to a therapist to help deal with her depression over a romantic breakup. Suddenly, she's accusing you of sexual abuse—something that never happened—and wants to cut off all contact with you.

+ Your adult child was sexually abused by a distant relative when she was a child. You suspect that this early trauma is a factor in her anger and distancing herself from the family in general. But every time you try to bring it up, she cuts you off, saying she doesn't want to talk about it.

+ As an adult child, you've come to dread family holiday gatherings because the warm memories everyone shares don't ring true for you. Everyone else remembers closeness. You remember pain and exclusion.

+ You're at odds with your parent (or your adult child) because your memories just don't match up—even when you're talking about the same event or events.

The Curious Nature
of Memories

When we think of memories, we often imagine mental snapshots or videotapes of a certain past. While we might admit that some memories may be enhanced by time—those "misty water-colored memories" of the way we were—we tend to believe, in general, that our memories are indisputable fact.

At the time of an experience, we may anticipate and reject the eventual softening of a memory over the years, clinging to the facts as we know them in the moment—determined to remember just how mean and unfair a parent was or how hard a situation was. Think for a moment about some of your own memories from childhood, adolescence, or your college days. Have the memories or the feelings they evoke changed over time?

When I was an undergraduate at Northwestern, weary of putting myself through school, the rigor of a challenging program, and the angst of being perpetually lovelorn, there was a moment when I was stomping through the snow on the way to class muttering to myself: "I will never forget how hard this was. Ever. I'll never become one of those nostalgic alums who thinks these years were great!"

Although I was adamant at the time that I would forever remember my college years as a time of hardship and existential loneliness (and I still recall that moment and those feelings well), my memories of my college experience have expanded over time, evaluated in evolving contexts. Now my memories of Northwestern are largely about life-changing lessons learned both in and out of the classroom and of special people from that era—some still close, lifelong friends—who are evidence that I was never really alone in facing the challenges of my young life.

Our memories are changeable, malleable, influenced by a variety of factors.

They can be influenced by the quality of attachment we feel to our parents or our children. In one study of seventeen-year-olds and their parents, the adolescents who had a secure attachment to their parents remembered interactions with both parents, including conflicts, more favorably over time. Those with insecure attachments showed less positive reconstructive memory. In the same way, the mothers of secure girls remembered conflicts more favorably over time, whereas mothers of insecure boys had less favorable memories. The fathers in the study, interestingly enough, showed no attachment-related memory bias.* Does this suggest that fathers are the most objective in terms of recounting past events? The researchers made no comment about this finding. To be sure, this would be an interesting topic for future study!

Memories can be influenced by a number of naturally occurring distortions. Prominent research psychologist Daniel L. Schacter has noted, "Memory is inherently a reconstructive process whereby we piece together the past to form a coherent narrative that becomes our autobiography. In the process of reconstructing the past, we color and shape our life's experiences based on what we know of the world."[†]

In his research, Dr. Schacter has identified several types of distortions common to our memories.

There is "imagination inflation." This can range from someone remembering a real event with some embellishments that they are certain did occur to having a false recollection of an experience that did not occur. Sometimes imagination inflation will shape a memory to match a person's current self-image.

---

* Matthew J. Dykas et al, "Do Adolescents and Parents Reconstruct Memories about Their Conflict as a Functional Adolescent Attachment?" *Child Development* 81, no. 5 (Sept–Oct 2011): 1145–1454.

† Daniel L. Schacter, Scott A. Guerin, and Peggy L. St. Jacques, "Memory Distortion: An Adaptive Perspective," *Trends in Cognitive Science* 15, no. 10 (October 2011): 467–474.

During a recent family gathering, for example, Sheila, at twenty-nine, the youngest child of an aging, widowed mother, quaffed a few glasses of wine and then tearfully recounted a traumatic family event that took place more than twenty years ago: the night her father, now deceased, flew into a rage and beat her brother Patrick so severely that he immediately left home and went to live with relatives.

The young woman, now a compassionate, caring nurse, recounted that night in a way that raised her mother's and two siblings' eyebrows. She remembered trying to defend her brother, empathizing with his pain and throwing herself between him and their violent father. But the reality, as other family members recall, is that the father's rage was triggered by a very young Sheila tattling on her brother. As the violence escalated, Sheila screamed for her father to stop. She tried to intervene but was pushed aside. Her guilt over her role in this pivotal family drama and her evolution as a loving adult have colored her memories to fit the person she is now. Although the memories of her tattletale behavior as a child have faded, it may well be true that she felt her brother's pain acutely and felt regret over her part in triggering the event as she tried to intervene. And though there was a little eye-rolling among other family members as they listened to her revised version of that night, no one challenged her memory.

"Why would I?" asks Patrick. "It was such a painful, chaotic time. I think she remembers what she felt then and how she feels now. And she was just a small child at the time. Why impose my reality on her? She remembers this the way she needs to remember it."

Remembering the gist of an experience—perhaps forgetting specific details but remembering the general event—is another memory distortion that Dr. Schacter and his colleagues have identified.

Melanie, twenty-six, and her father Eric have been at odds lately over her assertions that he never spent time with her when she was growing up. Hurt, he pointed out to her that he often took her to the zoo and to museums and that they had a Saturday ritual of going for ice cream after dinner. Melanie's memories are vague. "I do remember going places like the zoo and the Natural History Museum and that chocolate chip ice cream was my favorite. I just don't remember much specifically about my dad being part of that," she says.

Yet another distortion: post-event misinformation. If someone hears erroneous information along with a memorable event, that misinformation may become part of the memory.

When Christopher, now forty-one, was six years old, his parents split up, and his mother, who was ill and had few resources at the time, left him with his father. Her memory of that desperate time just before her departure includes holding Christopher on her lap and telling him how she loved him and how she would come back for him. Soon thereafter, his father and a paternal aunt told him that his mother didn't love him and was never coming back.

In his memory of the event, all Christopher can recall is the pain he felt when his mother walked out the door and being told that she didn't love him. This memory, forever altered by misinformation, has complicated their relationship for many years. Even though his mother did come back into his life when he was still quite young, even though she has expressed her love for him over the years, he has found it hard to trust and believe her words. He also finds trust and commitment difficult in romantic relationships.

Some studies have found that negative events and information are more likely to be distorted in memory than positive events. One study has proposed that this focus on the negative may be a means of enhancing an individual's ability to deal with such events should they recur.*

Other researchers have found that people's memories of their own parts in salient life events may be overly positive or negative, serving to inflate their current self-evaluation, and that this can be beneficial to current well-being.† This may explain Sheila's need, as we have seen, to remember that she tried to protect her brother rather than her role in triggering her father's violence that escalated into a family crisis.

Strong emotions can also shape our memories. We may have vivid recollections of events that were intensely frightening, sad,

---

* S. Porter et al., "A Prospective Investigation of the Vulnerability of Memory for Positive and Negative Emotional Scenes to the Misinformation Effect," *Canadian Journal of Behavioral Science* 42 (2010): 55–61.

† A. E. Wilson and M. Ross, "The Identity Function of Autobiographical Memory: Time Is on Our Side," *Memory* 11 (2003): 137–149.

infuriating, or otherwise devastating, but not all of the details we remember may be accurate.

Jon, thirty-four, has vivid memories of the day his beloved maternal grandmother died unexpectedly when he was fifteen. What compounded his grief and sparked anger at his mother was the fact that his grandmother's elderly dog Max, whom he loved greatly, was put down during a home visit from a vet on the same day. "How could you do that?" he recently asked his mother, with whom he has had an on-again, off-again estrangement since he has been an independent adult. "I would have taken care of him. You knew that and still you had him killed!"

His mother looked startled at these details. "But I didn't make that decision," she said quietly. "Your Nana, because of her heart condition, had written out instructions to family and friends in the event of her death. Her instructions had been that Max would go to you. But several weeks before she died, she added a P.S. to her instructions to Aunt Cecile, who, as you might remember, lived next door to her then. Nana had just discovered that Max had inoperable cancer and only weeks to live. She couldn't bear to put him down, but asked Aunt Cecile to have the vet come to the house in the event of her death to euthanize Max. In fact, by the time the news got to us that Nana had died, Max had already joined her."

Jon looked skeptical, repeating, "I would have taken care of him..."

Strong emotions about certain people and events in our lives can go far beyond misunderstandings. Some researchers have found that emotions can even increase a person's susceptibility to false memories.*

The concept of false memories—repressed and recovered memories—has been highly controversial in the past two decades. This controversy reached its peak in the 1990s, when a number of adults, often in therapy for common problems like depression or anxiety, were suddenly recalling instances of sexual abuse or satanic ritual abuse, memories they claimed had been buried until they were "recovered" during the course of their therapy. They experienced these "memories" as deeply and painfully as they felt other memories of remembered events in their lives. They often angrily confronted their parents with stunning accusations and initiated long-term estrangements.

The controversy centered on whether it was indeed possible to have total amnesia about such a painful event in one's life, and whether it was possible to recover such memories many years later. Many patients reported that their recovered memories had been accessed when a therapist did hypnosis or hypnotic exercises like guided imagery in therapy sessions.

Some of these therapists, though well-meaning, tended to believe that a huge variety of conditions, such as depression, anxiety, or eating disorders, invariably were signs that a patient had been sexually abused in childhood. Some of these therapists (as well as the authors of a few popular books of that time)

---

*   Robin Kaplan et al, "Emotion and False Memory," *Emotion Review* 8, no. 1 (January 2016), 8-B.

were or believed themselves to be survivors of abuse themselves. Identifying as victims of this type of abuse greatly influenced their work with patients.

In researching the phenomenon of recovering long-buried memories, noted memory researcher Elizabeth Loftus found that, in many instances, therapists were using highly suggestive techniques to help patients "remember" instances of abuse, leading patients to form emotional but false memories of events that never occurred.*

Professional organizations, such as the American Medical Association, weighed in with their own skepticism. The AMA stated that it considered recovered memories of childhood sexual abuse to be of uncertain authenticity, that such memories should be subject to external verification, and that use of recovered memories was fraught with problems of potential misapplication.†

Although the matter has largely disappeared from headlines today, some families are still being affected by those long-ago accusations and estrangements. And there are still some therapists, often unlicensed practitioners who specialize in hypnotic regression and other questionable therapies, who may trigger such "recollections."

Today, many more therapists believe that there are a *number* of possible contributing factors to patients' depression, anxiety,

---

*   E. F. Loftus and K. Ketcham, *The Myth of Repressed Memory: False Memories and Allegations of Sexual Abuse* (New York: St. Martin's Griffin, 1996).

†   American Medical Association, *Report of the Council on Scientific Affairs: Memories of Childhood Sexual Abuse*, C.S.A. Report 5, A-94 (1994).

eating disorders, or other concerns that prompt them to seek therapy. Therapists want to be supportive of patients who actually have experienced abuse, while not enabling false memories in patients whose strong emotions about certain family members or events may make them especially vulnerable to suggestion.

Researchers have found that people who have experienced trauma—from abuse to war experiences or having survived the Holocaust—tend to remember such events. Sometimes such survivors wish fervently that they could forget. They may be troubled by memories in recurring thoughts and in dreams, perhaps waking up with nightmares. They are unlikely to succeed in blocking these memories or to have amnesia.‡ A trauma survivor may maintain silence about the past, but it is still very much with them.

In the same way, a child who has been abused may not want to talk about his or her memories. He or she may want to talk about these experiences later in life—or not. But the memories have always been present, though often unexpressed for a variety of reasons.

Memories of childhood trauma, vivid and tinged with strong emotion, can evolve over time. Journalist Susan Faludi, who recounts her relationship with her father in her recent memoir *In the Darkroom*, recalls a parent who was frightening, explosive, and violent. After her parents divorced, she was estranged from her father for twenty-five years.

In that time, her father moved back to his native Hungary.

---

‡   D. L. Schacter, *Searching for Memory: The Brain, the Mind and the Past* (New York: Basic Books, 1996).

Initiating contact with her again all those years later, he stunned her with the news that he had undergone sex reassignment surgery and was now a transgender woman. They reconnected, and although some of their subsequent visits were uneasy and conflicted, Ms. Faludi came to understand her father and her past with him in a new way.

"The process of writing the book freed me from living with the caricature I had of my father," she said in a recent interview. "As a child, you don't see the vulnerability of your parents—only their power. Writing the book freed me from the demon I'd demonized. My father went, in my mind, from symbol to human."*

Our memories have great power to unite or divide us, and so much depends on how we handle differences in family memories and understand the emotional weight some memories bring to family relationships.

How to Avoid Divergent-Memory-Related Estrangement Triggers

Ideas for Parents

View divergent memories as a learning opportunity. If you and your adult child remember the same events in different ways, this can be a chance to get to know your son or daughter in a whole new

---

* 	Kathryn E. Livingston, "Reporting on a Father's Gender Transition: PW Talks with Susan Faludi," *Publishers Weekly*, June 20, 2016: 144.

way by tuning in to the way he or she views the past and how this has colored his world view. It can also be a chance to look back and understand when the conflicts that still trouble you may have started.

"I was stunned over the way my son Doug, who is now in his thirties, remembered our relationship during his high school years," says Pamela. "My memory of that time was that I encouraged his talents and interests. His memory is that I was always pushing and pressuring him. Knowing now that he felt that way helps me to understand some of the anger and resentment that has been there between us all these years."

Listen! Don't argue! As we have seen, memories are shaped by many factors, and it's not at all unusual to have some significant variations in family memories. Don't assume that your recollections are the ultimate truth and your adult child's are not. Honor his or her reality as well as your own by listening with love. This can create opportunities to better communication and mutual understanding.

It is much more constructive to say "I had no idea that you had experienced that time in the way you did" or "I'm so sorry. I didn't mean to hurt you. But I can understand now why you did feel hurt," instead of "No! It wasn't that way at all! You're wrong!"

The need to be right slams the door on loving communication and, once again, causes hurt.

Express wonder rather than anger or frustration over your divergent memories. This, too, can facilitate communication and help you and your adult child work through and get over some conflicts from the past.

It is so much more useful to say something like "Isn't it amazing how we can remember the same event in such different ways? I'm interested in hearing more about what you remember," instead of shutting the conversation down with "No! It absolutely never happened! At least not that way! End of discussion."

Defensiveness can be an understandable reflex when you feel that your adult child has misunderstood your motives, underestimated your love and devotion, or otherwise seen your parenting efforts in the past through a prism of ingratitude.

"I would just get enraged when my daughter, who is now thirty-four, would carry on about her memories of feeling lonely and left out when she was a child," says Jana. "She was the adored only child of two loving parents. What more could we have given her? But when I calmed down finally and asked her if she could remember why she felt the way she did, she told me that my husband and I were such a loving and close couple that she sometimes felt superfluous, like an intruder or a definite third wheel. I had no idea she felt that way. And she had no idea just how much she was loved. Once I stopped being defensive and listened, I was able to express my love for her, our love for her, that was always there, in a way that she could begin to feel it at last."

If an adult child brings up distressing memories of abuse or other childhood traumas that you know to be true, give loving support. When a family has weathered some deeply painful events, there is a tendency to not want to go there again. It can be tempting to say, "That was a long time ago. Why bring it up now?"

However, it's important to keep in mind that when a young child experiences a traumatic event, it may take years before he or she feels capable of speaking openly about it. It isn't that this memory is new. If she is like most victims of abuse or trauma, your adult child has had varying degrees of awareness and distress about the event for years and may only now have reached a point where he or she can begin to deal with it emotionally.

Marilyn, a long-ago patient of mine, suffered a traumatic loss when she was only nine years old, surviving an auto accident that killed her father. She came to me for therapy years later for help in dealing with the grief and guilt she was feeling suddenly and intensely.

She had never cried about her father's death as a child or adolescent. Whenever she would try, over time, to talk about her memories, her mom, believing that it was best not to revisit that devastating time, would tell her that it was best not to think back on that trauma. So Marilyn tried to push her memories back, to not think about all she had lost.

"I can tell you the minute I let those memories come back fully and my feelings burst through all the walls I had built around me to contain my grief," she said tearfully. "It was seven months ago, when my daughter was just a few weeks old. My husband and I were sitting up in bed and he was holding our baby, kissing her and speaking in such a soft and loving way. Suddenly, I felt this wonderful sense of family, of being safe, and could allow my memories and feelings to happen. I started to sob uncontrollably and kept saying over and over, 'My daddy! My daddy's dead...!'

Still holding the baby, Mark gathered me into his arms and told me how much I was loved. I cried for a long time—out of grief for my daddy and happiness that I had the love and the security now to let all my feelings happen."

Some deeply painful memories of past abuse may be more complicated to process as a family. Perhaps the abuse is something you suspected, but never knew for sure, and this revelation can have a devastating impact on certain family relationships.

Perhaps you behaved in an undeniably abusive way toward your child in years past—perhaps due to your own emotional or substance abuse problems at the time, perhaps in a momentary flashback to the way a parent treated *you* as a child—and this is something over which you feel immense shame and regret. Those feelings can cause you to react in a number of communication-blocking ways when your adult child brings up these memories. You might deny that it ever happened, in a desperate attempt not to revisit that time. You may react impatiently, saying something like "Well, I'm sorry. But why go back there and remember all that? There's nothing I can do about it now."

But there *are* things you can do: be supportive of your adult child as he or she experiences these distressing memories and, perhaps, suggest getting family therapy to deal with the issue together. And you can apologize for what was done or for not being as supportive as you could have been at the time. Showing your love in these ways can mean so much, and help you work toward healing strained relationships.

If your adult child accuses you or your spouse of abuse that you know never happened, try to put your shock and anger aside for the moment, to show love, support, and curiosity about what sparked such a memory. Although now this tends not to happen as often as it did twenty-five years ago at the height of the "recovered memories" controversy, it can still happen and be devastating to families.

As we saw earlier, this scenario can often occur when an adult child seeks therapy for any number of problems—from distress over conflicts with you to depression about a lost love relationship. Most therapists will work with the patient to deal with the problem at hand. But some—especially untrained, unlicensed "therapists" who offer regressive hypnosis and other therapies of questionable value—may invariably see any signs of depression or anxiety or anger at parents as symptoms of long-ago abuse and lead the patient in highly suggestive ways to believe that he or she has been abused, even if such events never took place. The practitioner has the power in the relationship, and the patient is highly vulnerable. It can be a volatile mix.

The young adult may be highly emotional and absolutely convinced that the abuse happened and that he or she must cut off all contact with you. And you may be left stunned—wondering how in the world your adult child could believe things that are so outrageously untrue.

This is one of the most heartbreaking situations a parent can face. Your options for getting through to your child may be limited at first, especially as long as the adult child continues to see that therapist. Estrangements over false memories can last for months or years.

In the meantime, it can be helpful to get family therapy for yourself, your spouse, and other affected family members, or to seek the support of an organization such as the False Memory Syndrome Foundation (fmsfonline.org).

Eventually, however, the adult child will end his or her work with the therapist—often when the money runs out or the child finally begins to question the newly recovered memories. Then, gradually, he or she might seek to reconnect.

Your best course of action is to tap into whatever love you have shared, to express your continuing love despite your confusion and distress over the current situation, and to keep the door open for your adult child to return to you. This may take a considerable amount of time, but there is hope as long as your son or daughter knows that your love is constant and your arms open.

Ideas for Adult Children

View divergent memories as natural, not a sign of disrespect. You may find yourself flinching when you hear your parents sharing family memories that differ so in either content or spirit from your own memories of the same events. However, if you can see these differences not as delusional or disrespectful, but as simply a view from a different angle, a different family role or life stage, tensions can ease considerably.

"My dad has this memory that his mother was a wonderful

person, but I remember her as just awful, really critical and mean," says Kimberly, thirty-one. "What's weird is that he talks about how mean she was to him when he was a child growing up alone with her after his father died. And yet he remembers her as wonderful. I used to get incensed with him over that. But then I tried to look at it from his point of view: maybe he needed to believe that she was wonderful just to endure living with her all those years. Who knows? Maybe she had her moments of wonderfulness when she was younger. The thing is that we've stopped fighting about it and insisting that we are right. And that has helped our relationship a lot!"

Agree to disagree. Instead of getting into conflicts about divergent memories—as in "No, Mom, it *wasn't* that way at all!" or "Why do you always put a negative spin on things? Those were happy times!"—agree to disagree, seeing each perspective as valid.

It may be that your parent remembers your childhood Christmases as wondrous times when you were excited about Santa coming and getting a real Christmas tree, while you remember uncomfortable family gatherings with drunken Uncle Fred and your dad getting into loud arguments and older family members you didn't know well wanting to hug and kiss you. Sometimes a parent holds onto a memory that they hope you share. Your parents may have wanted the holiday to be wondrous for you. And that's what they choose to remember.

It may be that what your mom saw as encouragement, you experienced as criticism, or that what your dad remembers as close, meaningful discussions, you recall as lectures.

Perhaps what matters most is what the memories impart—
your reality and theirs. Your mom wanted to encourage you and
your dad to communicate with you. However short you feel
their intentions and memories fall from matching with your own
impressions and memories, the realities—yours and theirs—
reveal good intentions and wanting to be close, wanting to
encourage, yearning for affirmation.

**If you're in therapy, and the therapist suggests that your
symptoms are a sign of abuse and, when you say that you don't
remember ever being abused, the therapist offers to do regressive hypnosis to "recover" these memories or otherwise pushes
you in the direction of believing you were abused, be wary.**
People who are dealing with depression, anxiety, eating disorders,
or grief over significant losses, for example, may have a number of
reasons for feeling and acting the way they do. Long-ago abuse is
not the default underlying cause of all emotional distress. As we
have seen, research suggests that people who have been abused
or traumatized have vivid memories of these events. They may
try unsuccessfully to forget. They may decline to talk about these
memories. But the memories are there.

While hypnosis sometimes can be useful in the hands of a
highly trained professional in a medical setting, being treated
with hypnotic techniques by someone with less training and
expertise can be risky. And memory work, especially in the hands
of a therapist who may guide you in the direction of believing
that you have been abused, is especially questionable. Through
the power of suggestion at a vulnerable time, false memories can

feel painfully real and be immensely destructive to your life and your family relationships.

If a therapist suggests strongly that you cut all ties with your family of origin, this is a red flag. While you may decide that you have your own good reasons to create distance from a difficult parent, it is a decision you need to make for yourself.

In general, therapists will seek to help you to integrate your feelings and experiences and to reconnect and resolve conflicts with your family. If a family member is truly abusive, you may choose to estrange yourself from him or her. But be wary of a therapist who insists that estrangement is your only option.

If you have ongoing painful memories of abuse, bring these up in a way that feels safe and healing. You may choose to talk with a supportive parent or other relative, or with a licensed therapist or medical professional. Or you may choose to have family therapy that may—or may not—include the family member who abused you. If you have been abused by a parent, discussing your memories and your feelings with that parent may or may not be healing.

Gary, whose single instance of molesting his young teen daughter (during a time when he was drinking heavily) came to light when the now-grown daughter confronted him twenty years later, expressed deep remorse and apologized to her repeatedly.

"In some ways, he seemed more distressed about this than I did," his daughter Samantha reports. "The memory has always upset me. And our silence on the matter was equally upsetting. But now that we've talked…well, I'd say it's better. At least he's sorry. That doesn't make what happened that time okay. But the tension of that unspoken memory isn't there between us anymore."

Try to enjoy family memories—divergent or not—as a communication bridge between you and your parents. Families and individuals all have their stories, the memories and beliefs that help to define who they are both separately and together.

Sharing stories, memories, and family jokes can help keep bonds strong, even when your life or the lives of your parents are in transition.

"I don't always agree with my dad," says Shelley, a twenty-two-year-old college student. "But I love the stories he tells about some of our family vacations and some of the crazy things that we've all done together. I can't imagine right now wanting to take an extended vacation with my parents or my brothers anymore. But I love hearing about our past adventures as seen through Dad's eyes. Some of his details…umm…I don't know… but they're great stories! Evenings when we just sit around and listen, or share some of our own fun memories of the past, feel very special, very close."

If, like Shelley, you can come to enjoy shared family memories that are positive and fun, and not get caught up in the accuracy or inaccuracy of another's interpretation of positive events in your shared past, this can be a great help in maintaining a strong family bond, even in otherwise difficult times.

It can also help, when your relationship is feeling strained by conflict or life transitions, to conjure up some happier memories about the person or persons with whom you are in conflict.

"My mother and I nearly became estranged when my husband and I got married," says thirty-six-year-old Rona, now married ten years and the mother of two children. "She wasn't sure she liked my husband and, even more, she was reluctant to give up her place in the center of my life. What helped was when I sat down with her and told her how much her support over the years had meant to me and also how warmly I remembered some of our special times together—like a trip we made, just the two of us, when I was a teenager. We flew from L.A. to New York City and spent a week seeing a bunch of Broadway shows and doing touristy things and talking up a storm. I shared my memories of that time together and told her how much it had meant to me, how I would never forget a minute of it. She smiled and told me that she would always remember that, too. And then I said that we would always have those memories and that now it was time to make new ones, with an expanded family, and that I hoped she would be part of these, too.

"I wouldn't say she changed her views about my husband overnight, but she began to adjust. Now she thinks he's great and, of course, she's totally in love with the grandchildren."

Our memories of time shared, of love and support, of overcoming challenges together, may help to bridge the emotional gap that can grow as adult children leave the nest and make lives of their own.

Even when specific details aren't a perfect match, focusing on the warm feelings these memories evoke can help parents and adult children through challenges and inspire hope for creating new memories of shared love in the years to come.

CHAPTER NINE

Mental Illness

Whether or not a family member has an official diagnosis, parents and adult children often present mental health issues as a major cause of family stress and conflict. In fact, in studies looking at reasons for parent-child estrangements, adult children are most likely to have cut off contact with parents because of "toxic behavior."*

Toxicity, by the way, is not a psychological diagnosis, but a description of personal traits that may cause conflict and estrangement between a person and his or her family members. While phrases like "toxic parents" or "toxic relationships" have been popularized in a lot of self-help books, these are terms

---

* Kristin Carr et al, "Giving Voice to the Silence of Family Estrangement: Comparing Reasons of Estranged Parents and Adult Children in a Nonmatched Sample," *Journal of Family Communication* 15 (April 2, 2015): 130–140.

that many people use to describe relationships that fuel so many negative feelings that estrangement begins to look the only option.

What does this so-called toxicity look like in both parents and adult children?

+ When you try to discuss your feelings over a crisis in your life with your mother, the conversation becomes all about her as she tells you about her own feelings or about her fears that your crisis will reflect unfavorably on the family.

+ Whenever you start to build some wonderful relationships with friends or experience a happy and healthy love relationship, your father flies into a rage and tries to alienate you from them with criticism and sarcasm.

+ All you can remember about your growing-up years is the family secret of your mother's major depression and how lonely and unloved you felt.

+ Your father fluctuated between delightful storytelling that went late into the night, depressions that kept him in bed for days, and terrifying moments of rage when he threatened to kill everyone in the family.

+ You make a harmless remark to your new daughter-in-law, and she immediately flies off the handle and wants to banish you from her and your son's life.

+ Your son returns from overseas duty in Iraq a totally changed person, and your whole family is in turmoil.

+ Your adult child has been diagnosed with schizophrenia and isn't taking his medications, but you can't talk with his doctor or therapist about it because he's legally an adult.

+ Your daughter, with whom you were close during her growing-up years, suddenly decides that you're totally toxic and is threatening estrangement.

WHAT MAKES PARENT–ADULT CHILD RELATIONSHIPS FEEL TOXIC?

A serious mental illness, addiction, or personality disorder in one family member can greatly affect the lives of the others and heighten the estrangement risk as parents and adult children all struggle with a myriad of feelings and challenges.

If you're the parent of an adult child with a mental illness or addiction, you may feel a combination of fear, frustration, guilt, and depletion as the active parenting phase of your life is extended. You fear letting go and, at the same time, yearn for your grown son or daughter to find the help he or she needs to live a healthy, productive life.

If you're the adult child of an alcoholic or mentally ill parent, you may have grown up with too little nurturing and too much responsibility, and feeling a confusing mix of shame, guilt, and anger that is extending into your adulthood. And you may fear that someday your parent's affliction may become your own.

Although these challenges can happen with a full array of psychiatric disorders, the following are some of the most common.

These descriptions of symptoms are summarized from the *Diagnostic and Statistical Manual of Mental Disorders* (DSM-V), published by the American Psychiatric Association, the primary tool that mental health professionals use for diagnosis of mental illnesses and disorders. Health professionals do not use these descriptions alone to make a diagnosis. They utilize their extensive training and observation, listening and spending time with a patient—usually over several sessions—before making a diagnosis.

These descriptions are included *not* for an instant, at-home diagnosis but to help you to understand what might be going on with your son, daughter, or parent. It's important to note that people can have a few symptoms of a disorder without meeting the diagnostic criteria for the disorder. Also, some symptoms that are abnormal in an adult may not be cause for alarm in an adolescent or an immature adult child (such as a few of the symptoms of narcissism—like fantasies of unlimited success). It is useful to know, however, possible reasons that your parent, adult child, daughter-in-law, or son-in-law may be acting or reacting the way he or she does. It may be a signal that a person in the family needs professional help or, at least, some extra measure of understanding.

Common Mental Illnesses

Major Depressive Disorder

Five or more of the following symptoms are present during a two-week period for those with major depressive disorder, with at least one of those either being a depressed mood or loss of general interest.

+ Depressed mood most of the day, every day. May report feelings of sadness, emptiness, hopelessness.
+ Diminished interest or pleasure in all or almost all activities most of the day, nearly every day.
+ Significant weight loss when not dieting or weight gain (more than 5 percent of body weight in a month) or decrease or increase in appetite nearly every day.
+ Insomnia or hypersomnia nearly every day.
+ Psychomotor agitation or retardation nearly every day (observed by others, not just self-reported feelings of restlessness or a sense of slowing down).
+ Fatigue or loss of energy nearly every day.
+ Feelings of worthlessness or excessive or inappropriate guilt (which may be delusional) nearly every day, not merely guilt or self-reproach about being sick.
+ Diminished ability to think or concentrate or indecisiveness nearly every day.
+ Recurrent thoughts of death (not just fear of dying), recurrent

suicidal ideation without a specific plan, or a suicide attempt or a specific plan for committing suicide.

These symptoms cause clinically significant distress or impairment in social, occupational, and other important areas of functioning.*

There are other disorders with depression as a major symptom, such as **persistent depressive disorder (dysthymia)**, which tends to be chronic, with depressed mood and other symptoms such as changes in appetite, sleep disorders, low energy, and fatigue persisting for at least two years.†

Bipolar I

In this disorder, a person has cycles of major depression and manic episodes. During a manic episode, the person has a period of abnormally elevated or expansive or irritable mood combined with persistently increased goal-oriented activity, lasting at least one week and present most of the day, every day.

In addition, he or she has at least three (four if the mood is only irritable) of the following symptoms:

+ Inflated self-esteem or grandiosity
+ Decreased need for sleep

---

* American Psychiatric Association, Desk Reference to the Diagnostic Criteria from *DSM-V*, 94–95.
† Ibid., 97–98.

+ Tendency to talk more than usual
+ Racing thoughts and ideas
+ Distractibility
+ Increase in goal-oriented activities (socially, at school, at work, sexually) or psychomotor agitation
+ Excessive involvement in activities that have a high potential for painful consequences (such as spending sprees or sexual indiscretions)
+ Mood disturbance sufficiently severe to cause marked impairment of social or occupational functioning or hospitalization to prevent harm to self or others*

Bipolar II

This disorder has one or more periods of depression and at least one hypomanic episode, lasting at least four consecutive days. Hypomania is a somewhat milder version of the mania described above.†

Cyclothymic Disorder

A person with this disorder would have both hypomanic symptoms and depressive symptoms that don't meet the criteria for either a

---

*   American Psychiatric Association, *Desk Reference to the Diagnostic Criteria from DSM-V*, 65–68.

†   American Psychiatric Association, *Desk Reference to the Diagnostic Criteria from DSM-IV*, 71–74.

major depression or a hypomanic episode, but these symptoms will be present for at least two years, occurring cyclically.[‡]

Schizophrenia

This brain disorder causes distortions in the way a person sees and experiences his or her environment. To be diagnosed with schizophrenia, a person must have two of the following symptoms for a significant portion of the time during a one-month period, and at least one of these must be one of the first three listed:

+ Delusions
+ Hallucinations
+ Disorganized speech (e.g., frequent derailment or incoherence)
+ Grossly disorganized or catatonic behavior
+ Negative symptoms (such as diminished emotional expression)
+ Level of functioning in one or more major areas, such as work, interpersonal relations, or self-care, is markedly below the level achieved prior to onset.

Continuous signs of disturbance persist for at least six months. This period must include at least one month of some of the symptoms listed above.[§]

[‡]   Ibid, 76.

[§]   American Psychiatric Association, *Desk Reference to the Diagnostic Criteria from DSM-V*, 50-52.

Post-Traumatic Stress Disorder (PTSD)

This disorder follows a traumatic event during which a person is exposed to actual or threatened death, serious injury or sexual violence. Symptoms, which must be present for one month or longer, include:

+ Recurrent, involuntary, distressing memories of the event
+ Recurrent, distressing dreams related to the traumatic event
+ Flashbacks in which the person feels or acts as if the event were recurring
+ Intense or prolonged psychological distress at exposure to cues that symbolize or resemble some aspect of the traumatic event
+ Marked physiological reactions to these external or internal cues
+ Avoidance of or efforts to avoid distressing memories, thoughts, or feelings regarding the traumatic event
+ Alterations in mood with two or more of the following:

  Persistent negative beliefs about oneself, others, or the world ("I am bad," "No one can be trusted," or "The world is completely dangerous")

  Persistent negative emotional state (fear, horror, anger, guilt, or shame)

  Feelings of detachment or estrangement from others

  Persistent inability to experience positive emotions

+ Marked alternations in arousal and reactivity associated with the traumatic event and including at least two of the following:

Irritable behavior and angry outbursts, with little or no provoca-
   tion, expressed as verbal or physical aggression toward people
   or objects
Reckless or self-destructive behavior
Hypervigilance
Exaggerated startle response
Problems with concentration
*Sleep disturbance (difficulty falling or staying asleep or restless sleep)**

PERSONALITY DISORDERS

The DSM-V recognizes a number of these, but the ones we clini-
cians tend to hear about or see most often in conflicted family
sessions include the following:

Borderline Personality Disorder

The person who is diagnosed with this disorder must have five or
more of the following nine symptoms:

+ Frantic attempts to avoid real or imagined abandonment
+ Unstable and intense relationships (these relationships may
   involve splitting—a tendency to idealize and then devalue a

---

*   American Psychiatric Association, *Desk Reference to the Diagnostic Criteria from DSM-V*, pp.
    142-146.

person, so a person with BPD may call someone "my new best
friend" and then, soon thereafter, contend that the person
isn't worth knowing)

+ Unstable self-image
+ Impulsivity (overspending, substance abuse, sex, reckless
driving, binge eating, and failure to plan ahead)
+ Unstable mood
+ Recurrent suicidal behavior, gestures, or threats, or self-
mutilating behavior (like cutting)
+ Inappropriate intense anger and difficulty controlling anger
(frequent displays of temper, recurrent physical fights)
+ Chronic feelings of emptiness and boredom
+ Transient, stress-related paranoid ideation or severe dissocia-
tive symptoms*

Obsessive-Compulsive Personality Disorder (OCPD)

Those diagnosed with this disorder have four or more of the
following eight symptoms:

+ Preoccupation with rules, order, lists, and organization to the
extent that the major point of an activity is lost
+ Perfectionism that interferes with task completion
+ Devotion to work at the expense of leisure and friendships

---

* American Psychiatric Association, *Desk Reference to the Diagnostic Criteria from DSM-V*,
325-326.

+ Inflexibility about matters of morality, ethics, and values
+ Reluctance to delegate tasks to others
+ Inability to discard worn or worthless objects that have no sentimental value
+ Rigidity and stubbornness
+ Miserliness toward self and others: money is to be hoarded[†]

Narcissistic Personality Disorder

People diagnosed with this disorder have at least five of the following nine symptoms:

+ Grandiosity (exaggerates achievements and talents, expects to be recognized as superior without commensurate achievements)
+ Fantasies of unlimited success, power, brilliance, and beauty
+ Belief that he or she is unique and special and can only be understood by, or should only associate with, other special or high-status people (or institutions)
+ Requiring excessive admiration
+ Sense of entitlement
+ Tendency to be interpersonally exploitive (takes advantage of others to achieve his or her own ends)
+ Lack of empathy

[†]   Ibid., 329–330.

+ Envy of others and belief that others are envious of him or her
+ Arrogant, haughty behaviors or attitudes*

Although it's common to label problematic people in our lives as narcissists or borderline, it's important, once again, to remember two things: first, an official diagnosis needs to come from a medical or mental health professional; and second, a person can have some of the traits of a personality disorder without actually having the disorder.

Sometimes a trace of a personality disorder can be a factor in success, such as when person has some obsessive-compulsive traits that include attention to detail and dedication to work (without the need for perfectionism that can stall a project) or when some narcissistic traits can propel someone into a challenging profession. Writing about narcissism in the *New York Times*, Jane Brody noted that a study in Italy found that narcissistic personality disorder traits were found in as many as 17 percent of first-year medical students.†

Of course, while narcissistic traits might help one in the competitive race to medical school, they might also prove an obstacle to becoming a caring and effective physician, since empathy is a major factor in providing good health care.

When we notice traits of a personality disorder, it is not usually in a positive way. Even without a full diagnosis,

---

*   Ibid., 327.

†   Jane Brody, "How to Recognize a Narcissist," *New York Times*, July 19, 2016.

having such traits can make a family member problematic to varying degrees.

A difficult daughter-in-law may exhibit the idealization/ devaluation behavior or the temper outbursts of someone with borderline personality disorder without the other symptoms. And most of us have a little of the narcissist in us, but manage to retain empathy for others. It's important to see ways that a family member's behavior or thought patterns may coincide with a mental illness or personality disorder and the ways in which he or she functions well.

Problems with alcohol or drug abuse can occur with a disorder. Some people drink in order to deal with depression or anxiety. For people with the risk-taking symptoms of bipolar disorder or borderline personality disorder, substance abuse may be part of their impulsive behavior patterns. And, of course, alcohol or drug abuse alone can be a primary factor in shattering family relationships.

The alcoholic or drug-abusing parent or adult child may exhibit some of the same symptoms of people with mental illness: they may explode in rage, lose touch with reality, or refuse to take responsibility for their behavior and mistakes, making a habit of blaming others instead.

What Causes Mental Illness or Personality Disorders?

Some disorders may include a genetic component. For example, some studies have found that those who have a schizophrenic parent have a higher risk of developing the disorder. While the lifetime risk of having schizophrenia is about 1 percent in the general population, it is ten times higher for those who have a parent with the disease. And if both parents have schizophrenia, the lifetime risk for their children is about 40 percent. With major depressive disorder in parents researchers have found that about 61 percent of adult children develop depression as well in their adult lives.[*]

A recent study found that those whose parents or grandparents have experienced depression face a significantly higher-than-normal risk of depression themselves. The researchers suggested that people with a family history of depression should be alert to depressive symptoms and seek professional help if they notice symptoms in themselves.[†]

In the same way, other studies have found that borderline personality disorder is five times more likely to occur if a person has a close family member (a parent or sibling) with the disorder.[‡]

---

[*]   Fritz Mattejat and Helmut Remschmidt, "The Children of Mentally Ill Parents," *Deutsches Ärzteblatt International* 105, no. 23 (2008): 103–108.

[†]   Myrna M. Weissman, Obianuju O. Berry, and Virginia Warner, "A 30-Year Study of Three Generations at High Risk and Low Risk of Depression," *JAMA Psychiatry* 73, no. 9 (2016): 970–977.

[‡]   National Institute of Mental Health, https://www.nimh.nih.gov/health/topics/borderline-personality-disorder/index.shtml#part_145388.

There may well be factors other than genetics involved in developing a mental illness. For example, as the child of an impaired parent, you may have grown up with environmental factors that contributed to your current depression. A lack of nurturing, needs going unmet, criticism, and chaos can all have a long-lasting impact on one's emotional health.

There are studies showing some environmental (home life, lifestyle) influences in developing a disorder. For example, researchers looking into the origins of narcissism found that parental overevaluation could be a factor. The children seemed to acquire narcissism, in part, by internalizing parents' inflated views of them. With those who had healthy self-esteem, on the other hand, parental warmth, rather than overevaluation, was key.[§]

If a loved one is showing definite signs of a mental illness or personality disorder, there is help, and there is hope. There are medications that can be helpful for those with bipolar disorder, major depressive disorder, and other depressive disorders, as well as schizophrenia. Cognitive behavioral therapy (CBT) and exposure therapy with a competent, well-trained psychotherapist can help those with PTSD.

Research has also found, in recent years, that an acceptance-based treatment such as dialectical behavior therapy (DBT) can be useful in treating borderline personality disorder. Like CBT, DBT focuses on changing the thoughts and behaviors that

---

§   Eddie Brummelman et al, "Origins of Narcissism in Children," *PNAS Early Edition*, February 12, 2015.

maintain a disorder or problem with skills training (like communication or problem solving), becoming aware of patterns of thoughts and beliefs and working to change those, and learning calming behaviors. DBT goes further to emphasize mindfulness and distress tolerance, and to enable emotional regulation with interpersonal effectiveness. The therapy may involve sessions that last several hours at a time, once a week, for six months to a year, with homework for the patient to complete in between. It has been found useful with many different disorders, but particularly with borderline personality disorder and suicidality.*

With some disorders, convincing the person to get help may be a challenge. For example, someone with narcissistic personality disorder may feel that life is just fine. We don't see a lot of people coming into therapy to deal with their narcissism per se. They may only seek therapy to deal with relationship problems or other difficulties that may be rooted in their narcissistic beliefs and behavior.

The impact of mental health disorders (and the substance abuse that can accompany some of these) on families can be devastating and long-lasting.

---

* Martin M. Antony, "Reasoning with Unreasonable People: Focus on Disorders of Emotion Regulation" (CEU Seminar for Health Professionals, Institute for Brain Potential, Mesa, AZ, October 5, 2016).

WHEN AN ADULT CHILD IS MENTALLY ILL

One of the first reactions parents may have is shock: *How could this happen to my child? To us?* If your child is like many others, he or she may not have shown obvious signs of a problem until he or she was grown—maybe in the late teens or the twenties.

"We thought everything was great with our daughter— that her future was assured—when she got into an Ivy League university," says Martha, whose nineteen-year-old daughter suffered what she describes as "an emotional collapse" during the second semester of her freshman year. "Now she is home and in therapy after she was hospitalized following a suicide attempt. Everything—from our daily lives to our hopes for her future— has changed. I can't believe this is happening to her and to us. I just want her to stay alive at this point."

Martha's surprise is echoed by many parents whose adult children suddenly show signs of mental illness as they transition to adulthood.

Research has found that many mental health disorders first appear in young adulthood. Studies have found that 75 percent of impulse control and substance abuse disorders begin by age twenty-four. The median onset age for mood disorders (such as major depressive disorder) is around twenty-five. Anxiety disorders also tend to begin around twenty-five.[†] Even disorders that

---

[†]   R. C. Kessler et al, "Lifetime Prevalence and Age of Onset Distributions of DSM-IV Disorders in the National Comorbidity Survey Replication," *AMA Archives of General Psychiatry* 62 no. 6 (2005): 593–602.

may begin earlier, such as schizophrenia, reveal themselves most clearly during emerging adulthood.*

When you see your adult child suffering, you suffer. And you may feel limited in your ability to help. Since your son or daughter is over eighteen, there are limits on what you can do to make sure they get treatment or take medications. Unless he or she signs a release for you to talk to his or her therapist, you can't call or go in and speak with the therapist or ask questions. And if your child is in denial—refusing to admit that something is wrong, refusing to get help—you can't insist and drag them in to treatment. Even an involuntary hospitalization is brief—and usually does little to improve your relationship.

It is at this juncture, when your adult child is angry, lashing out, and refusing to believe that there is a problem, that estrangement can happen. It may be that he or she storms off, cutting off all communication for a time. It may be that you feel you need to put distance between an adult child who is mentally ill and/or abusing substances in order to protect the rest of the family. You may have moments of anger and resentment as well as fatigue over your extended parenting duties, wondering when, if ever, your adult child will get well enough to function in the world and become independent.

"This was definitely not what my wife and I planned for our later years," says Bill, a seventy-one-year-old former retiree who

---

*   R. C. Kessler et al, "Age of Onset of Mental Disorders: A Review of Recent Literature," *Current Opinion in Psychiatry* 20, no. 4 (2007): 359–364.

has returned to work in a local supermarket. "Our son is thirty-five years old and has pretty severe OCD. He takes hourlong showers three or four times a day. He gets caught up in pointless activities. He is very picky about his food. He has never held a job, and that's why I went back to work. I want him out of the house. Enough is enough. My wife is scared [that] he'll end up living on the streets and that he doesn't have the wherewithal to make his own way in the world. But are we helping him like this? It can't go on forever. What will he do after we're gone? And what about our quality of life in the meantime?"

Some parents live in mourning for the life opportunities lost to their children, the dreams that are slipping away. Some live in fear of the ultimate nightmare: an adult child's suicide.

"As bad as things are with my daughter's bipolar disorder and her drinking, I know it could be worse," says Stella, fifty-seven. "I'm just thankful she's alive."

Parents who are estranged from a mentally ill or addicted son or daughter have many of the same fears, without the comfort of certainty that their adult child is alive.

"It's the not knowing that's especially hard," says Thea, the sixty-two-year-old mother of a son with PTSD and substance-abuse problems. "I have no idea where my son is or how to contact him. I'm worried sick every day that I'll get a phone call telling me the worst or, nearly as terrible, to just live the rest of my life with this not knowing."

Avoiding estrangement triggered by mental illness in an adult child can be a challenge as you seek to help your troubled adult child and, at the same time, to keep yourself and the rest of the family safe while your adult child may be in denial that anything is wrong, inconsistent about taking medications, or self-medicating with alcohol or drugs, and lashing out at you as you try to help.

Ideas for Parents

Stop arguing and judging, and start listening in a new way. Encourage your adult child to talk about his or her feelings, fears and what he needs to feel safe. If he is delusional, don't argue. Let him know you're hearing what he is saying. That doesn't mean you're agreeing with him, just letting him know that you are listening. This communicates caring and an honest attempt to understand—and that can mean much to a young adult struggling with a mental illness.

"My son felt deeply—loved deeply, hurt deeply—his whole life," says Aisling, a sixty-four-year-old divorced mother of two. "Sam's sensitivity was, at once, his greatest asset and his greatest flaw. He had so much to deal with at such a young age: a painful mix of criticism and rejection by several members of the family; an acrimonious divorce between me and my ex-husband when Sam was in middle school; and then there was mental illness. He had major depression. There was anxiety with panic attacks that made it hard for him to function in the working world. He began to try to soothe his tumultuous feelings with drugs, starting when he was in high school. I can't tell you how many times he was in rehab and how many times we all hoped and were disappointed when his life stalled just at the point of turning around. But the more we came to embrace him in all ways, the longer his periods of sobriety lasted. I tried very hard not to judge him. There were some terrible times for our family, times when we had to call the police, times when we had to get restraining orders. But these alternated with times when we talked about everything in the world and laughed together and felt our spirits very much in sync. And those are the memories of him that I cherish."

After a promising period of sobriety that lasted nearly a year, a family crisis that seemed to affect Sam only peripherally caused him to use just once more—and he died of a heroin overdose at the age of twenty-nine.

"What has made it hard is that people are quick to judge and categorize," says Aisling. "People came up to me at his memorial service or in the weeks after and told me they were sorry he had 'gone bad.' He was never bad. He was in pain. He was tormented with mental illness. While my story doesn't have the hoped-for happy ending that most parents of addicts long to hear, I would like to say that not labeling or judging your mentally ill and addicted adult child, but reaching out to the troubled person he or she is, can make such a difference in your relationship [and] the memories you make together and, I would hope, might make a happier ending possible for other families."

Accept your limitations and encourage your adult child to get professional help. You've always been there for your child. Your love has been constant. But your ability to help a mentally ill adult child is limited. Some conditions require medication or professional intervention for any improvement to happen. Sometimes your ability to help, even to give loving support, may be limited if there has been a lot of conflict and anger between you and your son or daughter. It may be that someone else in the family—your spouse, a grandparent, a sibling, a cousin—or a close friend may be able to get through to your child in a way you can't right now and encourage him or her to get help.

Set boundaries to safeguard the family and, possibly, to prevent estrangement. Your safety and sanity, and that of the rest of your family, is a top priority. If your adult child is verbally or physically abusive, let him or her know that this behavior won't be tolerated in your home. You might express your love, but set a limit.

"We had to do that with our borderline son," says Cynthia, fifty-eight. "He was always having these angry outbursts. I know that's part of his condition, but we were all getting battle fatigue. It was just too much. It was either call a halt to the tantrums or kick him out of the house. I didn't want to kick him out and risk losing him, one way or another. So I finally said 'Enough!' And things have improved. It isn't perfect, but he's trying. And I give him a lot of credit for trying. I know it's hard for him to control his anger. But it's so necessary for so many reasons, starting at home."

Threatening behavior on the part of the adult child and your need to protect yourself and other family members can, indeed, lead to estrangement. But a study of estrangement vis-à-vis setting boundaries concluded that setting and enforcing ground rules at home might be a realistic alternative to family estrangement.*

Be alert for life-threatening situations. In a heartbreaking number of instances, the suicide of an adult child appears to come with no warning, and there is nothing the devastated parents could have done to prevent it. Nevertheless, being alert to changes in your child's behavior can be lifesaving.

For example, if your adult child has been so depressed that he or she can't get out of bed in the morning or do much of anything, the time to worry most is when he or she begins to feel somewhat better. At the depth of depression, a young person may not have the energy to attempt suicide. However, when the mood is beginning to lift—the depression still present, but less immobilizing—the possibility of suicide can be particularly high.

If you notice that your adult child is cleaning his room for the first time in months and giving away treasured possessions, be alert.

Ask your child if he has ever considered taking his own life. Many parents avoid asking this for fear that they will put the idea into their troubled child's head or because it's just too terrible to contemplate, let alone discuss. But in raising the issue, you may learn important information. If your adult child has suicidal feelings *and a plan for carrying out a suicide*, the danger is high enough to insist on immediate help—whether this is getting him

---

*   Sanna J. Thompson et al. "Social Estrangement: Factors Associated with Alcohol or Drug Dependency among Homeless, Street-Involved Young Adults," *Journal of Drug Issues* 39 (October 2009): 905–926.

to call his therapist, taking him to an emergency room or, if the danger seems imminent, calling 911 for police and an ambulance.

Don't hesitate to ask for emergency help. Shame and fear of what might happen to a mentally ill child can keep many parents from picking up the phone and calling 911. But making that call, and asking if an officer trained in crisis intervention can be dispatched along with the ambulance, can make all the difference. It's better to risk overreacting than to live with regrets.

For several months, Jack and Helen, both in their late fifties, had been concerned, then fearful, about the mental state of their young son-in-law Gary, who was married to their eldest daughter Elaine. He would, in time, be diagnosed with Bipolar I disorder.

"Gary's parents had died tragically in an accident, and we loved him like a son," says Jack. "We had watched and worried as his depression increased over a period of two months, with times when he seemed happy, even ebullient, and then would crash into another depression. When he started talking about suicide, we got frantic. Elaine convinced him to start therapy, and his first appointment was set for a Monday. That Sunday, he was acting so hopeless and so bizarre that we urged our daughter to come stay with us that night and then pick him up the next morning for his therapy appointment. She said, 'I would never forgive myself if he committed suicide tonight. I need to be with him.' We talked about calling the police and an ambulance, but all decided that might be too drastic a move. That night, when Elaine was sleeping, Gary killed her by slashing her throat. He said he had to kill her because, with her love and her insistence that he get therapy, she was going to prevent him from committing suicide. I can't begin to express our devastation…and regret that we didn't call 911 that Sunday night."

Get help yourself. There are very few, if any, quick fixes when it comes to mental illness. Even some effective medications take a while to work, and psychotherapy, depending on the diagnosis, may be necessary for an extended period of time. In some instances, your adult child may appear to recover, to go into a remission from his troubling symptoms, only to relapse later on. There can be a frustrating, sometimes frightening unpredictability to life with a mentally ill adult child.

Getting psychotherapy yourself to deal with the full array of emotions that you may be feeling—depression, guilt, fear, and grief among them—can be helpful, as can connecting with a support organization. One of the best is the National Alliance on Mental Illness, or NAMI (nami.org). NAMI has chapters all over the country with educational materials, support groups, and lists of local resources for families dealing with the mental illness.

Getting help yourself can enable you to better help your troubled adult child—and also to feel less alone.

When a Parent Is Mentally Ill

Whether your parent is mentally ill or a substance abuser or both, there are aspects of growing up with an impaired parent that are similar, whatever the illness or addiction the parent suffered.

You may have shouldered responsibility for the household

and younger siblings at an early age. You may have felt shame and dread, never knowing what you would find when you came home from school. Having friends over was not an option.

You may have felt isolated, keeping the family secret of your parent's mental illness or addiction.

Looking back, you may feel that you missed so much: a happy, carefree childhood, high school years of fun and friends, and increasing freedom. And you're angry with your parent for his or her major part in that loss. When you decide to break free of the family dysfunction and illness, making a decision that is beneficial to you, your parent may react with rage, with frantic pleas and complaints about your selfishness.

"My going away to college was a huge deal," says Rebecca, a thirty-two-year-old journalist. "My depressed, alcoholic mother and my bipolar father had come to depend on me to care for my younger sister and run the household. I felt like I was suffocating. So when I got a full scholarship to a college nearly three thousand miles away, I felt so much hope and, at the same time, guilt about leaving my sister behind. My school counselor urged me to go. So did my pastor. An aunt who lived nearby also encouraged me to go and said she would keep an eye on my sister and help her. So I went, and it was my salvation. I made a new family of friends. I began to feel good about myself and my future. I'm not estranged from my parents, but I live on the opposite coast. We talk on the phone, email, and text. But I don't see them often. Maybe once every two or three years. I see my sister, who is married and has two kids and lives in the Midwest, more often—maybe twice a year. With some distance, I can view the whole family dynamic in a more compassionate way than I could when I was living in the middle of it."

Needing to put some distance between family dysfunction and yourself, to stop trying to feed the bottomless pit of your troubled parent's needs, to have some perspective and to have a life, many adult children of mentally ill parents choose estrangement. But there can be alternatives to totally cutting yourself off from your parents.

Ideas for Adult Children

Break the silence and learn all you can about your parent's condition. Many families maintain a strict silence about a loved one's mental illness, and children in particular are left to wonder what is going on, whether they are to blame for all the difficulties, or whether a parent's illness can afflict them. Even when you're an adult and no longer living at home, having as much information as you can about your parent's condition can help to assuage some of your own fears and make you better able to understand your parent.

"Until I understood that angry outbursts with very hurtful comments were all part of my mom's borderline personality disorder, I thought she was just a bitch, and I devoted so much of my life to fighting with her," says Casey, twenty-seven. "Now, when she has an outburst, I don't challenge her. And often things calm down. It's still not easy to be with her, but it's a lot better now that I know how this disorder affects her."

Make a decision about how much you can help, and stick to it. Growing up, you may have seen your mentally ill parent's needs eclipse everyone else's. You may have felt overwhelmed by too much responsibility too early in life. And you may feel your parent's continuing needs encroaching upon your independent adult life and your own spouse and children.

"My mom is bipolar and alcoholic and has horrible taste in men," says Mason, forty-one, married and the father of a teenaged son and daughter. "I spent my entire childhood taking care of her. It was us against the world. I was parent to my mother, and so many of my needs went unmet. But I survived. I'm happy in my marriage and with my children—who have been allowed to be children. But my mother's needs are like a bottomless pit. I could spend all my time trying to rescue her, but have had to face the fact that she can't be rescued. I hurt for her. I love her. I help her as much as I can. But there are times when I insist that she needs to call her therapist, take her meds, [and] check in with AA, and then [I] step back. I love her, but I can't make her whole."

It's okay to put yourself first. This may seem a radical concept when you've grown up taking care of a mentally ill parent, taking on household responsibilities at an early age, or staying invisible, in the background, while the focus of the family has been—always—on the mentally ill parent.

Like Rebecca, who chose to go away to college, putting a cordial distance between herself and her parents, Leanne recently made the decision to move into an apartment of her own despite a storm of parental protests.

"If my dad had his choice, I'd be living at home forever, catering to his need to be the center of all our lives," she says. "It's totally incomprehensible to him that I would want to live separately. He's a narcissist and a mean drunk. He yelled at me that I was only moving out so I could have sex. Well, yeah! But that's only part of it. Mostly, it's to live in peace and to have my own life. I don't feel that's asking too much."

Making decisions that are beneficial for you can help you to escape the fate that befalls all too many adult children of mentally ill or alcoholic parents: failure to make their own educational or vocational goals. Studies have found that adult offspring of mentally ill parents are less likely than the general population to have a high school diploma. Some 31 percent, in one study, lacked either a diploma or a GED.*

This situation can happen for a number of reasons. Growing up in a family that is fraught and chaotic and low on nurturing can make it hard to believe in yourself, to do homework on time, or to see much hope for the future.

When you make your own well-being a priority, you might seek help and encouragement from other family members or someone outside the family—like a special teacher. And when the chance comes to improve your situation—whether it is going away to school or moving away from home to establish an independent life or to devote more of your time to pursuing a

---

*   Carol T. Mowbray et al, "Psychological Outcomes for Adult Children of Parents with Severe Mental Illness: Demographic and Clinical History Predictors," *Health and Social Work* 31, no. 2 (May 2006): 99–108.

long-held dream for the future—saying "Yes!" to such opportunities is not selfish, but a matter of sanity and survival.

Seek help yourself, and work toward finding your own definition of normal. That can mean getting therapy to deal with feelings from the past and difficulties in the present—perhaps having trouble trusting others, feeling like an outsider, or still wondering just what is normal in relationships.

It can also mean feeling less alone by joining a support group of peers whose life experiences are similar to yours—like an Adult Children of Alcoholics group or one affiliated with or recommended by NAMI.

Stop blaming yourself. Self-blame is a very common reaction to parental problems.

When you were a child in a chaotic home with a parent you didn't know how to help, it was natural—from a child's point of view—to blame yourself for the situation. That might have made things feel a bit more manageable. You may have thought: "If I'm really good and take care of Mom, everything will be okay."

Only it wasn't, and you blamed yourself.

Or, perhaps, a parent blamed you for his or her mental distress. "My dad, who was schizophrenic and alcoholic and more than a little narcissistic, used to blame everyone else for his problems, especially me," says Ellie, thirty-nine. "When he was acting outrageous and seeing things that weren't there, I'd be there, just blown away, and he'd say 'You think I'm crazy? Well, you'd be crazy, too, if you had a daughter as horrible as you!' I knew, on one level, that was his illness talking. But on another level, I accepted the blame more than I realized."

Four years ago, her father died of a heart attack. That day, her mother was sitting with Ellie, riffling through a file of family papers in search of her husband's military papers for veteran's funeral benefits. Suddenly, from deep in the file, Ellie's mother grabbed a small manila envelope and handed it to her. "Take this home and read it," she said quietly. "I think it's important that you read it."

The contents of the envelope: a deposition from her father's first wife, to whom he was married briefly, long before Ellie was born. It was part of the court proceedings for their divorce. In the deposition, the ex-wife described behavior that was identical to his later behavior with Ellie and her mother. "My shoulders absolutely sagged with relief," Ellie remembers. "I had no idea how much guilt and self-blame I was carrying."

It's important to remember that, no matter what you felt back then, no matter what your mentally ill parent (or other relatives looking to assign blame) might have told you, your parent's mental illness is not your fault. It has nothing to do with you—even though it may have affected your life profoundly.

See the positive—as well as the challenges—in growing up as you did. There is so much emphasis—clinically and otherwise—on the difficulties of growing up as a child of a mentally ill parent. But researchers have found some positives as well: that children growing up with a mentally ill parent can develop valuable personal strengths such as enhanced awareness of their own compassion, sensitivity, resourcefulness, strength, and independence.*

Looking at the whole picture, you may be able to see positive aspects as well as pain. Reaching this perspective may not only enhance your own self-image, but also soften the anger and bitterness you might be feeling about the stresses and the losses that your parent's illness imposed on you through the years.

"Growing up with a bipolar mother who was frequently hospitalized and having to care for a developmentally disabled brother while my dad spent long hours running his small business was sure no picnic," says Noelle, now fifty-nine and the mother of a grown daughter. "I coped by taking responsibility, by being in charge and with dark humor that sounded flip at times—like 'Oh…Mama's going over the cuckoo's nest again…time to call the cops!' But I cared deeply about her and about my brother. I came to know their ways of thinking, their fears and pain. And it changed my life—and my daughter's life—in some positive ways. I grew up to become a special education teacher for emotionally disturbed children. My daughter teaches developmentally disabled adults. Seeing what we did—with my mother, her grandmother, and my brother, her uncle—gave us insight, compassion, and special motivation to try to make a difference to those suffering from mental illness or a developmental disability—perhaps at a time of life when it matters most!"

---

*   Michelle D. Sherman, "Reaching Out to Children of Parents with Mental Illness," *Social Work Today* 7, no. 5 (September/October 2007): 26.

Allowing yourself to see the full spectrum of your early experience—the positive as well as the painful and ugly—can make a real difference in how you deal with a difficult past. It doesn't mean denying feelings of anger and resentment. It doesn't mean that you don't sometimes grieve what might have been had you experienced a less stressful childhood. It means that you're open to the full range of feelings that come up as you remember the past and reflect on the present—sorrow for what was, for all of you, and love and compassion from the safe distance of your independent adulthood.

CHAPTER TEN
Echoes of the Past

The echoes of the past can include painful memories of a parent who was critical, cold, abusive, and unresponsive to your needs when you were growing up. The echoes can also be bittersweet: memories of a simpler, happier time when your child was young and sweet and trusting, and you were at the center of his life. Whether painful or bittersweet, these memories, these echoes of experiences that linger in your mind, your feelings and your actions can be a trigger for estrangement—with blame power struggles, guilt, and deep regrets.

Do any of the following scenarios sound familiar?

+ It's like your own personal horror movie: in times of conflict and stress between you and your adult child, you open your mouth and hear your mother's words tumble out, and you can't seem to stop sounding just like her.

+ You survived an abusive childhood and, admittedly, don't handle stress well, getting upset in instances that might not bother someone else. But your daughter, who has known nothing but love and advantages that you never had, has the same sensitivity to stress, and it drives you crazy. You see yourself in her—and feel so guilty.

+ Your dad really enjoyed the good old days when you were little, and you looked up to him so much. Now that you're a young adult and moving toward independence, he keeps trying to turn back the clock by making personal comments ("Are you still getting pimples?") that rankle or vehemently opposing your plans to take a job in a city several hours away. You want to tell him "I appreciate everything you've done for me. But it's time for me to make my own decisions..."

+ Your mother is critical, especially of you, and inflexible to the max. Whenever you try to open her mind, she snaps, "That's just the way I was raised!" And it makes you want to scream.

+ You know vaguely that your mom had a very difficult childhood, and you feel bad for her. But, in your mind, that doesn't begin to excuse the way she has treated you.

How the Past Impacts the Present

Our past plays a major role in our present. This influence isn't found just in memories, whether happy or painful. It is also found in experiences not remembered but nevertheless a part of who we are, such as the attachment we had—or didn't have—to our mothers in our infancy.

It can be in long-ago traumas of another generation leaving a genetic mark. It can be a genetic link to a mental illness or disorder. And it can be in role models, perhaps reviled in memory but unconsciously mimicked in our own parenting.

Attachment Styles

Optimally, attachment is a bond between parent and infant that creates a safe and warm environment and, according to John Bowlby, the father of attachment theory, this creates "internal working models," a sort of template for gauging the reliability and value of future relationships.[*]

Children who have a secure attachment—with the primary caregiver in tune with and meeting their needs and creating a feeling of safety in their world—grow up at ease in social situations and are more likely to have warm and lasting friendships and love relationships. Children who have insecure attachments—when perhaps the parent has problems with depression or substance abuse or other issues that impair the parent-child bond—may grow up with a sense that attachment is valuable, but not reliable or easily achieved, and this can cause anxiety in childhood and later on. In the same way, an attachment that is alluring but

---

[*]   J. Bowlby, "Attachment and Loss: Retrospect and Prospect," *American Journal of Orthopsychiatry* 52, no. 4 (October 1982): 664–678.

frightening can teach a child to fear future attachments. The child whose parent just doesn't connect may not learn the value of closeness with another.[†]

"I swore I would be different with my own kids," says Janice, the forty-eight-year-old mother of two young adult children. "My mother was so withholding of her affection. I don't think she ever told me that she loved me. I told my kids every day how much they were loved and wanted. And yet, I know I had my failings— even without their constant reminders. When they were little and crying incessantly or having tantrums in grocery-store lines, or later on when they were teenagers and challenging me on every rule, I would get easily overwhelmed. Sometimes I cried myself. Sometimes I couldn't take it and just withdrew from them. I'd shut out their arguments and walk away. The thing is, I guess it's hard for me to give them what I wasn't given myself. And yet that feels like a really lame excuse for not being the parent I wanted to be."

Those whose early attachment to a primary caregiver was insecure may not only struggle with future relationships but may also have greater difficulty separating from the parent and growing toward independence.[‡]

Looking back over our attachment styles, it's easy to blame parents. But it's important to remember that insecure attachment may have been a sad family legacy for generations.

---

†   Corinne Rees, "Childhood Attachment," *British Journal of General Practice* 57, no. 544 (November 1, 2007): 920–922.

‡   Mokhtar Malepour, "Effects of Attachment on Early and Later Development," *British Journal of Developmental Disabilities* 53, part 2, no. 105 (July 2007): 81–95.

Genetic and Biological Legacies

As we saw in the last chapter, mental disorders such as schizophrenia and depression can have a genetic link. But trauma?
Recent research has found that traumas suffered by our parents
or grandparents may have led to genetic or biological changes
that can be passed on to future generations. These are called
epigenetic changes. They are markers added to or removed from
the genetic structure (DNA) that causes certain genes to be
expressed in specific areas of the body. Trauma can modify the
function of a gene and, in doing so, can alter a person's response
to later traumatic or stressful experiences.* There is evidence that
these epigenetic changes can be passed on to future generations,
making offspring of those who suffered the trauma more likely,
for example, to have a highly sensitive response to stress with a
higher risk of post-traumatic stress disorder.†

One of the most prominent researchers in the area of
epigenetics is Dr. Rachel Yehuda, professor of psychiatry and
neuroscience and the director of the Traumatic Stress Studies
Division at Mount Sinai School of Medicine in New York. Early
in her career, as she focused her research on stress hormones, Dr.
Yahuda made a fascinating discovery: while the stress hormone

---

*   Adrienne VanZomeren-Dohm and Rowena Ng, *How Trauma Gets under the Skin: Biological
     and Cognitive Processes of Child Maltreatment* (University of Minnesota Children's Mental
     Health eReview, March 2013), PDF.

†   T. B. Franklin et al, "Epigenetic Transmission of the Impact of Early Stress across
     Generations," *Biological Psychiatry* 68, no. 5, (2010): 408–415.

cortisol is usually high in those reporting symptoms of stress or depression, Vietnam veterans suffering from PTSD showed that they had *lower* levels of cortisol than the average person.

In a recent interview, Dr. Yehuda emphasized that when she speaks of high or low levels of cortisol, she is speaking about the high end of the normal range or the low end of the normal range. She added that cortisol helps to bring down the high levels of adrenaline that are released during our "fight or flight" response to stress. When, in a certain subset of people with PTSD, the cortisol level is lower than usual, there may not be enough cortisol to help the person calm down, partially explaining the formation of traumatic memory or generalized triggers.[‡]

After her work with veterans, Dr. Yehuda immediately decided to test Holocaust survivors in Cleveland and New York to see if their cortisol levels were also low. She found surprising similarities between the two groups. Not only that, but the cortisol levels of the *children* of the Holocaust survivors were also low, signaling that this hormonal abnormality had been transmitted from parent to child, putting those children at greater risk for developing post-traumatic stress disorder when encountering stressful or traumatic situations in their own lives.[§]

[‡]   Shaili Jain, "Cortisol and PTSD, Part I: An Interview with Dr. Rachel Yehuda," *Psychology Today*, June 15, 2016, https://www.psychologytoday.com/blog/the-aftermath-trauma/201606/cortisol-and-ptsd-part-1.

[§]   R. Yehuda et al, "Influences of Maternal and Paternal PTSD on Epigenetic Regulation of the Glucocorticoid Receptor Gene in Holocaust Survivor Offspring," *American Journal of Psychiatry* 171, no. 8 (August 2014): 872–80; R. Yehuda, "Biological Factors Associated with Susceptibility to Posttraumatic Stress Disorder," *Canadian Journal of Psychiatry* 44 (1999): 34–39.

Dr. Yahuda observes, however, that the epigenetic changes transmitted in this way are not all necessarily negative. "The purpose of epigenetic changes is simply to increase the repertoire of possible responses. I don't think it's meant to damage people. It just expands the range of biologic responses, and that can be a very positive thing when that's needed," she says. "I mean, who would you rather be in a war zone with? Someone who has had previous adversity [and] knows how to defend themselves? Or someone who has never had to fight for anything? There is a wisdom in our body."[*]

While cortisol levels tend to fluctuate throughout the day in most people, ending up with levels stuck at the higher end or the lower end of the normal range may signal cortisol imbalance.

Other researchers have noted that PTSD appears to hasten cortisol imbalance, possibly because a prolonged stress response can cause hypothalamic-pituitary-adrenal (HPA) axis dysregulation and, in the process, alter cortisol levels. Higher-than-average cortisol levels can impact the immune system, increasing susceptibility to infection. Sustained lower-than-average cortisol levels, possibly the result of chronically high stress exhausting the HPA axis, can make a person more susceptible to autoimmune diseases, depressed mood, sleep disturbances, and fatigue.[†]

---

[*]   R. Yehuda, "How Trauma and Resilience Cross Generations," *On Being* podcast, July 30, 2015.

[†]   Eileen Delaney, "The Relationship between Traumatic Stress, PTSD, and Cortisol," Naval Center for Combat & Operational Stress Control, 2016, https://pdfs.semanticscholar. org/0dd2/b268811ce0e3312390467ca73e65be6af1c9.pdf.

Other studies have found that a parent's earlier trauma can also affect the parent's health, lifestyle, and parenting styles, thus impacting yet another generation.

A landmark study was conducted of 17,000 middle-class Americans in 1998. This study found, among other things, that adverse childhood experiences—such as emotional, physical, or sexual abuse, emotional or physical neglect, or household substance abuse—could cause chronic or toxic stress in the child, contributing significantly to negative adult physical and mental health outcomes as well as reduced parenting capacity in the future. The study noted social risk factors, reduced ability to respond to stressors in a healthy way, and perpetuation of adverse childhood experiences in parenting style and by transmission of epigenetic changes.[‡]

If any of this rings true for you, it's important to keep in mind that you're not a prisoner of your genetic legacy. You may have a heightened natural response to stress, but knowing that and finding ways to soothe yourself and to tap into the resilience that may also be part of your body's wisdom can turn a troubling legacy into an opportunity for growth and enhanced compassion and empathy.

[‡]   Vincent J. Felitti et al., "Relationship of Childhood Abuse and Household Dysfunction to Many of the Leading Causes of Death in Adults," *American Journal of Preventive Medicine* 14, no. 4 (May 1998): 245–258.

Role Models and Habits

There are some things we do without much thought that can be a vivid reminder of the past. My cousin Caron talks and laughs much like her late mother—my beloved Aunt Evelyn. I walk like my childhood role model—my much adored Aunt Molly—as well as following in her footsteps as a professional writer. I speak with a trace of my mother's eastern Kansas accent and acquired a love of storytelling from my loquacious Irish-American father. But there are other, less benign aspects of our own past that we may bring to the present.

More than a century ago, Sigmund Freud coined the phrase "repetition compulsion" to describe the attempt of our unconscious to replay unresolved issues in our lives in an effort for some sort of resolution. His contemporary Carl Jung also observed, "Whatever does not emerge as consciousness returns as destiny." Without meaning to do so, we may find ourselves reacting to our own children, events, or situations in familiar ways that echo the past.[*]

Brooke, for example, grew up in a wealthy family living on New York's Upper East Side. Her childhood home was filled with servants waiting to meet any possible need. And prevailing over the household with her sharp tongue and little silver bell was Brooke's mother, whom everyone—family and servants alike—called "The Queen."

---

[*]   Mark Wolynn, *It Didn't Start with You: How Inherited Family Trauma Shapes Who We Are and How to End the Cycle* (New York: Viking, April 2016).

Brooke was often summoned for an audience with The Queen to discuss ways that she fell short of her mother's expectations. One of her greatest transgressions was her tendency to put on weight—in part due to her penchant for sweets, in part because of her disinclination to engage in any kind of physical exercise.

"To my mother, putting on even five pounds was like a major crime," says Brooke, more than sixty years later. "She was so focused on the superficial. She treated people like things. She was awful. It used to drive me crazy. I vowed never to be like her."

While Brooke insists that her parenting style with her own semiestranged adult daughter has been much warmer and more affirmative, I saw The Queen come imperiously back to life recently, when her newly divorced daughter visited from New York. The daughter, still grieving her marital split, had put on a bit of weight since their last visit. Still, she was only slightly overweight.

But Brooke was mortified. "She looks disgusting," she muttered to me within hearing range of her daughter. "I can't believe it. She is *so* fat! I don't even know what to say to her!"

Although Brooke managed to exorcise The Queen long enough to comfort her daughter, I could see some of the roots of their intermittent estrangement in The Queen's brief reincarnation.

Ann, who has two married sons, also had an imperious matriarch of a mother who doted on her son and devalued her daughter, telling her that a college education would be a waste and that her best prospect in life would be to marry well. Ann deeply resented being ignored, dismissed, and expected to play a lifelong supporting role to her husband—and her mother.

All these years later, Ann brings her mother's imperiousness to her fraught relationships with her daughters-in-law, pointedly ignoring them during visits, undermining their authority with their children, and dismissing their professional accomplishments. She doesn't see that she is repeating her mother's behavior. When pressed on the specifics, she shrugs and replies, "Well, that's just the way I was raised. Take it or leave it."

Not surprisingly, her sons and their families have moved to another state and see Ann and her husband only occasionally for tension-filled family reunions.

How to Prevent Echoes of the Past from Triggering Estrangement

Ideas for Parents

Reflect on your past pain. Bring what happened long ago into your conscious awareness. You might do this on your own or in psychotherapy. Think about how what happened affected you then and how it continues to bring pain to you and others in the present. Think about the ways that what happened has limited you in your present life. Think about ways that you have managed to prevail over your early experiences. Some of these insights can help you to begin to make positive changes in the way you treat yourself and others.

Having new insights into the pain of your past can also help you to prevent or to understand some parenting mistakes of your own. For example, if you were raised by abusive or neglectful parents, you may have been determined that your own children would have a very different life. Maybe, instead of setting firm rules and boundaries, you treated them more like friends. Now you're wondering why they seem so dissatisfied with their growing-up years and are having some difficulty socially and at work.

The fact is, you can't remedy your own past by focusing on giving your kids the opposite experience. There needs to be a balance between love and limits. Understanding where your good intentions may have veered off course can help you begin to resolve some conflicts with your adult child.

If you find yourself grieving a happy past when your kids were small and resisting their move toward independence, examine your own past for answers. You may have had an insecure attachment to your own mother, growing up unsure whether relationships can survive separation. You may simply want to freeze time and enjoy your family as it once was, denying that it is evolving and expanding. Just as your child toddled away from you and then circled back, your adult child may still seek a loving and warm connection with you…if you can will yourself to let go.

If you find yourself treating your children as you were treated (in a negative way), realize that this has much more to do with you than it does with their behavior, either past or present. Let the pain begin to stop here and now. Get professional help to deal with your long-ago pain so that you can grieve it, resolve it, and stop visiting your pain and visiting it onto your children. There is no shame in admitting that this is a problem. The shame is in perpetuating the pain through yet another generation.

If your adult child confronts you with behavior of yours that has caused him or her pain, don't angrily deny or stubbornly defend your behavior. Lose the excuses. As hard as it can be, just listen. Create a path to new understanding by acknowledging your behavior and apologizing.

"But wait!" you may be thinking. "It took two to fire up that argument. My kid isn't blameless here..."

Concentrating on your own part in causing pain, without excuses, justifications, or counterblaming, can be the first step toward a fresh start together. Missing this opportunity can preclude a new connection between you for a long time...maybe forever.

To embrace this opportunity, you need to take responsibility for what has happened, listen to how your child perceived certain words or actions (even though you never meant to be hurtful), and tell him or her that you're sorry. You're sorry that this happened, that he or she was hurt. It can be the beginning of communicating on a whole new level and feeling a renewed surge of love for each other.

Contrary to that old saying from *Love Story*, love *does* mean saying you're sorry—over and over again—while searching for new ways to show your enduring love for each other.

Ideas for Adult Children

You're not doomed by your past or your parents' pasts or biology. Even if your parents have fallen far short in meeting your emotional needs, even if you and your mom have a history of intense conflict, there is hope. Even if your dad came back from Iraq visibly changed and, in ways, unknowable, there is hope. Even if you have a parent or grandparent who suffered abuse and who may have passed on to you a tendency to react strongly to everyday stressors, there is hope.

In understanding what has happened and what you need now, you can make peace with the past. You can find ways to soothe yourself when stress begins to get overwhelming, tapping the resilience that may well co-exist with the vulnerabilities you have inherited. You can stop old conflict patterns—by not rising to the bait with your mom, or by letting your veteran dad with PTSD know that you're trying to understand his distress instead of immediately jumping into an angry confrontation. Sometimes a small change in how you react can be the catalyst for major changes in family dynamics.

Bob's family has had a long history of intergenerational estrangement, being emotionally cut off, and very little physical or emotional affection. It was a major theme of his psychotherapy work. He longed to forge a warmer connection with his family of origin.

One Christmas, he decided to change the way he greeted his kin. Walking into his parents' home, he reached out to each one in turn—his mother, his grandmother, his younger brother, his stern father—and gave each a warm hug and said, "Merry Christmas...I love you."

The family dissolved in tears, hugging and kissing each other with long pent-up tenderness and love. From that time on, they were much more physically affectionate and emotionally open with each other.

"I was astonished at the power of a hug and loving words," Bob remembers. "I was hoping for positive change. But this really exceeded my expectations. I'm so glad I took the chance. Even my dad, who was always so cold and remote, warmed up more than a little."

Blame is a dead end: don't go there. We'll be talking more about this in the next chapter, but it's important to know that blaming, or putting responsibility for your current unhappy circumstances on another, gives you scant options for positive change. You can't mandate change in another person—even if it's obvious that they really need to make some major changes. But if you take responsibility for making your own life better, with or without the cooperation of a problematic parent, you have a good chance to heal your pain and build a happier future.

When discussing the past with your parents, concentrate on your feelings about the past and wishes for the future instead of having a major confrontation. Your parents may respond more positively—with openness to mending your relationship—if they hear your feelings rather than angry accusations.

"I had a talk with my parents recently about how it felt for me being constantly compared to my older sister who was, of course, perfect as far as they were concerned," says Paige, a twenty-two-year-old college student. "Even though she disappointed them by marrying right out of high school to a guy they didn't especially like, I've always felt like I wasn't loved as much, and that has hurt.

"I expressed it to my mother as a fear, like, 'I've always been afraid you didn't love me as much as you did Jennifer. Sometimes I've felt very much alone and unlovable.' Instead of getting mad, like I expected, my mom got tears in her eye and said, 'Oh, sweetheart. I'm so sorry you felt that way. We have always loved you. I guess you always seemed so independent we didn't think you needed the kind of nurturing and encouragement we gave Jennifer. But we were wrong. I'm so sorry! You've always been loved, and I'm so sorry you didn't know that.' It really helped our relationship to just talk and not argue."

It may also help to conjure up some happier memories from the past in a discussion with a parent. As difficult as the past may have been for you, there must have been moments when your parent did something right, something good, something meaningful that lingers in your memory. Sharing your stories about what went right can help create a warmer connection and make your discussion less contentious.

Listen to your parent's back story—even if you have to urge him or her to tell you—in order to better understand the echoes of the past that continue to resonate. This can be critical to making sense of the painful patterns, chaos, and volatility in your family dynamic. This advice hits close to home for me.

My father, Jim McCoy, was an enigma. On the one hand, he was loving, highly intelligent, a world-class story teller with a great sense of humor. From the time I was a small child, he encouraged me to do well in school, to get a good education, and to build a satisfying, challenging career. He told me that I was smart and talented and that he was proud of me. He often said that he loved me.

On the other hand, he was a monstrous, raging alcoholic, mentally ill, and a prescription drug abuser. He beat his three children. He threatened to kill us while brandishing a gun or a hypodermic needle filled with what he said was an instantly lethal substance. Fearful of being killed in our sleep, my brother, sister, and I would move furniture to block the door of our shared bedroom each night. He told us quite often that we had ruined his life by our mere existence.

We never knew which father we'd find when we came in the door.

I knew that he had had a difficult childhood. I knew that he had loved his gentle, scholarly linguist/attorney father, who had died when Jim was only eight years old. I knew that after his father died, his mother had moved the family from Tucson to Hollywood so that Jim could support the family by acting in silent movies and dancing in vaudeville.

But I didn't know, really know, the true horror of his childhood.

During a visit to my parents' house when I was in my late twenties, I was laughing with my father over the grim coincidence that he had received a call that very day, his sixtieth birthday, from Forest Lawn cemetery offering gravesites at bargain prices. Then, suddenly, he got tears in his eyes and covered his face.

I asked him if the sales call about a gravesite was an upsetting reminder of mortality on a landmark birthday.

He shook his head and finally said "No, it brings back a memory that is so painful, so awful, that I've never told anybody."

And, sobbing, he told me the story.

Leaving the house for the last time, when Jim was eight years old, his beloved father had told him that he was going on a business trip. But, in fact, he was very ill and going to Mexico to seek treatment. He died in Mexico a few months later. But his two children, Jim and Molly (only four years old), were never told about his death. Their mother, a volatile, alcoholic, emotionally unstable woman, quietly brought his body back to Tucson, and he was buried without ceremony. She simply told the children that his business trip had been extended...and extended. And she began making plans for the move to California.

Before they left, nearly a year after his father's death, Jim was facing some bullies on the playground of his parochial school one day. They taunted him over and over with a sing-song "Your dad is dead! Your dad is dead!"

Jim bristled. "No he's not!" he yelled. "He's on a business trip. My mom said."

Snickering, the other boys led him to the cemetery and showed him his father's grave with a newly placed headstone. In that instant, Jim's world fell apart. He collapsed, screaming, on his father's grave, with a grief so intense that the other boys got frightened and ran away.

When he went home, still sobbing, and confronted his mother, she beat him, told him to stop being a crybaby, and threatened to kill him if he ever told Molly the news. It was some years before Molly learned, from a visiting relative, that her father had died.

And so Jim spent the rest of his childhood supporting the family with his earnings from acting, dancing, sweeping the local market after closing, and selling newspapers. His mother, who drank away a large portion of his earnings, beat him if he didn't earn enough money to please her and criticized him for being a poor provider if he didn't get a particular role or vaudeville gig. He lived in fear, with constant emotional and physical abuse. And even just before his mother died (of alcoholic cirrhosis of the liver) when he was in his late teens, she was unrepentant. "I know you think I've been harsh," she said to him on her death-bed. "But I had to be both mother and father to you, so of course I was harsh."

"I loved her even though she was so cruel," he said, wiping his eyes. "And even though she has been dead for so many years, I feel her inside me, and it feels awful when I'm that way, too. It's like I don't know how to stop being horrible even though I love you kids. I really do."

I embraced him. Knowing the horrific details of his child-hood didn't make his behavior in adulthood, with his own family, suddenly—or ever—okay. But it did make who he was and what he did more understandable. And it did help to lift the burden of wondering what we had done to deserve such treatment or how we could have ruined his life.

There was great relief in knowing that it all had nothing to do with us, even though his abusive rages had impacted all of us greatly, in a variety of ways. Despite the fact that we've all had successful careers—my brother as a doctor, my sister as a nurse—and reasonably happy lives, some of the depression and issues with self-worth that came in the wake of our father's horrific childhood slipped down to our generation. We have dealt with anger too often suppressed and with feelings of total devastation when in serious conflict with or when rejected by someone we love. There are times, too, when we wonder how much easier, how much happier, life might have been had we not had this legacy of pain.

And yet, I feel great sadness and tenderness for that little boy named Jim, who lived inside the father I knew, and whose world was still in pieces the day he died, only a few years after telling me his story.

While my father's childhood and subsequent behavior represent a rather extreme case, many of us carry pain from the past that influences many areas of our lives. We have the best chance of stopping the patterns of pain by listening and understanding what has happened in a parent's past, by reflecting on our own challenges and strengths that have roots in family history well before our time.

It is this understanding—and making positive, conscious choices in our own lives—that can keep the past from becoming destiny.

CHAPTER ELEVEN
Stopping the Blame

"It isn't fair!"

There was both anger and anguish in her voice as Barbara reacted to the suggestion that stopping the mutual blame between her and her semiestranged twenty-eight-year-old daughter Jennifer could heal both their wounded hearts. She crumpled a tear-soaked tissue in her hand as she angrily rejected the possibility of listening to and then responding to her daughter's complaints with empathy.

"But she's wrong! I've done everything for her! I raised her mostly alone after my divorce, and it wasn't easy, but she always came first. Always! And now she's claiming to have had a miserable childhood, and I'm to blame, and that's just crazy. The only thing crazier is the suggestion that I should be the one to apologize!"

For many parents who have been bewildered and hurt by

their adult children's claims of having a less than optimal child-hood, by their chilly distancing and angry confrontations, empathy and apologies may well seem irrational and unfair. And adult children who feel wounded by parental choices, actions, and decisions may have similar feelings that being the first to reach out is inappropriate and out of the question.

But look at it this way: Blame is an emotional barricade. It can stand between you and any possibility of reconciliation. It can keep you from resolving your feelings of anger and grief over your adult child's or your parents' accusations and rejection. Blame, focused on the actions of others, keeps us from looking within and finding clues for positive change.

Stopping the blame is tough, especially when it's so clear to you that it's your adult child or your parent, not you, who is out of line. The decision to try something new may seem easier if you stop and ask yourself this question: Do I want to continue to be relentlessly right—or do I want a relationship with this person?

Healing your heart—and your relationship—isn't easy. The steps needed to stop the blame cycle are among the hardest tasks a loving parent or adult child will face. But the rewards can be life-changing.

Taking the first steps toward stopping the blame may mean sitting down to listen and to talk, agreeing to listen without inter-rupting, and asking that your parent or your son or daughter do the same. If feelings are too raw, or if you are totally estranged from each other, these first steps may be in a letter or email where you express love, empathy, and a willingness to hear the other person's point of view. Whether in person or via mail or online, respecting your parent's or your child's feelings is key to building a new understanding.

Keep in mind the following steps as you reach out and hope to make a difference.

Take the Initiative in Stopping the Blame and Healing the Relationship

Someone has to go first and, optimally, in most instances, it will be the parent. Why the parent?

Studies have given us both generational and cultural reasons: parents, in general, have a greater need for emotional connection with their adult children than their grown children have for connection with their parents.[*] And culturally, relationships in the U.S. are less likely to be bound by tradition and a sense of obligation, and more contingent on how these relationships *feel* to those involved. American couples are more likely to divorce if the relationship isn't fulfilling than are their counterparts in other countries.[†] In the same way, adult children are more likely to stay connected with parents who listen to, accept, and love them, who make them feel respected rather than diminished.

---

[*]   K. S. Birditt et al, "Tensions in the Parent and Adult Child Relationship: Links to Solidarity and Ambivalence," *Psychology and Aging* 24, no. 2 (2009): 287–295.

[†]   Joshua Coleman, "How Parents Can Start to Reconcile with Estranged Kids," *Greater Good* (guest blog post), August 25, 2010, http://greatergood.berkeley.edu/article/item/how_parents_can_start_to_reconcile_with_their_kids.

This doesn't mean that adult children shouldn't make the first step toward reconciliation if it feels right to them.

Chris, who recently turned thirty-five, had been estranged from his parents for the eight years since his marriage. The estrangement began when his wife insisted that his parents, who did not share their faith but who accepted his wife's beliefs, "are not godly people and don't belong in our life!"

After time and reflection and after hearing of his mother's deteriorating health, Chris called to make amends. "I was wrong to let our religious differences come between us, and I'm so sorry," he told them. "I know there has been a lot of hurt and we need to talk about it. But I just want you to know that I love you and I do want to be close again."

Whether it's the parent or the adult child who is the first to reach out, showing a willingness to listen and to resolve your painfully strained relationship can go a long way toward healing the pain between you.

Someone needs to go first. Let it be you.

Listen to What the Other Is Telling You, and Accept Their Reality without Getting Defensive

This is a tall order. As you listen to a perspective that may be different from your own, there will be a great temptation to fall into old reactions:

"It didn't happen that way!"

"I can't believe you're saying this: it's a total distortion of reality!"

"I did the best I could, and raising you wasn't exactly easy!"

"This is just lies, all lies!"

"How dare you talk to me that way?"

"You so don't understand!"

These comments fuel the fury and keep conflict going. On the other hand, listening without diverting your attention from what is being said in order to plan a response, offering empathy rather than defensiveness can, little by little, lead to new understanding:

"I never realized you felt that way…"

"That must have been so painful for you…"

"I can see how you would hear that in a different way than I meant…"

"I'm hearing such sadness, such a feeling of being left out…"

These comments are easier when you focus on what the other person is saying instead of planning a response. Make eye contact. Concentrate. Try to really hear what he or she is telling you, not just the obvious but also subtle meanings, the feelings between the words.

When a person feels heard, when her feelings are accepted, not angrily challenged, she may be more receptive to what you have to say, for your perspective on those growing-up years or a particularly painful conflict between you.

A word of caution: changing an established pattern of blame can take time. Your parent or your adult child may need the reassurance of a number of instances of your listening without judgment to trust that you value his or her perspective, respect her feelings, and want to heal your relationship. If the initial reaction to your first attempts at listening is dubious or worse, don't give up. Keep trying.

Take Responsibility for Your Part in the Current Conflict or Estrangement

This is the key to stopping the blame. Taking responsibility for your own behavior and choices interrupts the blame cycle.

If you're an adult child, this may mean owning some of the choices and behaviors you have previously overlooked while you were focusing on your parents' flawed behavior that hurt so much.

If you're a parent, this may mean fighting the tendency to protest that you always acted with love; that you made enormous sacrifices for your child; that you kept him or her housed, fed, and educated despite daunting challenges; that children expect too much and give too little; that a walk in your shoes would change his or her mind right away; that adult children owe their parents love and loyalty no matter what.

Your adult child's perspective is uniquely his or her own, arrived at via a variety of life experiences, both as a child and as a young adult. It is impossible for him or her to know exactly how you experienced certain life events, though his general understanding of your experiences and feelings may grow if you show respect for his or her point of view.

It's important, however, not to get mired in self-blame. Especially if you're a mother, you're susceptible to this pattern. Studies show that mothers are more likely to blame themselves for any difficulties that their children have, while fathers tend to blame external circumstances—or mothers!*

There is a big difference between taking responsibility for your *part* in the estrangement from your adult child and taking *total* responsibility for your difficulties. In the latter, you exempt your adult child from taking responsibility for her own behavior, choices, and life.

On the other hand, a refusal to acknowledge that you weren't always a perfect parent (or son or daughter) prevents any constructive, meaningful discussion and makes reconciliation much less likely.

How much it can mean when a parent says to an adult child:

"That was a mistake, a painful mistake, on my part…"

"I should have realized how much it meant to you to keep in touch with your dad after our divorce. I let my own anger get in the way of your need for him."

"I guess I thought that all that business travel and all those hours at the office made me a better provider, when it would have felt better for you if I had been there, just been available to you as a dad, more often."

---

* K. S. Birditt et al, "Tensions in the Parent and Adult Child Relationship: Links to Solidarity and Ambivalence," *Psychology and Aging* 24, no. 2 (2009): 287–295.

Accepting and admitting the ways that you weren't perfect as a parent over the years is not an exercise in humiliation, but a way for you and your adult child to grow in understanding and mutual respect. After all, it takes courage to look at those imperfections. And some imperfections are inevitable, no matter how much you have loved your children or how much you wanted to be the perfect parent you didn't have yourself.

The same is true for an adult child. Having the courage to examine and admit your own contributions to the conflict and your own imperfections as a person and as a child can go a long way toward easing the tension and making real communication possible.

Apologize for Your Mistakes, Misunderstandings, and Missteps

While the thought of this may make you choke with indignation when you're faced with an adult child whose attitude feels inappropriate and obnoxious—or with a parent who is relentlessly righteous or unrepentantly intrusive—this is a critical step to rebuilding your connection with each other.

It may be as simple (and difficult) as saying:

"I'm so sorry."
"I never meant to hurt you, but I can see that I did, and I apologize…"
"I can see now that what I said was inappropriate and I'm sorry."

Make an Effort Not to Take Accusations and Complaints Personally

How is that possible?

It's possible to hear what your adult child or your parent is saying in a new way if you listen to the feelings behind the accusations.

As a parent, listen to the impressions of that child from years ago that are prompting today's anger.

As an adult child, listen to the context of your parent's feelings and beliefs.

Hear their words as observations rather than personal attacks. Keep the focus on the other person, not on you.

For example, when your daughter says bitterly that you cared more about your work than about her when she was growing up, listen to the pain and longing behind those words instead of rushing to insist that she has it all wrong.

Making an effort to understand the feelings from her point of view can help to decrease the defensiveness that can keep blame going on and on. Invite her to talk about the incidents that stand out in her memories.

Maybe it was that school play you missed because of a business trip that couldn't be changed. Maybe it was the times you worked long hours and missed meals with your child for days at a time. Maybe it was when you were too busy to make or buy cupcakes to take to her classroom for her birthday—a ritual that everyone else's mother observed. In your busy life, perhaps these all seemed minor at the time, but one by one, all of these experiences added up to your daughter's feelings of not being important to you.

As difficult as it can be, listen to how life has seemed for your daughter, without judging whether this assessment of her growing-up years is accurate from your perspective. Asking her to be specific in telling you what was hurtful to her communicates several things: that you do care, that her feelings matter to you, that you're willing to listen. Apologizing for the specific ways that your daughter was hurt can be a step toward healing.

Acknowledging that you can't go back and make it okay for the nine-year-old whose school play (or dance recital or sports competition) you missed years ago, you can tell this young adult that you understand now why she feels angry and that you're sorry for causing her this pain.

In the same way, hearing a parent's perspective without judgment can help you to understand better what has transpired between you.

"I'll admit that I've done most of the pushing away in my relationship with my mother in the past few years," says Ashley, a twenty-eight-year-old administrative assistant. "All my life, she has been critical, put pressure on me to be a success on her terms, and left me feeling that whatever I do, it's never enough. But in talking with her the other day, I got the picture from her point of view: she didn't want me to have to settle for the kind of life she has had—stuck in a bad marriage, with no college degree or special skills to support herself were she to leave. She was terrified that I would end up like she did, and she wanted something better for me, even as I was insisting that relationships mattered more and falling in love with this boy and that instead of concentrating on my school work. I can understand why she got frustrated, though I still value relationships first and foremost. Hearing her concerns has helped me not only to understand better where she has been coming from, but also I have been thinking about how to upgrade my skills to get a better job, to seize my power—the power she has always wanted me to have—in my own way."

It's also important to understand that blaming can be a way to avoid taking responsibility for one's own life and choices.

When an aging parent is feeling lonely and that life has passed her by, it's easy to blame her adult children for their inattentiveness, expecting them to fill the voids in her life that she alone can fill with old and new interests, volunteer work, a part-time job, reconnecting with friends, or adopting a delightful cat or dog from a rescue shelter to add joy to her daily life. Blaming the kids for their selfishness and lack of caring is much easier than making major changes in her own life.

In the same way, if an adult child's life is not going the way she would like, it's all too easy to shift the responsibility from herself to her parents. Maybe she's angry because they were too critical and didn't encourage her enough when she was growing up, so she has reached adulthood with scant self-confidence. Or maybe she's upset because she feels that her inability to succeed in the workplace is due to her parents' coddling or lavish praise, leaving her unprepared for the demands of the real world.

Whatever the complaint, too many adult children remain stuck in anger and blaming mode, unable or unwilling to move to the next steps: understanding what happened and why in their childhood and adolescence; and moving beyond feeling like victims to taking responsibility and feeling empowered in their own lives.

Interrupt the Blame Cycle

Act and react differently. If you're a parent, this may mean stepping back and allowing your adult child to build his or her new adult life without requests or demands for closeness, expressing only your love and support. Your newly independent son or daughter may come back to you in time, encouraged by your love.

This may mean holding back venomous comments when your adult child is reacting to unkind comments or outrageous lies spread by your bitter ex-spouse or some other troublemaker in the family. Or it can mean keeping your cool when a daughter- or son-in-law tries to engage you in conflict or otherwise come between you and your adult child. Don't put your adult child in the position of having to choose between you and someone else. Refuse to play the game. Your kindness in the face of rancor may help to convince your adult child eventually that what is being said about you is wrong, or that you love him or her enough to hang in there even when the going gets tough.

If you're an adult child, interrupting the blame cycle may mean making an effort not to revert to old behaviors when your parent is being critical or intrusive. Again, refuse to play the game. Let your parent know that you will think about what he or she is telling you, but that you may eventually need to agree to disagree. Set a new boundary, and stick to it. For example, when Lisa's retired mother called her constantly at work, their old pattern was to hurl blame at each other:

"Mother, I can't talk to you now. You can't keep calling! You're going to get me fired from my job!"

"You just don't care! You never have time to talk! I never thought it would come to this. You're such a selfish person!"

When Lisa decided to stop blaming and change her behavior, the conflict with her mother eased considerably. "I told her that I would be happy to talk with her at a specific time, when she could call me or I would call her," Lisa says. "And it is always in the evening, always at home. I told her, in a calmer moment, that my boss takes a very dim view of personal phone calls during work hours and that, barring a life-threatening emergency, she needs to stop calling me at work. Once she realized that we had a special time to talk, she stopped calling me at work. So far, so good."

For both parent and adult child, interrupting the blame cycle can mean listening instead of denying, and acknowledging differing perspectives with love and respect. You know that you did the best you could, that you raised your child with love. He or she knows that whatever you gave didn't feel like enough or was overshadowed by life events, like divorce, or personal challenges, like alcohol or drug abuse or an anger management problem. And what you each know is the truth of your own perspective.

Tom, the widowed father of Kayla, thirty-two, remembers the sad days after his wife's death, when Kayla was only fourteen. "I was so sad and shocked because Jean's cancer death was quite fast, just two months after diagnosis," he says. "I knew how hard it was for Kayla to lose her mother, and my goal was to be there for her in every way. But, of course, I fell short. I had my own grief to deal with. I drank too much. But I love Kayla unconditionally and tried to be a good parent most of the time. At the same time, I understand how she could feel the way she does, and I accept that. No arguments. No excuses. No blaming the situation—or Kayla for her criticisms of me. It hurts, of course, to hear her version of our life together, and it hurts inside that I wasn't a better parent to my grieving child."

Kayla is trying to dial back the blame. "I've been angry for so long," she says. "I really resented how he was in those few years after Mom's death. He worked long hours. He drank a lot. He wasn't there for me. At least in the way I needed him to be. So when I was through college and on my own, I really didn't want to know him. Whenever we talked, it seemed like we'd end up arguing and blaming each other for being insensitive. We're trying to get past that now. I'm tired of being so angry, and I respect my dad for being the first to suggest a fresh start and to apologize. I want a dad again—and a grandpa for my baby son. Little by little, we're getting there."

Change usually does come gradually, little by little, as you find your way past anger, resentment, guilt, and blame.

Changing the way you act and react with your adult child

isn't easy. There will be times when you slip back into old patterns of behavior.

There will be times when you need to pause, take a deep breath, and think before you speak.

There will be times when your adult child doesn't react as you had hoped to your willingness to listen, to your apologies and to your openness to change. During such times, you may feel once again that your grown child's anger is unfair and unjustified, that his or her long silences are cruel and unnecessary. That feels true from your perspective, while the need to stay away or to hang onto anger right now may be top priorities from your adult child's perspective.

This doesn't mean allowing yourself to be targeted again and again, to become a victim of the other person's rage and abusive behavior.

If he or she is being abusive or is too angry to hear you, stop the conversation with a comment like "I want to understand what you're saying and resolve this, but right now this is nonproductive. Let's talk again after we have both calmed down."

There is a difference between hearing and accepting the other's anger and allowing yourself to be verbally abused with no immediate hope of a meaningful discussion. Always leave the door open, but don't hesitate to walk away when the blaming escalates and the other person stops listening.

Remember that you only have control over your own behavior, and that your goal here is to stop the blame. Stopping the blame on your end may eventually cause your parent or your adult child to stop, reflect, and change his or her blaming behavior as well. Or maybe it won't. There are instances when even one's best efforts result in more recrimination, silence, and rejection.

Celia, who is estranged from her twenty-five-year-old daughter Misty, has tried many times to stop the blame cycle that has escalated during the past three years.

"We used to be close, and now nothing I do or say is right," she says sadly. "I have listened to her accusations about defects in my character. (She thinks I'm selfish, too critical, and too demanding.) I've tried very hard both to look at all of this from her point of view and also to change my own behavior. I admit that I have been too quick to criticize, correct, and rush in with unsolicited advice in the past. I admitted that all to her and I apologized. I've made an honest effort to do better. I've tried to show her how much I love her. But so far, it hasn't made much difference. She questions my motives. She says I'm being manipulative. I call her. She doesn't pick up. I text her. No answer. Same thing with emails. And I wrote her a letter of love and apology that she sent back to me unopened."

For some, the blame and anger go on and on. There is no easy resolution. There is no happy ending. While we will address ways that parents and adult children can deal with rejection and long-term estrangement in chapter 14, it may help right now to know that you tried your best to reconcile. There is always that bit of hope that, in time, the other person will hear you as you have endeavored to hear him or her and that this will lead eventually to a more satisfying relationship for you both.

Stopping the Blame and Healing Your Relationship Requires Understanding the Past in Order to Create a Happier Present

Resolving old pain can have benefits far beyond lessening the tension between you.

It may help to look, once again, at John Bowlby's attachment theory, which takes the position that babies and young children who feel insecure attachments to one or both parents reach adulthood with deep insecurities about whether they deserve to be loved and nurtured—and that this has an impact on their ability to love and to form healthy romantic and parenting relationships.

Studies by Carolyn Page Cowan and Philip Cowan found that children of parents who described attachment difficulties in their own childhoods had problematic behavior at school and in their relationships. They observed that those with insecure early attachments struggled to control their emotions, soothe themselves when distressed, or express tenderness with others, which impacted relationships both with their partners and with their children.

The researchers came to the conclusion that understanding the past and moving beyond anger to a more compassionate view of how and why parents acted the way they did is essential to establishing an empowered (rather than victimized) self-view. It is the key to stopping not only the cycle of blame but also the multigenerational cycle of insecure attachment, so that intimate and healthy relationships become possible with partners and children.* That's why admitting your imperfections as a parent and sharing experiences from your own earlier years can help your adult child to understand better some of the ways you nurtured her—or didn't.

Making a commitment to understand the past can make a major difference in one's ability to grow past the blame and anger toward compassion and empowerment. The path to reconciliation, however, isn't likely to be a swift or smooth one. Keeping to your plan to stop blaming can be a special challenge when all you get in return is more blame. But it can be critical to keeping alive that spark of hope that this will not always be so.

For many others, the scenario can be more promising. With time, with patience and with love, change may happen for both of you. It's important you both to have the time to grieve what was, to accept what is, and to find new ways to be together.

---

*   Joshua Coleman, Carolyn P. Cowan, Philip A. Cowan, "The Cost of Blaming Parents," GreaterGood.com, December 23, 2014.

CHAPTER TWELVE

Learning to Live with Differences

The contentious 2016 presidential election was the final straw for the ongoing conflict between Taylor and her conservative parents. "They are unrepentant Republicans, and our political differences have always been a problem," she says. "We would go months without speaking after a battle. But this past election did us in. Truly. I was so horrified at their stubborn allegiance, even veneration, of Trump. I still can't believe it. It made me question their sanity and wonder if I ever want to be in the same room with them again. They seemed suddenly like strangers—even though they've always been pretty conservative and we've never voted for the same people. This was different. I don't know when, if ever, we'll call a truce."

What sparked the estrangement of Joe and his son Ben two years ago was a double whammy: Joe and his wife Teresa divorced after thirty-two years of marriage and, not long after, Joe came out as gay. Ben, who is deeply religious, was shocked at his parents' divorce and disgusted with his father's sexual orientation and decision to come out. "If he could be married and not act on his homosexual desires for all those years, why couldn't he keep doing it?" Ben asks. "The Church is clear on this. They don't condemn gay people. But acting on gay desires is sinful and wrong. I'll never agree with his choices. I don't want to see him or talk to him and hear all about his new life. Spare me."

These are just two of the many instances I've seen where parents and adult children find themselves at odds—with differing opinions, lifestyles, and worldviews—that have led to painful estrangements. What can you do to begin to live with your differences and come back together again?

The first step in healing estrangement stemming from fundamental differences is to ask yourself: "What do I want?"

If what you want is for a parent or an adult child to agree with you, you may have a long wait. You're entitled to your opinions and choices. So is your parent or child. So the most important question may be "Do I want to put my parent or child first, before my opinions, beliefs, or convictions, and learn to accept our differences?" The answer to that question may well determine whether or not you're able to heal your estrangement and move on.

Living with Differences
Means Letting Go

When you make the decision to give your relationship with your child or your parent a higher priority than your differences, there are several ways you may need to let go.

+ **Let go of old roles:** This is important for both parents and adult children. For parents, it may mean rethinking who you are as a parent. If your children are now adults, you need to let go of the tendency to give unasked-for advice or give or withhold approval. Once your child is an independent adult, you no longer have a vote of approval on how they live, where they work, whom they choose to love, or how they raise their kids. You're not the center of their lives anymore. You have a supporting role—and if you actively choose to be supportive rather than directive, you may be able to heal the rift in your relationship.

   For adult children, it is also important to let go of old roles. If you're still dependent on your parents for financial help, or you expect them to babysit at a moment's notice or make your life easier in other ways, you're not truly independent and can expect them to feel entitled to weigh in on financial decisions or child-rearing. Expecting your parents to do things for you takes you back to childhood. When you can do for yourself, but appreciate their support at certain times, the scenario shifts. A mutually appreciative, reciprocal

relationship between parents and adult children is the foundation of a healthier and happier bond.

+ **Let go of the need to be right.** Would you prefer to be right
or to have a relationship with someone you love? There
are times when you can't have both. Take a long look at
the point of your contention. You and your loved one may
have parted ways over political or religious beliefs, over
lifestyle, over choices when faced with an unexpected life
event. Your parents' Republican (or Democratic) views,
your adult child's stance on climate change, your parent's
seemingly rigid religious beliefs, your child's defection
from your faith and choices that violate your beliefs: all of
these are crisis points in your relationship. And these are
times when you need to reflect on what matters most: your
relationship with your parent or child, or your opinions,
beliefs, and convictions.

"When my son and his girlfriend moved in together, I was
really against that and let him know," says Mara, fifty-nine and
the mother of three adult children in their thirties. She was
estranged from her son for a little over a year because of her
objections to his cohabitation. "I was so caught up in my own
beliefs and what other people in the family and among our
close friends might think. I came to the conclusion, during
some very lonely times without hearing from him, that he
was more important than my beliefs or the judgments of
other people. I wrote him a letter saying I was sorry. I didn't
hear anything for weeks. Then he called me. But it was very

tense for a while. We were walking on eggshells with each other. We're a little more comfortable now. Things are taking a long time to get better. But I'm hopeful."

While saying "I'm sorry" and making the first move to make amends is a step in the right direction, a rift that has led to estrangement isn't instantly (or perhaps ever) resolved. It takes time to trust again and to believe that you can live with your differences and that positive change is possible.

+ **Let go of the need to have the last word.** If you don't, your battles or tense silence could go on and on. Take a deep breath and consider the advantages of a *supportive* silence in healing your estrangement. Listen instead of talking. Don't give advice unless it's asked for, and don't ask for advice unless you're prepared to hear the other person out.

"My mother and I really got hung up on her tendency to be so quick with opinions and advice," says Melissa, twenty-six, single and a paralegal with a large law firm. "She felt she had the right to tell me anything at all about my appearance, my friends, or guys I was dating because 'I'm your mother!' From my point of view, we weren't exactly estranged, but talking to her was such a pain when she was busy being an expert on my life that I just stopped calling her or taking her calls. I'd send a text saying I was okay, just busy. That went on for well over six months. She was really upset with me. I finally told her that her unasked-for advice was coming between us. At first, she argued and justified it with motherly love. I finally said 'Could you just listen to me? Please? Without feeling you have to say anything or fix anything for me?' She's trying—and I give her lots of credit for that. I'm still vigilant, though…"

Again, habits of a lifetime can't change overnight, but being willing to listen to what your adult child (or your parent) is telling you is a good start toward positive change.

Your Differences Are Natural, Normal, and Okay

Many of us think that because we're family, because we shared so many years of our lives in close contact under the same roof, our beliefs and interests should be the same. But, even when we share a genetic heritage, we all have our own worldviews, shaped by friends, teachers, and our own experiences outside the family. We grow up to have a vast array of feelings and beliefs. Some of these may coincide with the values and beliefs of those we love. Some, however, are very much our own.

One of my dearest friends is an identical twin, as genetically close as a person can be to another. He and his twin brother spent the first eighteen years of their lives together before going off to different colleges. Even though the most dramatic differences between them became more noticeable from that juncture on, there were differences growing up: one excelled at sports; the other was more academic. They found ways, even in their earliest days, to grow into distinct individuals.

In middle age, they have vastly different careers, lifestyles, and political beliefs. They no longer look quite so identical. There are times when their philosophical and political differences come between them. For months before and after the 2016 election, they were at serious odds and went without speaking for a time. "But I never lose sight of the fact that I love him deeply and forever," my friend told me recently. "I may not like or agree with some or most of his views. We may get exasperated with each other for a time. But the love is there, always. Knowing that and feeling that makes all the difference."

There may be times when a loved one makes life changes that are, at least initially, jolting and disconcerting and take some major adjustments on your part. And it isn't always an impulsive young adult who is at the epicenter of such a family crisis.

Erwin, "Baldy" to his friends and family, was a hardworking mechanic who was devoted to his wife Jean and daughter Catherine. He had always had a touch of eccentricity—usually expressed with passionate interests and areas of study that were quite different from his work and daily life. He delved into a study of medieval history, then into little-known facts about each U.S. president. In time, he became passionately interested in geology and the geological features of the United States. Later on, that passion expanded in another direction: the care, feeding, and domestication of quail.

A few years ago, Catherine was shocked at her parents' retirement plans: to sell the family home and split the money evenly between them. Her mother happily moved into a small, neat condo nearby. Her father bought a battered old Volkswagen van, with plans to become a permanent RVer. He hit the road, off to explore the lower forty-eight continental states, with four of his favorite quail in tow.

"I was horrified," Catherine remembers. "I thought he had totally lost his mind. I freaked out when I saw that cluttered van with quail running loose in it. I argued with him and probed into his personal matters maybe more than I should have. It caused a brief estrangement. We didn't speak for several months. I meant well. I wanted to be sure he was okay, that he wouldn't become some homeless guy living on the streets, having blown all his money. I was upset that my parents were parting, even though their split was amicable. It just didn't seem right. But my mother set me straight. She said, 'Look at him. He's a happy man. He has worked so hard all his life to provide for us. This is his time to just enjoy his life. And I'm enjoying my clean, uncluttered condo. It works for both of us. So don't knock it.' I guess I had been having this fantasy that he would be a sweet, full-time grandpa to my two sons. But that wasn't him. When I let go of my own fantasies about how he should be and could accept his choices, Dad became kind of a legend to my sons. We keep a map and track his travels—from his postcards and letters—all across the country. That wouldn't be the kind of life I'd choose, for sure. But he's happy. The quail are all thriving. He is having a good life."

Letting go of our fantasies of what life could—or, in our minds, should—be like for a beloved family member, and instead accepting, even celebrating, their dreams, can make a major difference in healing an estrangement.

Boundaries and Limits Help
to Build New Closeness

There are times when emotional clashes between parents and adult children spring from needs to create space, privacy, and limits. Adult children, especially, may feel that, in order to become truly independent adults, they need to create distance from their parents.

"My mother constantly invaded my territory, both literally and figuratively," says Cherilyn, a twenty-nine-year-old editor at an educational publishing house. "She would drop by my apartment anytime she felt like it. No warning. No phone call. Nothing. And she felt perfectly comfortable commenting on my life as she found it: the boyfriend coming out of the bathroom, drying himself from the shower, just after she arrived, or the state of my housekeeping. It drove me crazy. I felt I had no privacy. I finally told her that she needed to call before coming over and that if I wanted her opinions or advice on my life, I'd ask, and to otherwise spare me. She didn't speak to me for months. I felt bad, but frankly, the silence was a relief. I finally called her, and we talked. Things are better now. We take it day by day. So far, so good."

As close as we feel to our family members, there are some questions we do not ask, some comments we do not make out of respect for each other's privacy, some challenges we don't make to the right of an independent adult to make decisions. There comes a time, particularly for parents, when our comments need to shift from directive to reflective, accepting differences of opinion and lifestyle choices as a natural part of the family's evolution. Once our children are independent adults, we're not in a position to give or withhold approval of an adult child's choice. To continue to believe that we have a right to judge can be a giant step toward estrangement.

Even in instances when we feel the need to intervene in an adult child's life—for instance, when an adult child is struggling with an addiction—there are times when we have to will ourselves to step back and allow the adult child to own and to resolve the struggle.

"We went through hell together with our alcoholic son," says Irene, a newly retired sixty-two-year-old. "He was in and out of our home, living with us for long stretches, promising to get sober and get a job. When I would try to help with advice or pleas, or with ads for jobs, he'd get furious. When he kept drinking, I'd get furious. He stormed out of the house one night, and we didn't hear from him for a year. I can't begin to tell you how terrible that was. I didn't know where he was, whether he was dead or alive. I'd go to therapy and cry, to Al-Anon and cry. He had to hit bottom on his own and make the decision to get sober on his own. And he did. I'm grateful for every day of sobriety he has. I no longer nag or remind or judge. It's his struggle. We're behind him all the way. But he is responsible for maintaining sobriety."

Maintaining healthy boundaries can bring you closer together. When a loved one knows he or she can enjoy being with you without risking battles over autonomy, the loved one is much more likely to want to share time, opinions, news, and experiences with you.

Dale, who enjoys an excellent relationship with his thirty-five-year-old daughter Katie, was recently asked if he had given her any advice about a career setback she appeared to be having. He looked surprised, then smiled. "She hasn't asked for my advice," he said. "But she knows that she always has my support whatever decisions she makes. She's my beloved daughter, but *she's* the expert on her own life."

BE THE FIRST TO REACH OUT AND APOLOGIZE

The differences that caused your estrangement may have been deep and fierce. You may have believed, beyond all doubt, that you were right and your family member was wrong. But if you really want to begin to get past your differences and heal your estrangement, you may need to be the first to say "I'm sorry."

It may seem a tall order, especially at first.

"My daughter Angie left for college and never looked back," says Bev, who became the mother of three children upon her marriage to Allen, a widower whose wife had died when the youngest, Angie, was still an infant. "Over the years, I became quite angry and impatient at the distant relationship she had with us, especially when her dad became ill. I was so righteous. Of course, she lives nearly two thousand miles away. She has her own husband and children. I know she cares. But it hurt when she would rarely call or visit. Then I started looking at things from what I guessed must be her perspective: when I married Allen, she was nine years old and thrilled. And I was so immature at the time, and so wanting just to be a wife and not knowing how to be an instant mother. I tried, but my efforts fell way short of her needs. Of course, she was wounded. Of course, she needed to keep a distance. So during a rare, recent visit, I apologized to her for not living up to her needs for a loving mom, for all the ways I had disappointed her. She ran over to me and fell into my arms in a long and tearful embrace. We told each other we loved each other—as her own wonderful, deeply loved teenage daughter sat grinning in the background. The apology was a new beginning that she accepted with the generosity of her heart and it opened a whole new chapter in our lives."

No matter what has transpired, it is often the parent who needs to make the first move to apologize. As we have seen in previous chapters, parents are more likely to want and seek closeness with adult children. Particularly when they approach middle age and are busy with careers and families of their own, adult children may have less of an emotional investment in maintaining ties with their parents. In the end, apologizing and calling a truce may fall to whoever most wants to end the estrangement.

"My evangelical parents have been distraught, angry, and rejecting since I came out to them as a lesbian," says Lori, twenty-seven. "I have apologized to them for my hurtful words to them when they first reacted—horribly—to my news. I have invited them to my wedding. I want to keep the door open. So far, they have been rejecting. And that hurts. I hope they find it in their hearts to be part of my wedding. But I'm not counting on that. But here's the thing: I feel like I've done the right thing by apologizing first, even though that seemed outrageous before I decided to do it. I did it for them. But I also did it for me. I want to feel that, even though we're estranged, I've done what I could to leave the door open a crack for us to be together again in a new way."

As Lori points out, an apology is not always an instant answer to estrangement. There may need to be many apologies. Healing the estrangement may take a considerable amount of time. Full healing may never happen. But if reconciliation is ever to happen, someone needs to take the first step. Why not you?

FIND COMFORTABLE WAYS
TO BE TOGETHER

Think of what you do share, despite your differences. Maybe it's a love of sports, or theater or music. Maybe you enjoy chess or hiking or volunteer work with animal rescue or with your local food bank.

What could you do together that you would both enjoy and be able to put your differences aside, at least for a while?

"My friend gave me this advice and, at least at first, I totally rejected it," says Julia, a thirty-one-year-old publicist. "I was so angry with my mom over the fact that these days we can't seem to agree on anything. She doesn't approve of anything in my life, and I don't agree that she has the right to approve or disapprove.

We hadn't spoken for several months. But then I started thinking about things that were really fun to do with her, like going to plays, especially musicals, which she loves. So I called her and apologized. And then I told her that I wanted to treat her to *Beautiful*, the musical about Carole King. It was coming to our town the next week. Even though she was a bit cranky at first, she began to get excited about the show within a few days. She's a big Carole King fan. We went and had a great time together. I think that it reminded us both that we can still enjoy each other, even if we differ in a lot of ways."

Julia's insight is an important one. You can disagree in many ways with someone and still be close. What you don't share is much less important than what you do. And what matters most is love.

CHAPTER THIRTEEN

Breaking the Silence through Better Communication

Estrangement is uniquely painful in an age of instant communication. It isn't just that the phone never rings. You may find yourself texting or emailing into a void. You may be watching your grandchildren grow up via Facebook posts. What can you do if silence hangs heavy, or when what little contact you do have with your parent or your adult child seems to spark further conflict?

FIVE FACTS ABOUT BREAKING THE SILENCE OF ESTRANGEMENT

1. **The sooner the silence is broken, the better.** When researcher Dr. Karl Pillemer interviewed elderly parents who were estranged from their adult children, they urged

other parents to make peace sooner rather than later. He observed that, with time, the viewpoints of both parties can harden, and it may become easier not to make an effort to reconnect.* Some parents and adult children decide that time may be healing. That can happen when the immediate anger and pain of a confrontation begin to cool. But there is a danger in waiting too long, hoping that time alone will heal the pain.

In her studies of family estrangements, researcher Dorothy Jerrome observed that "a striking feature of these cases was the tendency for estrangement to go on unchallenged. Assumptions were made, conclusions were drawn, and the ensuing stalemate could last for decades."†

So as soon as possible, be the first to apologize, to seek reconciliation, even if you've been feeling wrongly accused. If you want to keep that connection, reach out as soon as you feel able to do so without continuing the conflict.

2. **The person to break the silence will probably be the parent.** As we have seen previously, a number of studies have noted the "generational stake hypothesis," which contends that parents, especially as they age, may have a greater stake in maintaining close relationships with their adult children

---

*   Karl Pillemer, "Parents of Estranged Children Offer Advice," Huffington Post, April 12, 2012. www.huffingtonpost.com/karl-a-pillemer-phd/estranged-children_b_1267734.html.

†   Dorothy Jerrome, "Family Estrangement: Parents and Children Who Lose Touch," *Journal of Family Therapy* 16 (1994): 241–258.

than the children, who may have formed their own families, have in keeping in close contact with their parents.*

How you break the silence can determine whether you'll reconnect or whether your estrangement will deepen.

3. **The parent will probably be the one to make concessions.** No matter how unfair that seems, it's a fact. This isn't just because you, as a parent, may have a greater emotional investment in reconnection, but may also be due to differing reasons for estrangement.

    While each painful parent and adult child estrangement has its own unique back story, there are certain themes and trends that researchers have found in reasons that parents and their adult children give for their estrangement.

    For example, researchers have discovered that parents tend to blame estrangement on sources outside of themselves— most significantly, on relationships that they find objectionable or the influence a certain relationship may be having on their son or daughter. In contrast, adult children attribute estrangement to personal characteristics of their parents— such as toxic behavior or seemingly unchangeable personality characteristics—or to a general sense of feeling unloved.

    In the latter instance, parents were uncertain about their role in creating these feelings, while children were explicit

*   K. S. Birditt et al, "Tensions in the Parent and Adult Child Relationship: Links to Solidarity and Ambivalence," *Psychology and Aging* 24, no. 2 (2009): 287–295.

about their reasons for feeling unloved, attributing these, once again, to stable and internal characteristics of their parents.[†]

Looking at the matter this way, you may be faced with a tough choice: to change your behavior or attitude, or risk losing your adult child. This can mean accepting that the decision to maintain a relationship, even when you object, is theirs to make. It can mean that helping him or her to feel loved does not include arguing that, of course, you always loved him. Instead, it can mean listening to what she is saying and finding new ways meaningful to *her* to show your love.

4. **Remember: this is about reconnection, not defending yourself.** That doesn't mean that verbal abuse is okay. If a conversation is degenerating into abuse, you may need to call a temporary halt, saying that you want to hear the other person's point of view, but it's hard to hear when you're feeling attacked. That said, you may well hear some uncomfortable truths, from your family member's point of view, in your quest for reconciliation.

This isn't the time to refute what you're hearing. It's your family member's reality. In the interest of reconciliation, listen and then speak only of your continuing love and your desire to repair your relationship. This may be a message you need

---

† Kristin Carr et al, "Giving Voice to the Silence of Family Estrangement: Comparing Reasons of Estranged Parents and Adult Children in a Non-Matched Sample," *Journal of Family Communication* 15 (2015): 130–140.

to send in a variety of ways over time before reconciliation becomes a distinct possibility.

5. **The key to reconnection is listening...and love.** Whether you're an estranged parent or an estranged adult child, it's most important to listen. Listening can give you clues for repairing and rebuilding your relationship. It can give you new insights into what went wrong, the other person's desire and commitment to reconcile, and how you can begin to rebuild the loving connection between you.

It isn't always that easy, however. You may be in a situation where a parent is just too angry or too centered on his or her own pain to listen and try to understand your point of view. Or your adult child has simply stopped speaking to you and rejects all of your overtures to make peace: not answering your phone calls, texts, emails, or letters. You may be wondering how to break through that wall of silence, that anger and resentment, those old patterns of relating, to find a new way to be together.

There are no guarantees. Some estrangements last for years. Some are forever. But learning to communicate in a new way can bring hope for a happier resolution.

Strategies for Opening Conversations

However you plan to reach out, keep in mind that you have no control over what your parent or your adult child says or does. However, you do have the power to change your part of the conversation, whether it's in person, on the phone, texting, via email, or via social media.

The following are some tips and strategies for tackling that first conversation. Which method you choose for your opening conversation may depend on your own comfort level or, perhaps more important, on the best way to reach out to your adult child. While you may be most comfortable on the phone, your adult child might be most accessible via texting. Or if you're an adult child feeling that texting is the only reasonable way to communicate, ask yourself what might be the most effective way to get a conversation going again with a parent who might not have a smartphone. Give the matter some serious thought, weighing the advantages and disadvantages of various methods.

In-Person Conversations

Advantages: You can read body language, make eye contact, and have the chance to reach out and touch each other if that might enhance your connection.

Disadvantages: The immediacy of the conversation can be risky.

You may struggle to edit your comments if you feel attacked, rejected, or not heard, and your conflict can start anew.

What not to say:

"I think you owe me an apology."

"I'm really upset about this so stop being stubborn."

"Everyone in the family thinks you're being unreasonable."

"Have you thought about my objections and come to any decisions?"

How to say it better:

"I'm so sorry…"

"I was wondering if you could tell me more about how you're feeling."

"I'm curious about your thoughts on what I could do to make things better."

If you're a parent trying to reconnect with your adult child, remember that reconciliation may well be more important to you than it is to your son or daughter. The conversation, as difficult as it may be, needs to be about your adult child, not you. It needs to open the door for them to express their feelings and ideas. Until you know why they're estranging themselves from you—and many parents *don't* really know or understand why—it's hard to find ways to heal the rift. If your adult child says "You should know why," you might reply "I'm trying to understand this from your point of view. I really want to hear your thoughts on this."

Betty, the fifty-four-year-old mother of Penelope, thirty, has a further suggestion. "I would advise parents to arrange a meeting in a public place," she says. "That worked well for my daughter and me. I had tried meeting with her at her home, and it quickly went south. It was too easy for her to tell me to get out and to stomp into her bedroom, slamming the door. I asked her to lunch at a place we both enjoy. It was neutral territory. We both had an incentive to behave ourselves and to talk in a more civilized way. We both felt more relaxed and conversation came more easily. I wouldn't say that we managed to solve all of our issues that day. But it was a start."

Telephone

Advantages: Immediacy. You can listen for tone of voice and respond warmly and supportively. Some people are able to talk better together when they're not making eye contact.

Disadvantages: Immediacy. You can slip into old conflicts and arguments, saying things that, in retrospect, you wish you hadn't. It's also not possible, unless you're doing FaceTime or Skype, to read body language.

What not to do or say: Same as an in-person conversation. Don't blame. Don't accuse. Don't make angry demands.

How to say it better: Same as an in-person conversation. Express a willingness to listen before saying anything about your desire to reconnect.

Special warning: One of the worst things you can do is to make repeated phone calls or to leave a series of distressed phone messages. The other person may feel harassed and thus more justified than ever in estranging himself or herself from you.

"Guilty as charged," says Joanna, fifty-two. "When my daughter stopped talking to me, I barraged her with phone calls at home and at work. I was desperate to end our estrangement. I wanted to tell her, over and over, how much I loved and missed her. I meant well. But it seems like I only succeeded in upsetting her even more. She was like, 'Enough already! Stop calling me, Mom! I don't want to talk to you right now.' I backed off and let her be. I sent her a birthday card. I texted occasionally to express my love. But I stopped calling. Eventually, she called me and we had a good talk. I still walk on eggshells with her, but I'm hopeful. It will just take time and restraint on my part."

Texting

Advantages: This is the preferred method of contact for many younger people these days. It has the advantages of immediate contact with the chance to think about and moderate your sentiments.

Disadvantages: This isn't a medium for pouring out your heart. It's best to keep your message brief and to the point.

What not to say: Anything negative or that could be construed as critical. These short, immediate messages can have a real impact. Choose your words carefully. Don't text when angry.

How to say it better: Express love, support, and hope. Utilize texting to simply stay in touch in a nondemanding way when your adult child or parent isn't talking to you. It's best to say something like "Thinking of you. Hope you're okay. Just know that I love you." And leave it at that. As with phone messages, don't barrage the other person with texts. Just send one occasionally to let the other person know that the door is always open and that your love is constant.

Email

Advantages: This also has immediacy, with the advantage of editing your thoughts to express your sentiments clearly and most effectively. You can always go back and read each other's responses, even printing them out for later reflection.

Disadvantages: Some young adults see email as a somewhat antiquated form of communication, even though it may feel cutting-edge to the parental generation. If your adult child gets many emails at work or is particularly angry, there is the danger that your email could be overlooked or, worse, deleted without being read.

What not to say: Don't start off with a negative heading or begin your email with an accusatory tone.

Subject:

   "*Enough!*"

   "*Stop This Nonsense!*"

   "*Very Upset*"

Beginning:

*"Okay, you've made your point and managed to ruin my
    weekend."*

"I can't believe it has come to this."

"I can't stop crying."

How to say it better: Express your love, your positive commitment to change, and your openness to hear your child's or
your parent's perspective:

Subject:

"So sorry!"

"Good Point"

"Love You"

Beginning:

"I'm so sorry that I reacted the way I did."

*"I've spent time thinking about what you said and think you
    have a good point. I want to hear more..."*

"Please know that I'll always love you."

For some parents and adult children, the immediacy of email,
along with the chance to think and edit one's thoughts, can work
well in resolving disputes and estrangements.

Not long ago, I saw the magic of email work wonderfully to
mend a brief rift in our own family.

Ryan, now thirty-three, was only nine when he and my
husband Bob were matched in the Big Brothers program in Los
Angeles. The relationship has been a blessing to all of us over the
years, as Ryan has become like a son to us. We cried happy tears
at both his college graduation and when he received his master's

degree in social work. We're thrilled that he is now in a job he loves, as a licensed clinical social worker, bringing valuable help and much-needed therapy to an underserved population. His phone calls brighten our days.

Nevertheless, we tend to worry like parents when we hear about challenges he faces and see him make some mistakes that are typical in the young-adult years.

During a brief weekend visit with Ryan not long ago, I was delighted when he and Bob decided to go out to dinner together, just the two of them. But I was alarmed when they both came back visibly upset and, uncharacteristically, didn't want to talk about it. Ryan went quietly to his room well before his usual bedtime. Bob sat silently in his chair.

When Ryan got ready to catch his flight back to Los Angeles the next day, he made light of the conflict with "Well, Bob, I think we're doing better. Only one major argument in four days. I think that's a record for us!"

We all laughed. Since he was a bright, opinionated nine-year-old, Ryan has felt free to disagree with Bob about everything from film choices to politics. But this time was different. This time I could see the pain lingering behind their smiles.

That night, Bob sat down and wrote a heartfelt email to Ryan, apologizing for his barrage of criticism over dinner. What had set Bob off was Ryan's casual comment about an outstanding parking ticket. This had led to an impassioned discussion about financial responsibility and then branched off into an emotional debate about how he spent his free time and over yoga (Ryan's new passion) versus aerobics (Bob's preferred method of daily exercise). In his email, Bob told Ryan that he was sorry he had been so critical, that the criticism was out of line. He said that he had simply been a jerk, was sorry, and loved him very much.

The response from Ryan was prompt and also heartfelt. He told Bob that he had been stung by the criticism because Bob's opinions matter immensely to him and because he felt that, given his recent life circumstances—the breakup of a five-year romantic relationship and the stress of beginning a demanding new job—he felt that he had been doing pretty well. He acknowledged that he could have handled the parking ticket matter better and would in the future. He expressed his love.

"I felt it could have become a rift that kept growing between us," Bob says. "And though we usually talk on the phone, I knew that a phone call wouldn't work in resolving this. He would joke about it as he did when he was leaving. I knew he was deeply hurt. I wanted to send an immediate apology. I did act like a jerk. I needed to say that. And it made a difference."

Now they're back to life as usual, with long phone conversations several times a week.

While the dispute between Bob and Ryan was brief and less disruptive than a family estrangement, the power of email in overcoming their usual defenses, resolving the matter, and bringing them back together again is instructive.

Even if it isn't your preferred method of communication in less contentious times, email can be an effective way of communication if used wisely.

Social Media

Advantages: This is a way to see how adult children or parents are doing even though you may be not speaking at the moment.

Disadvantages: Watching their lives go on without you can be heartbreaking. It can be especially difficult to see grandchildren growing up and family celebrations going on without you. It can also be a minefield with the danger of ill-advised comments or self-disclosing blog posts or tweets.

What not to do: Do not air your differences or the fact of your estrangement on social media. It could embarrass or enrage the other person, deepening your estrangement, and it also could bring a number of family members and friends into the middle of it, with unsolicited advice or judgments.

If you choose to make a comment on your adult child's or parent's Facebook page, keep it neutral or positive. Don't leave a comment that could sound reproachful or guilt-inducing. For example, instead of commenting on a picture of your little granddaughter with "I sure do miss my beautiful grandbaby!" try "Beautiful!" or "Beautiful! Love to all!"

If you're a blogger, it's best to refrain from writing posts about your problems with your family member or your feelings about your estrangement, particularly if you have hopes of reconciliation. If self-disclosure is a major feature of your blog, it may be best to keep the spotlight on yourself—perhaps blogging about some important self-discoveries such as your finding that unsolicited advice can be heard as a vote of no confidence by an adult child, or your resolve to let go and only give advice when it's asked for. Publically disclosing your difficulties with your parents or with your adult child before you're able to resolve the conflicts between you can be counterproductive.

Better use of social media: Quietly keeping up with an estranged family member's life via Facebook. Blogging with careful thought and discretion in order to help others. Optimally, blogs about your estrangement would follow a solid reconnection, with the knowledge and consent of the other person. Some parents or adult children, however, holding little hope of reconciliation, may blog about their estrangements in order to help others in similar situations feel less alone.

Snail Mail

Advantages: Old-fashioned cards and letters via U.S. Postal Service have a number of advantages. They're fairly unique these days. One can't help but be intrigued by a personal letter or card amidst the bills, advertisements, and junk mail. There is a wonderful permanence to a card or letter. One can keep it to read over and over. One can set it aside and think about it for a time before sending a reply. It can also be a concrete reminder of how your relationship veered off course and how committed the other person is to resolve your differences.

Disadvantages: Regular mail is much less immediate than electronic communication methods. Mail can be discarded, torn up, or returned to the sender. And, while a carefully, lovingly written letter seeking to make amends, or a birthday or Christmas card with a brief, loving message, can warm the heart, a nasty, critical, or self-pitying letter can do lasting harm.

How to make snail mail work for you: If you're feeling angry, deeply hurt, and emotional, go ahead and write a letter. Then put it in a drawer and let it sit awhile. Tear it up. Burn it in the fireplace. Don't send it. Give your letter a lot of thought. Edit it. Sleep on it. Keep the tone positive, talking about what the relationship means to you and your willingness to listen and to work with the other in resolving the issues that divide you. And know that this may only be the first of many olive branches you extend.

Dr. Joshua Coleman, a San Francisco area psychologist, the author of the excellent *When Parents Hurt*, and an expert in parent–adult child estrangements, has a terrific online seminar series at drjoshuacoleman.com for estranged parents, including special instructions on how to write an effective letter of amends.

It could well be that despite your best efforts to break the silence between you and your loved one, the estrangement continues. It may be that time and continued, well-considered communication efforts on your part will bring about reconciliation eventually. Instant, neat, happy endings are common in Hollywood films and television shows, but not so much in real life.

You may reconnect only after numerous attempts—or not at all. Despite your best attempts to reach out, you may find only silence or rejection, and face the challenge of living with that reality. You may always keep, in your heart, a spark of hope for the wonderful surprise of a phone call, a letter, an email, a text. But you no longer plan your life around it.

SECTION THREE

WHAT CAN I DO?

CHAPTER FOURTEEN

Living with Rejection

There may come a time when, as hard as you have tried to show your love, your empathy, and your desire to reconcile, your parent or your adult child is not feeling it. Rejection has become a fact of life. Estrangement is a front-and-center part of your daily reality. This can happen in a number of ways.

It may be that your parent or adult child refuses to accept who you are and to reach a loving compromise regarding your differences. For a variety of reasons—perhaps a late-life divorce, perhaps your coming out as gay, perhaps clashing religious or political beliefs—he or she no longer wants to know you.

"I tried so hard to convince my parents that I'm still the same person they said they loved before they knew I was gay," says Joseph, twenty-seven. "But they just can't deal. They told me when I change, I'll be welcome home again. Until then, I'm not to call or visit or attend family holiday gatherings. I've been hoping, these past two years, that they would miss me and change their minds. Now, after two years of their rejection, I wouldn't go there for Thanksgiving or Christmas if they begged me. So I guess what we have here is permanent."

It may be that your estrangement is partial, but ongoing. It may be not as much rejection as exclusion.

"That's how I feel: excluded from the life of my son and his family," says Carol, a sixty-three-year-old widow and the mother of Don, forty, who is married and has two young sons. "After my husband died four years ago, I moved from Chicago to Phoenix to be near my son and his family. I didn't want to hover, so I bought a small house in a retirement community about half an hour away from them. I have a lot of interests and have made new friends in my community, so I don't expect a lot from my son. But I had hoped to see them more than I do. It seems that whenever I call and offer to take the grand-kids for an evening or weekend, it's not convenient. They call me and ask me to babysit with little notice and always when the kids are already asleep. I told them I'd love to spend time with the grandkids when they're conscious! The hardest thing is holidays: they say that Thanksgiving and Christmas are 'family time' for them and that, as extended family, I can't be part of that. They always invite me over on December 23 for a few hours—never a meal—so I can bring presents. Otherwise, I'm not welcome for the holidays. It's hard to understand. We haven't had arguments. I'm always nice to my daughter-in-law.

They're all I have in terms of family—and yet, they don't consider me part of their family."

Sometimes the reason for your parent's or your adult child's rejection and estrangement remains a painful mystery.

"I really don't understand what happened," says Jane, widowed and sixty-eight years old. "My daughter Ashley and I always got along. We were always close. Then, shortly after she got married, everything changed. She called me, sounding like someone I don't know. She was angry and said she wanted me out of her life and then she hung up on me. I can't tell you the nights I've been awake, crying and wondering what I ever did to deserve this. Did she always hate me and just not show it? Did her husband influence her in some way? I can't claim to know him well, but I've always been cordial and accepting of him. I was happy about their marriage. My late husband and I made huge sacrifices that we never mentioned to Ashley so that she was able to graduate from college debt-free. I just don't know what all this could be. She has refused to talk to me for several years now. She won't take my phone calls or answer my emails. All my letters have been returned, unopened. Now they've moved and I have no idea where my daughter lives. It's like my heart got ripped out of my chest. Unless you're a parent in this situation, you can't begin to know how devastating this is. It's like…how do I go on with my life? Does the pain ever stop? Will I ever stop crying and wondering?"

Rejection by a loved one—particularly an adult child or a parent—is uniquely painful. You may grieve, cry, and wonder for a long time. If the estrangement turns out to be permanent, the grief can be forever. More often than not, you won't be able to change the way that your parent or your adult child is behaving. You can only change how you react to it. And your choices right now can make a huge difference in your quality of life. Even when the pain of rejection threatens to take over your life, there are ways to soothe the pain and inject some hope and moments of happiness back into your life.

Allow Yourself to Grieve

The loss of your relationship with your parent or your adult child is a profound one. Allowing yourself to go through the grief process can be somewhat healing. As you grieve, you go through stages of bargaining, denial, anger, and depression on the way to acceptance. All of these have a purpose. Denial can give you a rest from your pain. Anger can clarify some of your feelings, give you more energy, and perhaps help you to feel less of a victim.

As painful as it can be, the grief process moves you forward. Getting stuck in sadness and depression can keep you mired for months or years in hapless victimhood, reliving the rejection over and over.

The term "closure" has been much overused in self-help circles. It assumes that you get past pain and move on. It is more likely that, in time, you will make some kind of peace with what is, never forgetting the pain, but beginning to see new possibilities.

"My parents' rejection will always hurt," says Joseph. "But I've started to see it in a different light. I've lost my parents. But they've lost a son who had so much love to give. I'm a good person, a good friend, a good partner. I was a good son, could still have been. It's so sad. But I'm choosing to let goodness shine in my life, in relationships and how I treat people."

Don't Ruminate about Your Misfortune

Some people misunderstand this warning. One client protested: "Don't dwell on it? How do I not? My only child has cut me out of her life and I'm not supposed to think about it?"

In a very real sense, she was right: when you're facing rejection from a parent or a child, it's horrible. There's no way it won't come to mind most days. The pain never totally goes away.

But there is a difference between having this be a part of your life and rumination on what has happened. In ruminating, you go over and over the same scenario, the feelings of pain and outrage over your rejection playing in an endless loop in your mind. Your emotional wound grows as you are re-injured time and time again in an ongoing emotional downward spiral.

Interrupt those thoughts. How do you do that? You can tell yourself to stop, substituting a happier thought of friends and family who *are* loving. You can reach out to those others. You can do some physical exercise or listen to music you've always loved. All of this can help. Stopping this cycle of pain doesn't mean trivializing what has happened, but allowing yourself time to breathe, to reflect, and to begin some healing.

"I never thought I would heal from the pain of being rejected by my daughter after my wife and I divorced three years ago," says Jerry, fifty-six. "My son wasn't thrilled, but he came around. My daughter still isn't speaking to me. She doesn't return my calls or texts. We had always been close. I wasn't looking for the kids to take sides or to be happy about the divorce. But I never expected this. For months, I kept going over and over her rejection, feeling worse and worse. I was so worked up that if she had called to make peace, I would have botched it for sure. So I stopped myself from going back to that dark place and started looking ahead. I'm taking better care of myself physically. I'm concentrating more on my work, which I enjoy, and my relationship with my son. I still hope very much that my daughter and I will reconcile at some point, but I'm giving it a rest for now. I would welcome her with open arms. But I'm trying to accept what is at the moment."

Reimagine Your Life with This New Reality

Right now, it may seem impossible to think about life going on without your loved one. Moving on with your life doesn't mean giving up the hope that, someday, reconciliation will happen. But it means embracing life as is and appreciating all the love you do have in your life at the moment.

"I'm so thankful for the love of my other two children, my husband, and my sister, who also happens to be my best friend," says Cecile, fifty, whose twenty-six-year-old son has disappeared into a marriage with a woman from a much more affluent family. Saying that his family "just doesn't fit" with his new life and in-laws who look down on his parents' modest lifestyle, he has aligned firmly with his wife's family and left his own behind. "His rejection hurt tremendously," Cecile says. "And I do hope he rediscovers the value of love and remembering where he came from. But, in the meantime, what can we all do but love each other, enjoy our lives as much as possible, and just go on?"

For Carol, the widow who relocated to Arizona to be near her son, only to find herself excluded from family holiday celebrations, going on with life has meant creating her own meaningful celebrations.

"I spend Thanksgiving with some of my friends here in Sun City," she says. "All of us are far away—usually geographically, but in some cases like mine, emotionally—from loved ones. So we celebrate our friendships as we give thanks together, either at someone's home or going out to a nice restaurant. It's always a busy, fun day that I've come to look forward to. And Christmas Eve and Christmas? I've made those days very special. On Christmas Eve, I have friends over for dinner. Then I go to Midnight Mass, something I always wanted to do but my husband and kids never did. So I didn't either, until now. I love the candlelight and Christmas music and the spiritual meaning of it all. Christmas Day is a day of total indulgence! I sleep in, stay in my pajamas, and read all day. After all the years of cooking and cleaning and trying to make Christmas merry for my family, this day is now just for me! I might warm up some take-out Chinese food or some homemade soup or make myself some cinnamon toast. Whatever sounds good to me at the time. Now my friend Irene, who is totally estranged from her only child, spends Christmas volunteering with her church group to feed the homeless. She loves that tradition. I may try that, too, in time. But right now, total self-indulgence, doing exactly what I want for the holidays, soothes my spirit."

Jane, whose daughter Ashley has disappeared angrily and mysteriously from her life, has also found a way to go on. "My life has become more about the love I have—from my sister, my nephews, my friends, than the love I have lost," she says. "I never thought I would be able to say that. I'm still heartbroken. But I realized that I had to stop crying and start living again."

Keep the Door Open

When your efforts at reconciliation are consistently rebuffed by a parent or adult child, there can be a temptation, fueled by deep hurt, to lash out in kind and reject your rejecting loved one. As difficult as it may be, step back and let things be. You've done what you could to resolve your differences and prevent an estrangement. Now you wait it out and get on with your life, while leaving the door open just in case.

As hopeless as your relationship with your loved one appears right now, there is always hope if you stay open to the possibility that someday things may change. Maybe when you least expect it.

Claudia and Ray endured a fifteen-year-long estrangement from their son Clark. He had married a deeply conservative, religious woman who was estranged from her own parents and who quickly took issue with the fact that her new in-laws were liberals with no religious affiliation. Forced to choose between his parents and his wife, Clark chose his wife, stopping all communication with Claudia and Ray except for annual Christmas cards with a form letter of family updates inside.

"We told ourselves that at least we had an address and a kind of generic update on their lives," says Claudia. "We were deeply hurt and mystified, of course. We had never criticized their religious beliefs or touted our beliefs or lifestyle as superior in any way. I ached to hold the two grandchildren who were growing up without us and way too fast. But I just quietly hoped and went on. I would send Christmas and birthday cards to all, expressing only our best wishes and love. No pleas to reconcile. No arguments. Only loving feelings. This went on for years. Then, one day, everything changed."

The phone rang. It was their son. He apologized for the long estrangement, telling them it had not been their fault at all, only his. He expressed hope that they could be a family again and put the pain of the past behind them. There were happy tears and words of love.

"The reconciliation was as mysterious as the estrangement," Claudia says. "I don't know what moved him to call. It may have been that he was nearing a landmark birthday, his fortieth. It could have been getting a copy of a lovely family history picture book that Ray put together for all four children. Maybe he saw that family history, filled with people he had so loved, and decided that he wanted to be actively part of the family again. But I'm not asking questions and wondering why. I'm just so thankful that he and his family have come back to us. And I'm so glad we left the door open instead of writing him off."

• • •

Even if today looks hopeless, tomorrow, next year, or the next may bring a surprise that will make the pain of rejection a sad memory rather than a daily reality. And even if that phone call or email or text never comes, it's possible to build a good life for yourself. By avoiding the emotional dead end of rumination; by letting the grief process carry you beyond victimhood; by re-imagining your life filled with good times, good people, and love; by keeping the door open to your estranged loved one, you can build a full and satisfying life, balancing the pain of estrangement with ongoing love and hope.

CHAPTER FIFTEEN

Perfectly Imperfect: Living with What Is and Creating a Life of Your Own

She sat in my office, staring out the window and trying to hide her sudden tears. Diane was a new client with a familiar story: she was estranged from her two children for reasons neither she nor her husband understood. Her husband had shrugged the situation off with the sentiment, "Someday, they'll come around. In the meantime, hell with them if they want to be like that."

For Diane, the situation was more complicated. She couldn't understand how this could happen when the family had been so close as the kids were growing up. She missed her son and daughter terribly. She couldn't imagine life going on through holidays and birthdays without them. "My life used to be so perfect," she said. "But now…"

But now life is different. There are empty chairs at holiday celebrations. The phone doesn't ring. Life is all about loss and uncertainty, guilt and anger, shock and sadness.

And, like Diane, you may be thinking back to a time when life seemed perfect.

It may seem perfect only in retrospect. For most of us, life evolves in a series of perfectly imperfect ways.

How can you begin to build and savor a perfectly imperfect life?

Forgive Yourself and the Other Person

That may seem an impossible task. How can you begin to forgive someone who has hurt you so much? How can you forgive yourself for your part in making the estrangement happen? The latter task may be the hardest. So much of the shame that people, especially parents, feel about a family estrangement is the sense of failure. Be gentle with yourself. Tell yourself, "I did the best I could at the time. Maybe that wasn't very good. I've made mistakes. I take responsibility for my mistakes. And I will do better in the future. I will do everything I can to heal my heart and, if possible, the relationship with my parent (or adult child)."

"I was stuck in bitterness," says Marcy, estranged from her adult daughter for two years. "I was in major blaming mode, insisting to anyone in the family who would listen that I had a very ungrateful daughter. Then, as the estrangement went on, I started thinking. I thought about what she had said to me, her complaints, and how some of them made a certain amount of sense. I realized how we hadn't expressed our feelings clearly and well with each other. I forgave her and have been working on forgiving myself. It isn't an easy or fast process. I'm still working on it, but I feel so much lighter and happier most days. I sent her a letter expressing my feelings, and she texted me back, thanking me. It's our first communication in two years, so I feel hopeful, cautiously hopeful. And it all started with forgiveness. That load of anger and bitterness was just too heavy to carry any longer."

Don't Let Your Pain Define Your Life

That is easier to say than to do. But it's an important step toward reclaiming your life. The feelings of devastation, hurt, and anger that accompany an estrangement will be part of your life. But if you allow these negative feelings to overwhelm you and to set the tone in your daily living, this will only deepen your pain and isolation.

Emma found this to be true in the first year of her estrangement from her parents. "I was all about anger and bitching about my parents," she remembers. "I wasn't much fun to be with. All but my two best friends started to stay away. And one of my best friends told me that she was frustrated because she didn't know how to help me and that I appeared to be stuck in angry mode. That's when I decided I needed to add a little variety to my life and have fun with my friends again instead of dragging them down."

Give yourself and your friends a break. Focus on them and on having a good talk or fun evening. Don't overtax them or yourself with an unending litany of woe. This isn't to minimize the very real pain you're feeling. It's simply to remind you that there is much more to you than your pain and loss.

Break Your Isolation

The shame you may be feeling about an estrangement from your adult child or your parent can be immensely isolating. You may be keeping the fact of your estrangement from friends and acquaintances. You may be feeling that you're the only one who doesn't have holiday family celebrations. You may feel like a failure when you hear stories of adult children who do keep in touch, or when you see friends enjoying their grandchildren on a regular basis while you sit by a silent phone and watch your grandchildren growing up on Facebook. Or, as an estranged adult child, you may find yourself steering conversations away from family matters. You may fear judgment from friends because you're not in touch with your parents—or because you come from the kind of toxic environment where estrangement has seemed the only option.

There is a steep price you pay for maintaining isolation, however. Isolation keeps the pain going and makes you feel like a perpetual outsider.

Reach out in ways that feel safe: perhaps to a best friend or to a close family member. If you don't feel comfortable discussing what's going on with friends or other family members, think about getting therapy where you can talk freely about your feelings without the fear that the news might be spread beyond that room. Join an online forum for parents or adult children. Again, you can join one via Dr. Joshua Coleman's website (drjoshuacoleman.com) or check out two forums currently running on my blog (drkathleenmccoy.blogspot.com) connected with two popular posts "When Adult Children Become Strangers" and "Parents and Adult Children: Finding the Balance." Online forums give parents and adult children the chance to air their feelings, anonymously if they choose, to others who are experiencing similar situations. Reading about the experiences of others or reading their comments about your own posting can make you feel considerably less alone.

Not long ago, I received the following email from a mother estranged from one of her two daughters and struggling with a difficult relationship with the other. She had read several of my "Parents and Adult Children" blog posts and checked out the forums—and was feeling a surge of hope:

"I was struggling. Terribly. Then last night, I came across your blog about adult children," she wrote. "So at 2:00 a.m., after reading and really listening to what you were saying, I was able to write a sincere letter of apology to one daughter and start to understand how I need to have boundaries with another. As corny as this might sound, thank you for saving my life!"

Reaching out in whatever ways are most meaningful for you can, indeed, feel lifesaving. Knowing that you're not alone can mean so much.

Take Care of Yourself

When you're going through a difficult, painful time in your life, it's easy to let some priorities slip to the bottom of your list. You may be subsisting on leftover take-out, fast food, or comfort food—or not eating at all. You may be feeling too depressed to imagine getting up off the couch and taking a walk or hitting the gym. When you're feeling so alone, there's a temptation to say, "Why bother?"

But there's a very good reason to bother: stress can take a toll on your body, and you need good nutrition, exercise and social contact. You need to reintroduce fun into your life and practice good self-care. Instead of heading to McDonald's, make salads or home-cooked meals in advance in containers you can grab and have ready in minutes. Go to farmers' markets for fresh, local vegetables. Your parent or your adult child may not be showing much care for you at the moment, but this makes it even more imperative that you take good care of yourself.

"I've always greeted a negative turn in my life with a kind of comfort-food feeding frenzy," says Sally, who has weathered two divorces and a current estrangement from her son. "I was carrying all my pain on my body as extra pounds for all to see. This time, I just decided to treat myself better. I eat clean, mostly vegetables and fruit and some fresh fish a few times a week. I feel so much better. And I'm losing weight, too, though that wasn't my primary goal. What I want most is to take good care of myself and do all the good things I can think of: clean eating, walking every evening, and meditating. It all helps a lot!"

Accept What *Is* Right Now and Keep Your Mind Open

Instead of continuing to fight the estrangement or put angry energy into maintaining it, sit back, take a deep breath and accept what *is* right now.

"I have this mantra, this sentiment, that I say over and over each day," says Juanita, seventy, and estranged from her only daughter. "I say 'It is what it is.' I take a deep breath and say that, and it has been freeing for me. This moment, I don't need to do anything but accept what is. Of course, I'd be thrilled if my daughter and I could find a way back to each other. I can't help but think that accepting the situation as it is right now gives me a resting place to reflect and to just go on with my life. I find it soothing and comforting in a way that nothing else has been."

Coming to this point of acceptance isn't easy. But calm acceptance may take some of the desperation out of your attempts to reconnect or to keep a distance. It may give you the rest and the comfort you need to keep going—and keep hoping.

There may not be a neat Hollywood ending to this conflict.

Your relationship with your parents or your adult child may continue to be difficult, but you might discover ways to make peace with each other. You may find yourself living with a certain amount of pain and regret and anger for a long time. Whatever your relationship—or nonrelationship—accepting what is can help you start to go on with your life.

Let Love into Your Life

When you feel you've lost someone you loved most, it's a temptation to withdraw from and, perhaps, devalue the love that remains: from a spouse who may also be hurting, but in a different way; from other adult children or siblings; from extended family or friends who care deeply; from a beloved pet.

The love that surrounds you, even as you grieve your estrangement from a parent or an adult child, can soothe and comfort you, and reassure you that you are worthy of love and that there are others in your life who love and value you as you are. Each person, each offering of love, is a blessing that can help you to live well despite your pain and to feel so much less alone.

Find Ways to Let Joy Balance the Pain in Your Life

Living fully and well despite your ongoing crisis depends on keeping an essential balance in your life. The pain of estrangement, whether it feels like grief that never ends or a sense of emptiness where family love could be, needs to be balanced with love and fun and joy. If that sounds impossible, think about the alternative: a life of nonstop suffering.

Suffering is unlikely to change your estrangement situation in a positive way, and it certainly impairs your quality of life. But how do you begin to experience joy again when you're hurting so much?

I remember a wonderful conversation I had some years ago with a colleague when we were both going through major losses in our lives. Randi was recently divorced. I had lost both parents and my maternal grandmother to sudden, unexpected heart-attack and stroke deaths within a five-month period when I was only thirty-five. We were both feeling overwhelmed by the challenge of going on with our very changed lives.

"It occurs to me that going through a time of grief is like giving birth," Randi told me. "Sometimes the pain is just awful, but then it subsides for a while, and you can breathe freely, even laugh, and that makes you stronger for the next pain when it comes."

I remember making a vow then and there to laugh between my bouts of pain and just see what might happen. I was amazed and encouraged. I had new hope and optimism that I would survive this pain and live fully and joyfully once again.

Allowing laughter and love and joy into your life between your times of pain and grief can strengthen you for the next pain—and can make the periods of grief less frequent and less overwhelming.

Laughing between your moments of pain can add immeasurable comfort to the challenging times, and joy to those lovely, lengthening times in between.

Further Reading and Resources

BOOKS

→ *Adult Children of Emotionally Immature Parents: How to Heal from Distant, Rejecting, or Self-Centered Parents* by Lindsay C. Gibson, Psy, New Harbinger, 2015.

This is a terrific book with some very helpful insights and practical suggestions. Written by an experienced clinical psychologist, the emphasis of the book is not on blame but on healing and self-discovery.

→ *Healing from Family Rifts* by Mark Sichel, McGraw-Hill, 2004.

The emphasis in this insightful book by family therapist Sichel is on adults whose parents have shut them out. The author, who has been estranged from his parents, shares his own story as well as those of clients and others interviewed.

→ *Walking on Eggshells: Navigating the Delicate Relationship Between Adult Children and Their Parents* by Jane Isay, **Thorndike Press, 2007.**

This practical, well-written book focuses on the children of Baby Boomers and continuing conflicts around limit-setting and parent-child boundaries. The author, who is an editor and a seasoned parent, concentrates on conflict over developmental stages and offers sensible advice on maintaining a loving relationship through the adult child's emerging independence ("Keep your mouth shut and your door open").

→ **When Grown Kids Disappoint Us: Letting Go of Their Problems, Loving Them Anyway, and Getting On with Our Lives** by Jane Adams, PhD, Free Press, 2003.

This important book, written by psychologist Jane Adams, addresses the problem of parents emotionally battered by angry adult children. She also looks closely at the importance, for a parent who has been enmeshed in the chaos of an adult child's life, of standing back, letting go with love, and separating from the child's problems without separating from the child. The emphasis here is on adult children who are not living up to parental hopes for them, who are failing to launch into productive adult lives, and who are quick to blame parents.

→ *When Parents Hurt: Compassionate Strategies When You and Your Grown Child Don't Get Along* by Joshua Coleman, PhD, **Harper Collins, 2007.**

This is a wonderful book, offering insight, empathy, and perspective to parents who are mourning the loss of a harmonious relationship with an adult child who is troubled, angry, or distant. There is a particularly helpful chapter offering tips on how to write a letter of amends.

Online Resources for Estranged Parents and Adult Children Comprehensive Services

→ **Daily Strength for Estranged Parents**

dailystrength.org/groups/estranged-parents-of-adult-children-seeking-help

→ **Estranged Parents Forums on my *Living Fully in Midlife and Beyond* blog**

drkathleenmccoy.blogspot.com

Although my blog is for midlife adults in general, there are forums attached to my two most popular posts about estrangement and conflict between parents and adult children. Both have hundreds of comments that have become ongoing forums with both parents and adult children participating.

To access these forums, visit my blog and then scroll down past the most current blog posts to the "Popular Posts" list. At the top of that list, you will find:

✦ "When Adult Children Become Strangers," August 17, 2012.

✦ "Parents and Adult Children: Finding the Balance," February 6, 2011.

→ **Estranged Stories (for both parents and adult children)**

estrangedstories.ning.com

→ **Joshua Coleman, PhD**

drjoshuacoleman.com

This site, maintained by Dr. Coleman, the author of When Parents Hurt, *includes a number of valuable resources:*

+ *The Coleman Report.* This is a free newsletter with advice on parental estrangement, Parental Alienation Syndrome, and parent–adult child conflict. It is published online several times a week.

+ Free weekly webinar: *Q & A for Estranged Parents.* This is offered through the website every Monday at 11:30 a.m. PST (2:30 p.m. EST).

+ Webinar series online that offers topics such as "Five Most Common Mistakes of Estranged Parents," "Making Amends," "Should I Keep Trying or Just Give Up?" "How Do I Cope With the Pain?" "Does My Adult Child or Their Partner Have Mental Illness?" "Is Your Child's Therapist the Problem?" and "Should I Cut My Estranged Child Out of My Will?"

+ Forums for both parents and adult children.

RESOURCES FOR FAMILIES DEALING WITH MENTAL ILLNESS OR ADDICTION

→ **Adult Children of Alcoholics**

adultchildren.org

This site offers help finding a local meeting and also offers meetings via phone, Skype, or online.

→ **Al-Anon**

al-anon.alateen.org

This organization offers strength and hope for families of problem drinkers. (Those who have family members with other addictions may also find this useful.) The site offers links to local meetings or to phone and online meetings.

→ **Borderline Personality Disorder Center**

bpdcentral.com

This site offers help nationwide in finding a therapist in your area who is knowledgeable about borderline personality disorder and also the DBT therapy that appears to be most helpful in treatment.

→ **bpdfamily.com**

This site offers advice that could be helpful for estranged or conflicted families as well as those with diagnosed BPD.

→ **National Alliance on Mental Illness (NAMI)**

nami.org

NAMI has local chapters nationwide and, on its website, offers educational materials, support groups, and a list of local resources.

Resources for Families with an LGBTQ Adult Child

→ **The Marin Foundation**

themarinfoundation.org/resources

This site offers support and resources for Christian parents and adult children with an emphasis on embracing both faith and growing love for and acceptance of each other.

Services include a National Parent List with contact information enabling you to speak with other Christian parents who have LGBTQ adult children and who have embraced both faith and their children. There are also online support groups for parents and two private Facebook groups. These include Serendipitydodah for Moms and FreedHearts Fathers Group. There are also in-person support groups nationwide (there is a link to the list of these on the Marin Foundation site).

→ **Parents and Friends of Lesbians and Gays (PFLAG)**

pflag.org

This site offers information, help, and support with links to local groups.

TO CONTACT DR. KATHY MCCOY

→ **drkathymccoy.com**

Click on the contact page on the site to send me a confidential email. I would love to hear from you!

Index

D

E

Acknowledgments

My special thanks to...

Tim Schellhardt, my dear friend, who is an award-winning journalist and, even more important to him, the loving father of four amazing adult children. Tim contributed greatly to this book with his research assistance, his daily encouragement, and his wonderful insights into parent and adult child relationships.

My husband, Bob Stover, whose constant encouragement, excellent proofreading skills, willingness to do more than his share of housework and errands while this book was in progress, and ongoing independence were all a major help during my work on this project.

My agent Stephany Evans of Ayesha Pande Literary for believing in me and this book—and for her warm encouragement and excellent suggestions when it was in progress. I am also grateful to her colleague June Clark of Get There Media for her media consulting and much-appreciated help at various times along the way with this book. And special thanks to Susan Ann Protter, my longtime, now retired, agent, for putting me in touch with both of them!

My editor Anna Michels, who has taken such an avid interest in this project, gave me excellent suggestions and support as it progressed. I am also grateful to Grace Menary-Winefield, who graciously stepped in to work with me when Anna went on leave to welcome her first child, Alice Kathleen Michels, into the world!

Family, friends, and colleagues who offered support and encouragement during my work on this project: Mary Breiner, LMFT; John Breiner; Mike McCoy, MD; Jinjuta Kunthep McCoy; Tai McCoy; Caron and Raymond Roudebush; Joshua Coleman, PhD; Rachel Wahba, LCSW; Michael Scavio, PhD; Andrea Cleghorn, MSW; Carl and Judith Anderson; Pat Hill; Georgia Watson Boelhan; Sharon Zurawski Hacker; Jeanne and Jimmy Yagi; Sister Rita McCormack; Kim Tuomi; Marsha Morello; Pat and Joe Cosentino; Bruce and Mary Jo Scace; Debora Grady; Ruth Woodling; Jack Hill; Jeanie Croope; Alan David Nesbitt, LCSW; David Michael McFarlane; Maurice Sherbanee; Barbara Ferrell; Charles Wibbelsman, MD; Cindy Lockwood Miller; Michael Polich; Diane Moishe; Candy Yekel; Debra McDermott; and Arthur Vergara.

Some wonderful adult children who are an inspiration and delight: Ryan Grady, LCSW; Kelly Grady Callarman; Mary

Kate Schellhardt and Matt Palka; Chris and Eliza Schellhardt Yarbrough; Stephen Schellhardt and Devin DeSantis; Doyle and Laura Schellhardt Armbrust; Sharon Scace; Virginia Scace Lynch, PhD; Catherine Woodling; Matt Breiner; Liz Rowland; Katie Elliott; Brian Hacker and Carrie Goyette; and Sabrina Tate.

About the Author

Dr. Kathy McCoy is an award-winning author, journalist, and blogger as well as a psychotherapist specializing in work with troubled and estranged families.

She has written for a variety of national publications including *Redbook*, *Reader's Digest*, the *New York Times*, *Family Circle*, *Woman's Day*, and *Glamour* and has been a frequent guest on national television shows, including numerous appearances on the *Today* show and two on *Oprah*. She has also been interviewed as an expert on family relationships by *USA Today*, *US News and World Report*, *Psychology Today*, and online publications such as the Huffington Post, AARP.com, and Today.com.

Dr. McCoy is a contributing writer and blogger for

PsychologyToday.com and also has her own popular blog, *Living Fully in Midlife and Beyond*, that features a series of posts for parents and adult children. She also hosts the podcast *Living Fully with Dr. Kathy McCoy*, which is available on iTunes, Stitcher Radio, and Podcastpedia. Her blog and podcast can also be accessed through her website, drkathymccoy.com.